Choice in Education

THE NATIONAL SOCIETY
FOR THE STUDY OF EDUCATION

Series on Contemporary Educational Issues
Kenneth J. Rehage, Series Editor

The 1990 Titles

Choice in Education: Potential and Problems, William Lowe Boyd and Herbert Walberg, editors

The Educational Reform Movement of the 1980s: Perspectives and Cases, Joseph Murphy, editor

The National Society for the Study of Education also publishes Yearbooks which are distributed by the University of Chicago Press. Inquiries regarding all publications of the Society, as well as inquiries about membership in the Society, may be addressed to the Secretary-Treasurer, 5835 Kimbark Avenue, Chicago, IL 60637. Membership in the Society is open to any who are interested in promoting the investigation and discussion of educational questions.

Choice
in
Education

Potential and Problems

Edited by **William Lowe Boyd**,
Pennsylvania State University

and **Herbert J. Walberg**,
University of Illinois at Chicago

McCutchan Publishing Corporation
P.O. Box 774
Berkeley, California 94701

ISBN 0-8211-0138-2
Library of Congress Catalog Card Number 89-63477

Printed in the United States of America

Contents

Contributors

Ann Bastian, The New World Foundation
William Lowe Boyd, Pennsylvania State University
James Cibulka, University of Wisconsin, Milwaukee
Suzanne Davenport, Designs for Change
Denis P. Doyle, Hudson Institute
Richard Elmore, Michigan State University
Chester E. Finn, Jr., Vanderbilt University
Charles Glenn, Massachusetts Department of Education
Thomas H. Jones, University of Connecticut
Tim Mazzoni, University of Minnesota
Mary Metz, University of Wisconsin, Madison
Donald R. Moore, Designs for Change
Joe Nathan, Spring Hill Center
Barry Sullivan, University of Minnesota
Herbert J. Walberg, University of Illinois at Chicago
Joseph Weeres, Claremont Graduate School

Introduction and Overview

In *A Nation at Risk*, the National Commission on Excellence in Education (1983) riveted public attention on our serious educational problems and the critical need for reforms. Despite an extraordinary variety of substantial reforms, the achievement of the nation's school-children still fails to satisfy many parents, citizens, and legislators. In a new wave of reform, Republican presidents Ronald Reagan and George Bush, Democratic governors Rudy Perpich (Minnesota) and Michael Dukakis (Massachusetts), and many other politicians and businesspeople have called for more choice in education. Polls show that a clear majority of the public endorses choice in education.

More than twenty state legislatures and many school board members are considering the institution of choice plans that allow students to attend public schools outside their neighborhoods. Pioneered by Minnesota, state choice plans would allow secondary school students to attend any public school in the state; state funds would follow students to their chosen schools. Though seemingly revolutionary, such plans have precedents in decades-old schools, such as the Bronx

School of Science, that draw specialized students from beyond their immediate neighborhoods, and in interdistrict financing in New Hampshire that allows students to cross district lines for special programs. Abroad, Holland provides full national funding for schools inaugurated by parents of as few as three dozen students. The more immediate precedents, however, are voluntary desegregation plans. Federal courts have increasingly employed specialized magnet schools to attract students across school boundaries rather than ordering mandatory and often unpopular transportation arrangements and school district consolidation.

Advocates of parental choice believe that it unleashes strong incentives for school improvement. When consumers can "vote with their feet," educators get clear signals about their performance. Without such signals, advocates say, spurs for improvement remain weak, and monopolistic indifference thrives. Choice also benefits educators. When teachers have more voice and choice about what they teach, and the kind of school or program with which they are affiliated, their professionalism, creativity, and commitment to their work are enhanced. Choice for both teachers and students creates communities of shared values, which foster effective schooling. Even those who would impose a state or even a national curriculum can leave the means of organization and teaching to local decision making.

Clearly, proposals for choice hold exciting potential for consumers and producers. But, like other substantial reforms, they threaten the status quo. Some critics of choice, for example, say that it exacerbates inequity. Magnet schools, they contend, have negative side effects on nonselective schools; students who remain in ordinary neighborhood schools may lack the stimulation of bright or specialized classmates. Teachers in ordinary schools, it can be argued, may lack the professional stimulation of entrepreneurial colleagues. Such concern has led to yet another variety of choice—"schools within schools"—in which teams of like-minded colleagues can develop unique programs, yet benefit from daily contact with other groups.

Choice clearly raises provocative questions and stimulating policy issues. This book is intended to introduce readers to the potential of choice and to possible problems. The authors are well-known experts, and they approach the subject from distinctive angles. Some see great value in choice; others have serious reservations.

Chester Finn begins with "Why We Need Choice." He gives six reasons. In brief, the alternative, no choice, is incompatible with U.S.

ideals. Choice, moreover, fosters equality of opportunity; helps parents play their proper role; and stimulates school autonomy, teacher professionalism, and principal leadership. Choice, a potent mechanism, encourages greater learning. Finn elaborates on how each of these can work to improve our educational system.

In "Options for Choice in Public Education," Richard Elmore presents a systematic discussion of the large variety of possible ways of organizing public education. He outlines a wide range of options for enhancing or constraining choice. A key point he makes is that "policies affecting choice must be evaluated from both the demand and supply sides." Thus, "providing consumers with greater educational choice, while at the same time constraining the ability of educators to respond to consumer preferences will only increase dissatisfaction with schools."

James Cibulka's chapter, "Choice and the Restructuring of American Education," presents a discussion that follows logically from Elmore's analysis. If there is a variety of ways of organizing choice in education, how do these options mesh with other contemporary ideas for reforming U.S. schools? The Bush administration has endorsed choice as the key to restructuring and improving our schools. But other agencies and actors have strongly advocated a variety of other measures for restructuring our schools. Cibulka considers how choice plans might complement or conflict with a variety of restructuring measures that he classifies as core and ancillary strategies for reform.

In "Parent Choice in Four Nations," Charles Glenn attributes to France the "myth of the common school": that the nation should mold students to a single set of political loyalties. The Netherlands most successfully challenged this idea by fostering parent choice of schools—perhaps to the widest degree among affluent nations. Although traditionally least likely to use schools to promote national unity, Great Britain, under Margaret Thatcher, promotes parent choice to attain efficiency through competition. Canada, finally, provides choice in response to language and religious diversity. Although U.S. choice plans seem revolutionary to Americans, they seem tame compared to the tradition of the Netherlands and the present initiative in Great Britain.

Denis Doyle, in "Teacher Choice: Does It Have a Future?" draws on several recent works by economists and sociologists. They reveal the power of freely chosen, voluntary commitments to enhance human satisfaction and effectiveness. Doyle shows how such commitments might professionalize teaching. Under a "public practice option," for instance, teachers would control the school budget and would be free to organize schools in radically different ways. They might decide, for example, to substitute capital for labor by using computers, or to hire two aides instead of one teacher.

In "Magnet Schools and the Reform of Public Schooling," Mary Metz addresses choice in the context of school desegregation. Her case studies of three magnet middle schools suggest that they can serve apparently contradictory purposes such as excellence and equity, and collective and individual purposes. Still, such schools can be abused by elitist parents who want superior education for their own children alone. Magnet schools can be attacked, moreover, as inequitable because they are by definition non-standard. She concludes that reformers not only must take such benefits and pitfalls into consideration but must also engage the full support of parents, educators, and community leaders.

In "School Choice: The New Improved Sorting Machine," Donald Moore and Suzanne Davenport report on the implementation of choice plans in Boston, Chicago, New York, and Philadelphia. Disturbingly, they find that black, Hispanic, and low-income students and those with special learning problems and limited English proficiency tend to be further concentrated and excluded from some programs. Although some of these problems may be attributable to flaws of design and implementation, the authors are not sanguine that choice can provide an effective solution to the problems that beset urban schools.

In "Legislating Educational Choice in Minnesota," Tim Mazzoni and Barry Sullivan describe the pace-setting efforts of Governor Rudy Perpich and the state legislature. A 1985 enactment, for example, allows parents to send eligible senior high school students to public and private colleges and other post-secondary institutions part-or full-time at state expense. Another enactment allows dropouts and at-risk students, ages twelve to twenty-one, the right to seek enrollment in schools and postsecondary institutions outside their resident districts. Mazzoni and Sullivan describe both the policymaking and the implementation of these and other inventive choice programs.

In "School Choice: Unwrapping the Package", Ann Bastian first shares her view of private school choice as a threat to public education. She then raises critical questions about choice within the public sector. She attributes the success of poor and minority youngsters in the East Harlem school district less to choice than to teacher autonomy in developing small, personalized programs with a distinctive emphasis in the context of substantial decentralization in the district. Her reservations about Minnesota are that a small number of students take part in the program and that good results may be more attributable to the state's favorable circumstances than to choice.

In "Is More or Less Choice Needed?" Joseph Weeres views tuition vouchers and interdistrict transfers as neither necessary nor socially desirable. He argues, nonetheless, that site-based management of schools offers greater decision-making choices for school professionals aiming to be maximally responsive to the distinct needs of students in their communities. He explains further how superintendents and state officials can promote such professional management and responsive choices.

In "The Politics of Educational Choice," Thomas Jones argues that the comprehensive school has not worked for a variety of reasons. Among the consequences of its failure is the increasing racial and social class segregation recently attributable less to educational policies than to housing patterns. Choice offers several attractive features to solve current problems, raise achievement, and increase citizen satisfaction with schools. But Jones believes that many programs are likely to proceed slowly and fitfully at the state and local levels until their effects are better understood and documented.

Finally, in "Progress, Problems, and Prospects of State Educational Choice Plans," Joe Nathan addresses four topics: citizen interest in public school choice, the state and federal government responses, new research on existing programs, and prospects for expanding choice. Nathan's detailed analysis of choice legislation in fifteen states shows that the general notion of choice is being applied in diverse ways to solve particular problems of states and regions. He also shows how choice has worked in St. Louis, Milwaukee, and East Harlem.

In sum, the contents of this book illustrate both the rich potential of choice as well as the challenging issues it raises. As editors, we have tried to assemble a variety of viewpoints; and we hope the reader will be left with a more informed and thoughtful vision. Such a vision, indeed, combined with the reader's critical and creative faculties, may provide a key to the needed renewal and improvement of U.S. schools.

William Lowe Boyd
Herbert J. Walberg

Part I
The Dynamics and Potential of Choice in Education

CHAPTER 1

Why We Need Choice

Chester E. Finn, Jr.

Six compelling reasons argue for public policies that foster choice among schools. Let me state them briefly, then examine each a bit more fully, then explain why I am unpersuaded by the more common arguments *against* choice, and conclude by acknowledging that choice alone is no cure-all for what ails U.S. education. (For further explication, see Finn, 1986a, 1986b, 1987, 1989; Doyle and Finn, 1984.)

I should clear away one issue at the outset. For the United States at this point in history, I'm referring to choice within the broad policy framework we know as public education. This context wasn't always appropriate. "Educational choice" was long thought to be a code phrase for government aid to private schools, many of them church-sponsored. I'm a long-time consumer—and sometime critic—of private education, and mindful that many private schools are today experiencing renewed enrollment problems that could well draw them back like moths to the flame of government assistance, as happened under similar circumstances two decades ago. I'm also aware that some respected advocates of choice—law professor John Coons (University of California, Berkeley) comes to mind—believe that social justice requires policies that afford people the full array of education options, including private schools (Coons, 1989). Other analysts, such as Chubb and Moe (1986, 1988) and Coleman, Hoffer, and Kilgore (1982), conclude that the very "privateness" of private schools confers on them many organizational benefits that provide better education for their students. I have been struck by the extent to which today's excellence movement has sought to adapt many private school features to the circumstances of public education (Finn, 1989). Obviously, choice is one such feature. Nevertheless, here I want to confine myself to the pros and cons of choice within public education, while noting that some historic distinctions between public and private schools are already blurring and that this tendency is apt to continue.

Here are the six reasons why we need choice:

1. The alternative is incompatible with American democracy.
2. Choice fosters equality of opportunity.
3. Choice helps parents play their proper roles with respect to the education of their children.
4. Choice stimulates autonomy among schools, professionalism among teachers, and good leadership on the part of principals.
5. Schools of choice are more effective educational institutions; that is, students learn more in them.
6. Choice is a potent mechanism for accountability.

First, we live in a democratic republic anchored to the principle that government exists to serve the citizenry, not the other way around. In creating government, we did not surrender our human and civil rights. We are committed to minimal coercion by the state. Only where public safety or national security demands are we generally sanguine about government telling people what they can and cannot do, making them go places they do not want to go, and barring them from places where they *do* want to go.

In primary and secondary education, our basic arrangement is a compromise. On the one hand, civilized society needs to have its new members possess certain skills and knowledge, habits and behaviors, values and attitudes, and we think that these are generally best imbued in people via some sort of "formal" education when they are young. That is why we tell them they must attend school during a certain age span and why we are prepared to exert some of the police powers of the state to enforce that dictum. At the same time, and on the other hand, we believe that individuals and (for children) their parents retain the right to determine, within quite broad limits, just what the specific nature of that formal education will be and where it will be acquired. They may not abjure it altogether. But neither may they be forced to imbibe a particular version of it that they do not like or cannot countenance. Indeed, if they insist, they can even provide it around their own kitchen table.

"The child," the U.S. Supreme Court affirmed in 1925, "is not the mere creature of the state." That dictum was promulgated at the time to assure parents the right to send their children to private schools—a situation having arisen where the state of Oregon was seeking to oblige everyone to attend government schools. But the dictum also applies in many other domains, barring the state from making decisions for and about what children must do and where they must do it.

In a free society, it is simply unconscionable—in other settings, I would call it a sin—to oblige a child against his or her will to attend a rotten school that he or she would flee but for the denial of alternatives and the coercive powers of the state. In a democracy, however, more is required than the protection of individual rights from an overly manipulative government. The state itself must follow policies broadly acceptable to the electorate, or else its leaders can be replaced. And in the United States in the late 1980s, educational choice is a policy strongly favored by an overwhelming majority of the population. Multiple polls and surveys can be cited as evidence, all showing essentially the same thing. Perhaps the most carefully phrased and recent of these was the 1987 Gallup education poll, which asked a national sample of the general public, "[Do you] think that parents in your community should or should not have the right to choose which local public schools their children should attend?" The reply was 71 percent affirmative; just 20 percent opposed (Gallup and Clark, 1987, p. 20).

Even though most school administrators—and, we've recently learned, most school board presidents—disagree with the public about this key proposition, the fact is that strongly held public opinions on such matters must over time be heeded (Feistritzer, 1989, Table 22, p. 52). Otherwise we would be living in a kind of society that we could not rightly term *democratic*.

Second, choice policies do the most good for—and are most urgently sought by—the least fortunate members of society and those worst served by the traditional arrangements. Overwhelmingly, it is poor, disadvantaged, and minority students who are trapped in the crummiest schools and least able on their own to break out of that trap. Well-assimilated and well-to-do members of a mobile society have all manner of options in practically every domain of their lives. If they don't like the neighborhood park, they can join a club or take a holiday in Wyoming. If they don't like the municipal hospital, they can join a HMO (health maintenance organization) or fly to the Mayo Clinic. If they don't like the subway, they can buy a car, take a cab, or hire a limousine. And if they don't like the public school to which their children are assigned, they have at least three options: they can enlist influential friends to raise hell with the superintendent and school board until Amanda and Alexander are permitted to enroll under another roof; they can pack up and move to a different suburb with public schools more to their liking; or they can, of course, pay tuition to send their pampered progeny to a private school of their choosing.

The middle and upper classes of U.S. society do this sort of thing all the time. They take for granted that their rights and prerogatives include the selection of a suitable school for their children, and their resources are such that they can follow through on those preferences.

Who can't? Those lacking resources, that's who. And in what schools are poor, disadvantaged, and minority youngsters most often found? They are found in the least effective and most troubled schools of all, the schools in which they are least apt to get the kind of education that will give them authentic upward mobility in U.S. society. Of course, we should do our best to revitalize those schools. But we should not imprison students in them while we labor to improve them. It is the students, after all, for whose benefit the schools exist, not the other way around. And as a matter of basic social justice, we need to confer on low-income and minority youngsters the same fundamental opportunity in the field of education that their prosperous age mates already have the wherewithal to exercise: the right actually to attend a school that they think will work for them, and to make a change if it doesn't. And, if need be, to make another and then yet another change.

We know that some schools are far more effective educational institutions than others. We know that some schools are safer than others. We know that some schools have strengths and specialties— art and music, say, science and math, perhaps technical training in particular fields—that are attractive to certain students but not to others. Schools have personalities and distinguishing characteristics. They have peculiar styles and methods. Some work better for certain youngsters, some for others. Round pegs still do not fit into square holes. The ability to make a comfortable match between student and school is often an essential prerequisite for obtaining a good education. That means choice. And that in turn means more than the "end run" genre of choice that the well-to-do and influential can already exercise. It means clear policies that say to everyone, especially to those most in need of good schools and least generously furnished with private resources, "You are invited to participate in selecting a school that will work well for your child."

It is, I submit, no coincidence that on all those polls and surveys, low-income and minority people most strongly endorse choice policies, for they are the ones least able to practice choice without such policies. Nor is it an accident that perhaps the single most popular and widespread form of public school choice available today, the magnet school, was conceived as a means of fostering racial desegregation without resort to coercion. Choice turns out to be entirely compatible with such traditional social policy objectives as integration—indeed to be a powerful catapult across the neighborhood, district, and even municipal borders that are now the primary barriers to greater racial and ethnic integration. That is why many liberals favor certain kinds of choice policies. That is presumably why Massachusetts governor Michael Dukakis has endorsed a "controlled choice" plan for his state. That is why I predict that the great beneficiaries of Minnesota's celebrated statewide choice policy will be the residents of inner-city Minneapolis and St. Paul.

Third, choice empowers parents by drawing them into deciding the most fundamental of all questions about the education of their children: Where will the youngsters attend school?

"Most of all," writes Minnesota governor Rudy Perpich, "choice has promoted greater involvement by Minnesota's parents in the education of their children. Ultimately, parents are the ones who must demand quality. They must know what is expected of their children at various levels of education. And they must help set the tone and the attitude of our children toward the value of education" (Perpich, 1989). Yet the most frequently heard lament of U.S. educators is that parents aren't doing their part—aren't instilling a love for learning in their children, aren't supervising homework, aren't giving the kids good habits and sound values, aren't even making sure that the youngsters attend school regularly.

There is surely some justice in this charge, probably a great deal. But if we seriously care about enlisting parents as more effective partners in the education of their children, we have to begin by including them in the basic strategic judgments: What kind of education will the youngsters get? Where will they get it, and on what terms? Then, and I think only then, is it reasonable to expect parents to play an active role on a sustained basis. Then and only then is it reasonable to hold parents to account for what happens.

As I have already noted, many parents now participate in the selection of their children's schools. There is ample evidence that, given the opportunity, more will do so. That is why we so often observe parents camping out on the front lawn of the school administration building for several days and nights before the time when magnet school applications may be filed. That is why, after enduring several years of such queues, residents of Prince Georges County, Maryland, protested that a lot of children and parents—single parents, those with demanding jobs, those with health problems, for example—were not getting a fair shake because it isn't feasible for them to unroll their sleeping bags in front of the superintendent's office. In this instance, the school board responded by allotting a portion of the magnet school openings via a "lottery" system (while continuing to distribute the rest on a first come-first served basis). The larger point is that in Prince Georges County, as in so many parts of the United States, the demand for choice exceeds the supply available, which gives rise to "rationing" problems but which also illustrates the ardor of parents for more such opportunities.

Precisely because the family is our basic social unit and because the child is not the "creature of the state," we expect parents to engage themselves deeply in their children's upbringing. We leave to parents such fundamental decisions as how and where (and if) the child will be housed, fed, clothed, and medically cared for. Religion, morality, ethics, and values are almost entirely in their hands. We also expect parents to determine (whether by their actions or inactions) what "role models" the youngsters are apt to emulate. Only in the most egregious cases of child abuse—usually at the level of great physical brutality—does the larger society intrude itself into the parent-child relationship.

We acknowledge that many parents do not do all these things as well as some of us would wish. We often ponder social policies that might serve to "strengthen" the family. Nobody in his or her right mind would knowingly embrace policies that serve to weaken it. Yet in public education that is often precisely what we do, never even considering that most parents have no say in the most fundamental education decision of all. That is why we need choice as a conscious public policy. Incidentally, that is also a large part of the reason why most conservatives favor the concept. The really intriguing feature of the politics of choice in the late 1980s in the United States is that, while they may pursue different paths, liberals and conservatives keep finding themselves converging at the same policy destination.

Fourth, choice is a nearly inevitable companion of what Albert Shanker (president of the American Federation of Teachers) sometimes calls the "second reform movement" in U.S. education, a "bottom-up" effort to improve the enterprise by restructuring it, devolving more decisions to the school building level, and enhancing the professionalism of teachers and principal. The essence of this strategy is acknowledging that the individual school is education's principal "delivery system"—business might term it a "profit center"—and that the team of professional educators within the building will ultimately determine how good a school it is. Hence incentive and managerial arrangements need to be crafted that stimulate more such teams to take actions apt to yield favorable results. This strategy is precisely opposite to the customary pattern, which regards the "school system" as the key policy-and-management unit, which imposes rules and goals from above, and which treats individual schools as bureaucratic subdivisions, the more alike the better.

For our purposes, the essential point is that insofar as the second reform movement succeeds—insofar as educators gain greater professional autonomy and make more decisions at the building level—to that degree will schools come to differ from one another. The differences may take many forms, but they are sure to include variations in curricular emphases, in school "specialties," in pedagogical style, in the climate of interpersonal relationships within the school, in the allocation of resources (time and space and people, as well as money), and in the density and type of ties between school and home.

As schools come to differ along these and other dimensions, it becomes ever more important that students and their parents be able to choose among them. If the family wants—and the child needs—a highly structured school with a strong emphasis on science and math, it would be dysfunctional to send him or her to an "open" school where the teachers regard themselves as resource persons, where the students shape their own programs, and where the faculty's greatest strengths and enthusiasms are in the humanities. And if there is a school not far away that provides what the family is looking for, it would be absurd to deny the family the right to make the shift. Similarly, if School A opens its doors only during the traditional hours while School B can look after youngsters from 7 to 7, a working parent whose progeny would otherwise be "latchkey" children is plainly going to be more satisfied with School B.

When students are assigned to schools without regard to their needs and preferences, we can be certain that the political and managerial dynamics of the system are going to press for maximum uniformity among schools. Else it will appear arbitrary and capricious, like giving people only one channel on their television sets but running nonstop game shows on one person's set and endless sitcoms on another's. People will endure this sort of coercion only if they are absolutely certain that the same thing is happening to their neighbor. Yet it is ridiculous to think of school site management and professional empowerment unless schools are to be able to differ from one another in significant ways. And this, in turn, means that their clientele must be allowed to make choices.

So, incidentally, should teachers and principals. The second reform movement will falter if school teams are composed of people who cannot stand one another, who agree on nothing, and who would rather be in other schools. Education professionals need the right to select their colleagues, just as much as students need the right to select the schools whose teams have produced the kind of education environment that suits them.

Fifth, it stands to reason that people are going to be more successful in situations they have sought out and where they have willingly placed themselves, than in places where they had no choice about being. The human animal takes badly to coercion and is not apt to bring much ardor to an unwanted task. About the most you can expect of someone in that situation is dutifulness.

In education, much research indicates that magnet schools and other "schools of choice" tend to be more effective educational institutions. They function better. People in them are more enthusiastic and contented. Above all, students appear to learn more (Esposito, 1988, Chapter 2, pp. 10–34; Raywid, 1984, 1985a, 1985b, 1989). The reasons for this are fairly straightforward: parents are more engaged, the educators in the school are more apt to collaborate with each other, the match between teacher strengths and pupil needs is improved, and the school itself becomes a self-renewing system that gets ample feedback from its clientele and has the capacity to adjust and improve what it is doing.

If one believes, as I certainly do, that the enterprise of education should be judged almost exclusively by the cognitive learning of the students passing through it, then a policy of school choice, even if it had no other virtues, would be entirely justified by the simple fact that more learning occurs when such a policy is in operation.

Finally, choice is a sound and needed policy because, in creating a sort of "marketplace" around schools, it renders them accountable in the most direct and unambiguous way for what they are doing and how well they are doing it. Assuming that potential "customers" possess adequate information about the various schools—and this is an essential element of any well-constructed choice plan—various families will find some schools appealing and others repugnant. Occasionally their reasons will be frivolous or bizarre, but in general a parent will try to make a rational decision about the welfare of his or her child. When such decisions are aggregated across a community, we will find that some schools are attractive to a lot of people, others manifestly less so. In an unconstrained marketplace, this would in time mean that the popular schools would grow or replicate themselves while the unpopular ones would shrink and perhaps vanish. I cannot imagine a more suitable fate for a school that nobody would willingly attend than for it to close down. But even where the choice policy is so constrained that unpopular schools continue to have students, any principal or superintendent worth his or her salt will be influenced by the "management information" yielded by marketplace preferences, will note that something is clearly awry in the school that nobody wants to attend, and will do something about the situation.

In point of fact, relatively few students are apt to change schools. No one is yet sure what the outer limit will be, but I predict that only under the most extraordinary circumstances (such as several schools quite close to one another) will more than 15 or 20 percent of high school students ever enroll in schools other than those closest to their homes. At the elementary level, the percentage will be smaller still. It is extremely unlikely that wholesale abandonment of particular schools will occur. The key to choice as an accountability mechanism is that it *could* occur. And those running and working in schools will know that.

Accountability for results is indispensable to the proper functioning of any enterprise. Choice can introduce such a dynamic into education just as it already does in every other domain where it is practiced. Imagine going to an attorney you'd rather not use, attending a summer camp that you find revolting, buying a suit that doesn't fit. If enough others share your judgment, in time the camp will improve or close, the suit-maker will shape up (no pun intended), and the attorney may seek work as a bricklayer.

Our higher education system functions as a marketplace. So do many other public and quasi-public sectors of U.S. society. Medicaid recipients can choose their doctor, food stamp recipients their dinner menu, welfare recipients their haberdasher. Elementary-secondary public education is a sort of policy ghetto in which paternalistic, monopolistic practices endure, in which peoples' preferences are actionable only if the people are wealthy or well connected, and in which even the most horrendous institutions are maintained on a "life support system" by virtue of the workings of the compulsory attendance law in tandem with the involuntary pupil assignment scheme. Is it any wonder so many of our schools are mediocre? They are insulated from the consequences—both good and painful—of their work.

I should think the reasons just given would convince anyone. But there are holdouts, most commonly found within the ranks of professional educators and local school administrators, who are wary, skittish, even hostile toward school choice. Accordingly to Emily Feistritzer's poll data, 60 percent of school principals, 68 percent of local superintendents, and 51 percent of school board presidents are opposed to public school choice (Feistritzer, 1989, Table 22, p. 52). Congressman Augustus F. Hawkins, chairman of the House Education and Labor Committee, recently held a hearing in St. Paul at which he termed choice a "diversion away from programs that have already succeeded" (Wehrwein, 1989). A Chicago group called Designs for Change, after looking at magnet school programs in four big cities, called for a "moratorium" on choice because, they said, it was "becoming a new form of segregation, creating multi-tiered and unequal educational opportunities" ("Moratorium on Public School Choice Plans Urged," 1989).

The overt arguments *against* choice, as I read them, fall under two major headings: that choice is disruptive, costly, and logistically cumbersome; and that choice ill serves poor, disadvantaged, and minority students. I say "overt" because it is variations on these two themes that one encounters in public discourse—in speeches, articles, testimony, and the like. At least one further argument, spoken sotto voce if at all, advances the preference of some educators for situations in which they will *not* be held accountable for their results, precisely because they have a "captive audience." And as choice programs spread, we may encounter two further genres of resistance—although I have not yet caught even a whiff of either. I refer to upper middle-class anxiety lest their children's protected educational enclaves be broached by those who do not live in the neighborhood, so to speak. And to the possibility that private schools, already facing enrollment shortfalls, will see their "competitive advantage" eroded by a pronounced widening of educational alternatives within the public sector.

But let us not borrow trouble. For now let us stick to the two categories of objections to choice that are reasonably widespread today. Each has some legitimacy. Each can also be responded to in theory and dealt with in practice.

The contention that choice is expensive, confusing, and upsetting is all too familiar. Essentially the same response has been made by school administrators to *every single reform idea* that has ever been suggested to them. Large-scale upheavals are off-putting to people who are accustomed to doing things a certain way, who tend to be risk-averse and rather conservative souls to start with, who inhabit the middle and upper reaches of a large and sometimes intricate bureaucracy, and who sincerely believe that all their present resources are fully consumed doing what they are presently doing and that anybody with a notion about doing something more or differently had better start by putting some more money on the table.

These responses have little to do with choice *per se*. They have much to do with the culture of U.S. public education and the way that culture responds to the prospect of nonincremental (and sometimes even incremental) change. We would encounter essentially the same response if we suggested opening the schools on Saturday, offering a foreign language to every student commencing in the fourth grade, instituting team teaching where there was none, or having the teachers elect the principal. And so forth.

I don't minimize the disruptiveness of installing a choice policy in an organizational environment that isn't used to it. But let us be blunt: if we were content with the effectiveness of the present organization, we wouldn't be proposing to alter its dynamics in fundamental ways. The underlying reason why choice is gaining adherents today is precisely *because* it portends a very significant change in the traditional patterns of school operation. Whether it will be a good change is worth discussing; that it will be a large change is, after all, part of the point!

As for costs, some start-up expenses are indisputably associated with any major policy shift. Well-conceived choice plans also have certain continuing costs, such as the provision of adequate public information about schools to those making choices among them, and the management of the selection system itself. These expenses are real but not large; the information about school performance ought to be gathered even without a choice system, and the managers of the selection system *could be* the same people who won't in the future be needed to redraw district lines and work out pupil assignments to particular schools.

The one large expense that choice may bring is in the domain of student transportation, but this is apt to be a major additional outlay only if the system is accustomed to neighborhood schools—and, of course, if the system shoulders the responsibility *and* the cost of getting its students to their schools. If the district already runs a large pupil transportation program, it will have to make alterations, no doubt about it, but the added cost may not be great. Although I personally would not favor this alternative, it is also possible to imagine a choice policy that does not provide for pupil transportation, that provides it under certain conditions or within specified limits, or that imposes a user fee for it.

A more serious allegation, in my view, is that choice policies are bad for poor, minority, and low-achieving students, for those with various problems, and for those with apathetic or absent parents. Let me be clear—I invite the reader to review the second and third reasons offered in *favor* of choice—that it is mainly in order to give poor and minority students greater opportunity for a good education that choice seems to me a desirable policy.

As I read it, several related concerns are entwined here. One is that schools of choice may operate discriminatory admissions policies, keeping out students most in need of help while "creaming" the best students in the system, who in turn will be lost to the company of their less fortunate classmates. Another is that making one's way through a choice system requires levels of information, commitment, and savvy that youngsters "at risk" and their families may not possess. Yet another is that schools of choice may offer fancy academic specialties beloved of elites but won't provide the services needed by disadvantaged, non-English-speaking, and handicapped youngsters.

The major point I want to make is that while any or all of these problems *could* arise under a choice system, every one of them is *soluble*. Indeed, if they are anticipated—here the critics perform a useful service—they can be nipped in the bud rather than allowed to blossom.

By far the surest way to discourage discrimination and "creaming" in admissions is to turn *all* the schools in the system, perhaps in the state, into schools of choice. At least four rather small schools systems (Cambridge and Fall River, Massachusetts; Montclair, New Jersey; and Local District 4 in New York City) have done precisely this. Larger communities, such as Prince Georges County, Maryland, are rapidly adding to their magnet schools and in time will, I predict, be fully "magnetized." The entire state of Minnesota is headed in that direction. So is Iowa. Other states will surely follow.

If every school is a choice school, there remain issues of how to furnish public information about them and how to manage the selection system, but those are management problems, not issues of concept or principle.

Providing students and their families with sufficient information, both about individual schools and about the workings of the choice system itself, is a very important element of any choice plan. It will likely involve "outreach" efforts aimed at disadvantaged and minority students and at parents who do not speak English. But because we want to engage such families as deeply as possible in the education of their children anyway, it seems to me that such outreach efforts are a good idea. Indeed, helping a family make its way through the choice maze is an admirable way for the education system to establish an initial relationship with that family. It also seems to me plain that the school system will be wise to enlist various intermediaries and deputies here: community leaders, religious leaders, the mass media, and so forth.

Services for children with special needs may or may not be provided in every school in the system today. Although mildly handicapped youngsters, for example, are characteristically "mainstreamed," those with severe and/or multiple handicaps are commonly sent to schools specially equipped for them. (Indeed, one could say that severely handicapped children already attend magnet schools!) The general principle seems to me clear-cut: all those services that can readily be provided in a neighborhood school can also be provided in a "choice" school, and should be. Moreover, insofar as possible the services should follow the child. This notion is not wild or unprecedented. A retiree does not lose his or her pension by virtue of moving from Connecticut to Arizona. A welfare recipient does not lose his or her bimonthly check when relocating from one side of town to the other. A disabled veteran getting physical therapy can do so in the Veterans Administration hospital in Nashville as readily as in Seattle.

It should be noted, however, that making fully portable such benefits as compensatory and special education services will entail changes in federal policies and often in state programs, too. Chapter I funds and special education funds are not distributed eligible child by eligible child. If they were, they would automatically "follow" the youngster from one school to another. Instead, they flow to the school system and sometimes into the school building according to a demographic formula. Under current law, therefore, it is possible that Jane Doe, who needs and is receiving compensatory education at the Jefferson School, will move to the Madison School and there find herself without such services. Only if eligibility is made child-specific will federal aid become fully compatible with the policy of school choice.

That, it seems to me, is an argument for changing federal (and state) programs, not for jettisoning the concept of choice. Even in the near term it is possible to point out—in the school information that will be provided to families—which schools in the system provide which kinds of special services. Such data are as pertinent to family decisions as information about school facilities, hours, curricular emphases, and test scores.

I do not expect in these few paragraphs to convince all the skeptics, critics, and naysayers. I seek only to suggest to open-minded readers that there *are* solutions to the problems associated with the execution of choice policies, and that these problems are not markedly different from, and no more serious than, those we encounter when embarking on any large policy shift in any large public sector enterprise. To echo an earlier point, if we thought the enterprise of public education were satisfactorily doing the job today, we wouldn't be seeking to alter its organizational dynamics in profound ways. It is because we think that the job public education is doing is, on the whole, woefully inadequate, that we are prepared to consider large-scale shifts. That these bring implementation challenges, unanticipated dilemmas, demands for corollary innovations, and a fresh array of administrative headaches seems to me wholly predictable and not particularly discouraging. Not, at least, when we remember the stakes.

One more thought: in much of the opposition to choice, I find an undercurrent of liberal paternalism and professional sanctimony. This undertone says (though never so plainly) that these folks just don't have what it takes to make optimal decisions about their children's education, that a well-informed and objective educator is better suited to determine how to meet the youngsters' needs. It suggests that larger social and educational goals are involved here than students and parents can possibly fathom, and that the sum of a great many individual choices is not necessarily equal to the best interests of the community as a whole.

People who think this way mean well. In individual instances, they may even be correct! But not so very many more steps down that path lies an Orwellian society that few Americans wish to inhabit. The essential genius of our social contract is the notion, developed in the Enlightenment, that individuals are basically self-governing, that they pool resources and make joint decisions only for limited purposes, and that they do not thereby surrender their natural right to make the other decisions for themselves. That does not mean their choices will always be provident and wise. It does, however, mean that they are entitled to make such decisions and, when so moved, to make different decisions. Even the least among them. It is well past time that this principle found its way back into our public education system.

Desirable as I think choice is, and unswayed as I am by the allegations of those in opposition, I have no illusion that the institution of a thoroughgoing policy of public school choice will speedily set right all that is wrong with U.S. education. It will not—cannot—substitute for clear norms and standards, for a sound curriculum, qualified and committed teachers, suitable instructional materials, a sufficiency of teaching and learning time, strong school leadership, sure discipline, adequate resources, good character, and upright values. It will, I believe, enhance most of those qualities and clear the way for some of them to happen, but it does not take their place.

We take for granted nearly limitless choice in such domains as restaurant dining. But the element of choice does not guarantee a good meal if no restaurant in town has a competent chef, if there is little energy with which to heat the stoves, and if the restaurant managers all buy mediocre ingredients and plan dull menus. Choice is not a sufficient condition for educational excellence, but it is a highly desirable one. And in time we will be so accustomed to it that we will wonder what they were debating back in 1989.

REFERENCES

Chubb, John E., and Moe, Terry M. "No School Is an Island: Politics, Markets, and Education," *Brookings Review* 4 (1986): 21–28.

Chubb, John E., and Moe, Terry M. "Politics, Markets, and the Organization of Schools," *American Political Science Review* 82 (1988): 1065–1087.

Coleman, James S., Hoffer, Thomas, and Kilgore, Sally. *High School Achievement: Public, Catholic, and Private Schools Compared*. New York: Basic Books, 1982.

Coons, John E. "Don't Limit 'Choice' to Public Schools Only," *Los Angeles Times*, 22 January 1989, Part V, p. 5.

Doyle, Denis P., and Finn, Chester E., Jr. "American Schools and the Future of Local Control," *Public Interest*, No. 77 (1984): 77–95.

Esposito, Frank J. *Public School Choice: National Trends and Initiatives*. Trenton, NJ: New Jersey State Department of Education, 1988.

Feistritzer, C. Emily. *Profile of School Board Presidents in the U.S.* Washington, DC: National Center of Education Information, 1989.

Finn, Chester E., Jr. "Decentralize, Deregulate, Empower," *Policy Review*, No. 37 (1986a): 58–61.

Finn, Chester E., Jr. "Educational Choice: Theory, Practice, and Research," *Equity and Choice* 2 (1986b): 43–52.

Finn, Chester E., Jr. "Education that Works: Make the Schools Compete," *Harvard Business Review* 65 (1987): 63–68.

Finn, Chester E., Jr. "Are Public and Private Schools Converging?" *Independent School* 48 (1989): 45–55.

Gallup, Alec M., and Clark, David L. "The 19th Annual Phi Delta Kappa/Gallup Poll of the Public Attitudes toward the Public Schools," *Phi Delta Kappan* 69 (1987): 17–30.

"Moratorium on Public School Choice Plans Urged," *Education USA*, Newsline. 28 February 1989.

Perpich, Rudy. "Choose Your School," *New York Times*, 6 March 1989, p. A 17.

Raywid, Mary Anne. "Synthesis of Research on Schools of Choice," *Educational Leadership* 41 (1984): 70–78.

Raywid, Mary Anne. "The Choice Concept Takes Hold," *Equity and Choice* 2 (1985a): 7–14.

Raywid, Mary Anne. "Family Choice Arrangements in Public Schools: A Review of the Literature," *Review of Educational Research* 55 (1985b): 435–467.

Raywid, Mary Anne. "The Mounting Case for Schools of Choice." In *Public Schools by Choice*, ed. Joe Nathan. St. Paul, MN: Institute for Learning and Teaching, 1989.
Wehrwein, Austin C. "Hawkins Hits Choice at Minnesota Hearing," *Education Week* 22 February 1989, pp. 15, 17.

CHAPTER 2

Options for Choice In Public Education

Richard F. Elmore

Should parents and students be empowered to choose among schools, or among programs within schools? Should educators be empowered to organize and manage schools, to design educational programs, to recruit and select students, and to receive public funds

This chapter is a revised and condensed version of a chapter in *The Politics of Excellence and Choice in Education*, ed. William L. Boyd and Charles T. Kerchner (New York: Falmer Press, 1988). I wish to acknowledge helpful comments of the members of the seminar on choice at the Center for Policy Research in Education (CPRE) and of the advisory committees on research and dissemination at that center. Special thanks are due to David Cohen, Jim Fox, Paul Hill, Helen Ladd, and Lorraine McDonnell, who reviewed an earlier draft and offered useful comments. The research on which the chapter is based was sponsored by the Center for Policy Research in Education and was funded by the U.S. Department of Education, Grant Number OERI-0086-90011.

for providing education to those students? These are the two fundamental questions of educational choice.

The first might be called the "demand-side" question. It poses the
issue of whether the consumers of education should be given the
central role in deciding what kind of education is appropriate for
them. The second is the "supply-side" question. It poses the issue of
whether the providers of education should be given the autonomy and
flexibility to respond to differences in the judgments of consumers
about what is appropriate education.

Although there is some variation in the finer details of structure
from state to state and from community to community, two structural
features of U.S. education cut across all locations and levels. First, the
money to pay for education flows from taxpayers to local school
boards and to administrators who decide how it will be spent.
Consumers do not directly "purchase" public education, either with
their own money or with their share of public revenue. Second,
decisions about who attends which school, who teaches in which
school, and what is taught in schools are formally lodged with local
boards and administrators, operating within a framework of state and
federal policy. In other words, finance, attendance, staffing, and
curriculum content are locally centralized political and administrative decisions, not private consensual decisions between consumers
and providers.[1]

The organizing principle of this system, then, is local centralization. From the national or state level, education appears to be a highly
decentralized enterprise, because most detailed decisions about the
conduct of education are delegated to the 16,000 or so local school
districts. But from the client's or teacher's point of view, the system
appears highly centralized and bureaucratic. Decisions about who
gets access to what kind of education are determined by centrally
administered rules and structures, rather than by the preferences of
clients and providers. To raise the supply-side and demand-side
questions of educational choice, then, is to challenge this basic structure of locally centralized administration and to suggest that if
parents, students, and school-level educators were given more choice
the system would perform better. The current debate on educational
choice is about this proposition.

The main points of the analysis can be summarized briefly as
follows:

- Policies affecting choice must be evaluated from both the demand and supply sides. Providing consumers with greater educational choice, while at the same time constraining the ability of educators to respond to consumer preferences, will only increase dissatisfaction with schools.
- Policies affecting choice must take account of the broader public aims of education, in addition to the individual preferences of consumers and providers. These aims include providing a strong basic education for every school-age person.
- Policies affecting educational choice can be broken into four discrete categories: finance, attendance, staffing, and content. Within these four categories, policymakers have a wide range of options for enhancing and constraining choice. Various combinations of finance, attendance, staffing, and content correspond to distinctive forms of organization. The current system of local bureaucratic centralization represents only one of a large number of possible ways of organizing public education.
- There is little evidence that greater choice for consumers and providers of education will, by itself, dramatically change the performance of schools. But there are still substantial reasons why policymakers might want to initiate experiments in enhanced choice.

The locally centralized system, according to advocates of choice, is a formula for stagnation, unresponsiveness, and mediocrity. "Public schools today are rarely permitted to die of unpopularity. Thus, their incentive to innovate is meager, and their capacity to terminate unsuccessful programs is as bad or worse" (Coons and Sugarman, 1978, p. 154).

Furthermore, critics argue, the absence of choice and competition works against the very ideals of equal opportunity that the public schools are supposed to embody. "The poorer the family, the less its ability to furnish home remedies for educational ailments; ... the more difficult it is to escape an underfinanced or mismanaged public school system by changing residence; and ... the less its ability to induce the public system to provide the alternative classroom or program it prefers" (Coons and Sugarman, 1978, p. 26).

These convictions are shared by others representing widely divergent political viewpoints. Stephen Aarons argues that the existing organization of schooling "provides free choice for the rich and compulsory socialization for everyone else"; it "confronts the dissenting family with a choice between giving up its basic values . . . as the price of gaining a free education in a government school or paying twice in order to preserve its . . . rights" (quoted in U.S. Department of Education, 1985). "Government-operated schools," argues Joel Spring (1982, p. 33), "are destructive to the political culture of a democratic society and are one of the major obstacles to the free development and expression of ideas."

James Coleman (1985) adds, "Public schools have become increasingly distant from the families of the children they serve, increasingly impersonal agents of a larger society." Schools have lost their capacity "to support and sustain the family in its task of raising children"; they have lost their claim to a community of interest with families. The restoration of schools, Coleman concludes, requires "abandoning the assumption of the school as an agent of the state and substituting an assumption [that] the school is properly an extension of the family and the social community . . . of which the family is part" (Coleman, 1985).

The common thread in these critiques is a profound disillusionment with what educational historian David Tyack (1974; Tyack and Hansot, 1982) has called "the one best system." This system of locally centralized political and bureaucratic control, Tyack argues, is an outgrowth of the municipal reform movement of the nineteenth century, which tried to substitute enlightened lay leadership and scientific management for political patronage as the organizing principle of public education. The basic structure that grew out of this period—a locally elected lay board of education, a large and functionally specialized central administration, and schools run by principals reporting to the central administration—persists to this day and has a resilience, Tyack argues, that far surpasses its educational effectiveness. Local centralization of administrative functions in public schools, the argument goes, creates a self-interested bureaucracy with strong incentives to maximize its budget, control its clientele and subordinates, and expand its domain of influence, but only very weak incentives to attend to the essential processes of teaching and learning (see Michaelson, 1981).

CHOICE IN THE EXISTING SYSTEM

An enlightened public school administrator, confronted with these arguments, would probably reply that they represent a gross carica-ture of the typical public school system and a complete misunder-standing of the role that parent and student choice play in that system. Many school systems offer a considerable array of choices within and among schools. Parents and students play an active role in the choice of these programs. In fact, our enlightened administrator might continue, community sentiment seems to be running strongly against greater choice and toward clearer, more uniform academic standards for all students, regardless of students' and parents' per-sonal tastes or preferences. The public doesn't always value choice above other possible objectives, the administrator might conclude.

There is considerable empirical and theoretical support for the enlightened administrator's viewpoint. Consider the array of choices confronting students and parents in the existing system. Some choices, like place of residence and public-versus-private schooling, are time consuming, costly to make, and costly to reverse once they are made. These might be called "lumpy" choices.

Many parents and students, however, make smaller, more manage-able educational choices. These choices require smaller expenditures of money and time, and are easier to reverse. They can have signifi-cant consequences for parents, students, and schools. They are some-what "smoother" choices. Public school systems frequently offer a range of programs within and among schools, for the academically talented, for the handicapped, for students with specific learning problems, for the artistically, vocationally, or scientifically inclined, and many more.[2] The availability of these options allows parents to exercise educational choice by influencing the assignment of their children to teachers, classes, schools, and special programs within schools or school systems. In some instances (special education, for example), school officials are required by federal and state policy to include parents in choices affecting the assignment of their children.

Some significant proportion of parents actively exploit these oppor-tunities; other parents accept the assignments they are dealt, either because they are unaware that they have choices or because they willingly delegate those choices to others. In some instances, parents and students are "active choosers,"[3] in the sense that they exploit their options. In other instances, they are "inactive choosers,"[4] in the sense that they defer to the decisions of professionals, they don't acknowledge or understand their options, or they are simply satisfied with what they have. Some parents and students may be consistently more active than others. Some may, by virtue of their background or economic circumstances, be less able to assert their preferences.

Although the critics of the "one best system" have a point about its relative unresponsiveness to the preferences of individual clients, the system presents a variety of choices to its clients. Some of the choices (changes of residence, for example) are lumpy, in that they entail large costs and risks, while some are relatively smooth (changing teachers, for example), in that they require small costs and risks. Some choices are programmed by the existing system (special schools and programs within schools), while some are unprogrammed and lie in the hands of consumers (work, study, leisure). Some clients take an active posture toward their choices; others take an inactive posture. Critics can argue about the appropriateness of the constraints that the system of local centralization places on choice, or about the differential impact of choices on different types of clients, but they cannot argue that the system offers no choice. Likewise, supporters can argue that the system offers a variety of choices, but they cannot argue that those choices are equitably distributed or that they necessarily contribute to the best outcome for all clients.

POLICY OPTIONS: CHOICE BY DESIGN

The central problem arising out of the choice debate, then, is how to use the elements of school organization—finance, attendance, staffing, and content—to affect the relationship between clients and providers in ways that are likely to enhance the responsiveness and performance of schools. Three sets of actors are central to this enterprise: clients, providers, and policymakers. Each brings a distinctive set of interests and resources to the common task of schooling.

Clients (parents and students) provide the raw material for schools and, by their choices, they deliver important signals about their preferences for what is learned in school. Providers (teachers and administrators) bring the expert knowledge of content and pedagogy

Table 2-1
Illustrative Choice Options

	School Organization			
Element	Local Centralization	School Site Decentralization	Cooperative Contracting	Regulated Market
Finance	Payment to districts; centralized budgeting	Lump-sum payment to schools; decentralized budgeting	Contracting with consumer or producer cooperatives	Payment to clients
Attendance and staffing	Central assignment with centrally administered exceptions	Centrally administered matching	School-level selection; minimum regulation	School-level selection; minimum regulation
Content	Central rule making; decentralized implementation	School-level planning; decentralized rule making and implementation	Examination driven	Consumer driven

necessary to capitalize on the talents and preferences of consumers. Policymakers (board members and legislators) hold the proxy for the public at large, providing the money and authority necessary to make the enterprise work. Policies are more likely to work when they complement and reinforce the distinctive interests and resources of these actors.

Table 2-1 suggests some ways in which the elements of school organization can be brought together differently by policymakers in order to change the relationship between clients and providers. The point of this analysis is to illustrate how, by examining a *range* of solutions to the problem of school organization, we can alter the relationship between clients and providers. The exact options discussed in the analysis are less important than the underlying message that (1) the existing system of local centralization represents a very limited view of the relationship between clients and providers; and (2) there are many ways of altering this relationship, while at the same time representing the broader public interest in the organization of schools. (This analysis owes much to my colleague, Peter May, 1981.)

Finance

Finance determines the flow of money through the system. Most analyses of educational choice treat finance as a dichotomous variable: either we allocate money to schools through centralized administrative systems, or we give money directly to parents, in the form of vouchers or tax credits, for the purchase of education. This dichotomy sharpens the political debate, but it considerably understates the range of forms that financing can take and the range of ways finance can influence the relationship between consumers and providers.

Between the poles of payment to districts and payment to individual consumers are at least two other financing arrangements, each with a different set of incentives attached. These alternatives are lump-sum allocations to schools and contracting. Lump-sum allocations are a form of administrative decentralization. Schools are treated as "revenue centers," receiving a budget based on a per-pupil allocation, presumably adjusted for special students. Schools are responsible for allocating those funds among various activities, with minimum guidance from central administrators. A school might, for example, choose to reduce the number of full-time teachers, and increase part-time aides, in order to free teacher time for special instructional activities, individual tutorials, or part-time administration. Decentralization would require some degree of flexibility on the part of central administration in defining what constituted a school, in order for schools to have the flexibility to design their internal structures along different lines. Some schools would choose the traditional structure with a full-time building administrator. Others might choose a completely different structure, such as one in which teachers assume administrative responsibility or hire a business manager. The tighter the restrictions on what constitutes a school, the more lump-sum allocations look like centralized financing.

Contracting could take a number of forms, but it is mainly distinguished from centralized or lump-sum allocation by the fact that the contractor isn't necessarily a subordinate unit of the contracting agency. Contracting arrangements might be made with producer cooperatives (groups of teachers wishing to form a school) or consumer cooperatives (groups of parents who organize a school and hire people to staff it) or neighborhood groups who might wish to take over the operation of their neighborhood school. Under these arrangements, the contracting agency, which would probably be a local school board, could stipulate conditions for contractors, such as adult-student ratios, staff qualifications, minimum hours, and performance expectations. The tighter these stipulations, however, the more contracting begins to look like central control. Contracting is a common form of financing for public human services other than education—day care, community mental health, employment training, and so forth.

Lump-sum allocations and contracting represent the use of finance to shift the locus of allocation decisions from central administrators to providers. Vouchers and tax credits represent a shift to consumers. The financing of consumer cooperatives is a hybrid—a mechanism for funding consumers in an organized capacity.

Attendance and Staffing

Attendance and staffing determine the allocation of people to classrooms and schools, and consequently the fit between consumers and providers. Under centralized attendance and staffing systems, as they operate in practice, students and teachers are centrally assigned to schools, but the system accommodates by making exceptions for certain purposes, such as racial balance or faculty seniority. At the opposite extreme from central assignment is the regulated market model envisioned by voucher advocates, in which students and teachers choose schools based on their preferences. In the regulated market model, only selected constraints are set on these choices, designed to limit the possibility of outright discrimination or monopoly. (See Coons and Sugarman, 1978, pp. 148–152, 194–211.)

Between these extremes lie a number of other possibilities. Education professor Richard Murnane observes that consumer and producer choice in education actually entail three distinct components: *matching* student interests and capabilities with programs; *choosing*, or the process of students and parents selecting among alternative programs; and *being chosen* from a pool of applicants to participate in a competitive program (Murnane, 1986). One alternative might stress centrally administered matching as a mechanism for establishing the fit between students and staff. Board members and central administrators could set a broad menu of themes within which parents, students, and teachers would be expected to find some common ground. Any group of consumers or providers could propose an academic program organized around one of the themes, or central administrators could assign groups of educators to develop academic programs around themes and offer parents, teachers, and students the option of affiliating with one or more programs. This kind of centrally administered matching maintains central control over the specification of content options and provides some means of justifying attendance and staffing decisions on the basis of educationally relevant criteria, but it allows for a sorting of educators and students according to mutual interests. It also allows for the defining of options in ways that cut across racial, ethnic, and neighborhood lines, increasing the likelihood that choice will result in diversity of student populations. Everyone—students and staff—would be required to choose, and the central theme would be making the closest possible match between the interests and capabilities of students and educators. Significant changes in district student and teacher assignment practices would be necessary, as would some preference-ordering system, since not everybody would get their first choice. These changes could be made either on a district-wide basis or by designating "free zones" within or across established attendance areas. Many desegregating districts have already moved significantly in this direction by liberalizing transfer policies, establishing magnet schools, and allowing students to move among schools during the school day.

Another alternative might stress school-level selection, or being chosen, rather than centrally mandated matching. Staff and student assignment could simply be delegated to the school level, in much the same way as these functions are performed currently within universities, by charging the chief administrator or the corporate board of the school with the responsibility for selecting staff and students within certain broad personnel procedures and a budget constraint. Parents and students would apply to schools, and between application periods would be allowed to switch affiliations. Likewise, teachers, after some initial sorting process based on voluntary affiliation or central matching, could apply to any school on a space-available basis. New teachers entering the system would have to be hired by a school before they could be hired by the system at large—the reverse of centralized hiring. Because of the universalistic nature of elementary and secondary schools, any system of school-level selection would have to include either centrally mandated enrollment quotas or generous financial incentives to assure attention to the needs of difficult-to-teach students.

Centrally mandated matching and school-level selection represent alternative ways of shifting the locus of responsibility for attendance and staffing from central administrators to parents, students, and educators. They constitute ways of removing these key decisions from impersonal, standardized systems and placing them in structures in which real people are required to make and justify choices. Because of this attribute, they are not likely to be popular, at least initially, with those established school administrators and teachers who are the beneficiaries of centralized assignment. The idea behind the shift toward school-level selection is that the act of affiliating with a group is, in itself, an important source of motivation for doing well in that group.

Content

Content determines what is taught and, indirectly, how it is taught. Existing policies and practices toward content are not easily captured by a simple formula. A multitude of state- and district-level prescriptions bear in one way or another on content—subject matter requirements, graduation standards, textbook adoptions, and the like. But there is also considerable evidence that these prescriptions have mixed and complicated effects on what is taught. The reasons are twofold. First, content requirements can be complied with in *pro forma* ways at the district and school level. A district or school may teach Algebra I, but may do so in a watered-down or souped-up way; it may use the prescribed textbook, but may finish only half of it or supplement it with more advanced materials. There is virtually no direct inspection of compliance with content requirements. Second, content requirements interact heavily with classroom teaching to produce distinctively different experiences for different students in a nominally standardized curriculum. Teacher A may require students to work in groups on projects designed around standard topics, while Teacher B may lecture and pass out ditto sheets. The existing system, then, is characterized by centralized rule making with highly decentralized implementation.

At the opposite extreme from this system is the one envisioned by voucher advocates, in which content decisions are market determined, with minimal or no central regulation. In the regulated market model, every centrally mandated content requirement is seen as compromising the essential principle of consensual choice between consumers and providers. (See Coons and Sugarman, 1978, pp. 167 ff.)

In one sense, the locus of content determination could be seen as the most basic issue of choice, because changes in finance, attendance, and staffing practices would have little effect on the array of actual choices for consumers and providers if everyone were teaching the same thing in the same way. But even in the existing system there is little central control over the implementation of content requirements and considerable variation in what is actually taught. Hence it is far from clear that central rule making on content results in uniform practice. A more realistic assumption would be that the environment surrounding content decisions can be modified in certain ways, but that many of the key content decisions under any arrangement of finance, staffing, and attendance will occur at the school and classroom levels.

One alternative to the existing system would be to decentralize rule making as well as implementation. Because many key content decisions are already made at the school and classroom levels, one could simply formalize that practice and make it more visible. A school might be required, as a condition for public support, to prepare a statement of content and learning objectives and to submit to periodic reviews of its plan and performance by an external review panel composed of other educators, citizens, and state or local policymakers. State and local policymakers could describe the minimum elements of a plan, but the actual formulation of content and pedagogy would be left to the school, in its corporate capacity, defined to include parents and students, as well as educators. State and local policymakers could exert influence or leverage over content in much the same way as they do now—by "jawboning," or calling attention to exemplary programs and deficiencies in the proposals and practices of schools.

Another option is to influence content by measuring performance. That is, all content decisions could be nominally left to consumers and providers, but state or local government would stipulate that in order to advance to certain levels, and ultimately to receive a diploma, a student would have to pass a series of examinations in specified content areas. In order to receive continued public financial support, a school would have to maintain a certain success rate on the examination. Exams could be administered by a central agency and evaluated by teachers from other schools against a template provided by the examining agency.

The amount of variability in content from one school to another would depend on the frequency, breadth, and detail of the examination system. A system that tested only for basic mastery of academic subjects—writing, mathematics, science, history—would permit wide latitude in both pedagogy and content. A system that tested for levels of proficiency, rather than only for basic mastery, would allow some schools to focus exclusively on rigorous training for the highest level of proficiency in academic subjects, while others might aim for basic mastery supplemented by training in the arts, technology, or vocational skills.

An exam-driven system might also allow for mobility among schools and programs. At the secondary level, some students might formally "test out" of certain subjects and move on to more advanced courses at the postsecondary level. Other students requiring remedial help might focus exclusively for some period of time on a single academic subject in which they are having trouble. At the elementary level, parents might choose, for example, to enroll their children in intensive summer sessions in a given subject in order to free up time during the school year for extra instruction in art or music.

The problems with exam-driven systems are fairly well known. Without more restraint than most policymakers are willing to exercise, examinations can quickly become at least as obtrusive as centralized rule making in specifying content. Under pressure to justify the rigor and fairness of the exams, the examining agency would probably graft more and more specific content areas onto the exam, resulting in less and less flexibility for the design of school programs. Under pressure from diverse educational interests, examiners might adjust the content of the exam to reflect the emphases of certain types of schools. Regardless of how careful the examining agency was in limiting the exam to only basic subject matter, some schools would still compete by selecting students with high aptitudes for the exam, by allowing the content of the exam to dominate their curriculum, and by advertising their success rates to prospective applicants. Exams that discriminate on the basis of proficiency in subject matter knowledge can also discriminate on the basis of other attributes, including race and sex, raising questions of equity. Any uniform exam system carries the implicit assumption that children follow more or less uniform stages of development, which is not an accurate reflection of the diversity of children's intellectual growth.

Both decentralized rule making and examinations entail many practical problems, but they could result in a significant shift in the incentives under which consumers and providers operate. Both force the locus of responsibility for content decisions to the school level. Decentralized rule making uses process—planning and politics—as the main mechanism for generating engagement and commitment. Examinations use performance. Both provide a significant degree of central influence over content, though by indirect means. Decentralized rule making exerts influence through central review and approval. Examinations use exam content and collegial norms. Both forms of influence are highly susceptible to recentralization, if policymakers are not committed to shifting the locus of responsibility, because both involve the creation of new bureaucratic structures with their own interests.

Organization

The range of options described in Table 2-1 is grouped around organizational themes. In local centralization, the classroom is the central focus of the system, and each successive layer that surrounds it—the school, the district, the state, and the federal levels—makes some claim on classroom activity. Different levels make different, often overlapping or competing, claims. But the dominant theme is centralization of administrative functions at the district level. The district, in its corporate capacity, is the main administrative unit; the classroom, nested within the school, is the basic provider of education.

At the other extreme is the system visualized by advocates of regulated voucher systems, in which schools act as small autonomous firms, operating under the minimum constraints necessary to prevent monopoly or discriminatory practices. Consumers are direct recipients of government financing, which they, in turn, use to purchase education from providers. Staffing, attendance, and content decisions are made by mutual consent among consumers and providers, with no central planning or control, other than the minimum necessary to assure that certain conditions of consumer access and market structure are met. Central influence, insofar as it occurs at all, takes the form of "market-enhancing" activities—such as the consumer information functions performed by the Better Business Bureau or the market-clearing functions performed by counseling and placement services.

Between these extremes we have defined two of a virtually infinite number of organizational possibilities, for illustrative purposes. One of these might be called school site decentralization, which combines lump-sum financing of schools, centrally mandated matching of students and teachers with programs, and school-level planning for content. Schools, rather than individual consumers, are the recipients of government funding. District-level administration consists of setting the menu of content options through a combination of consultation with the community and central decision making, making lump-sum allocations to schools, and running a district-wide matching system that pairs students and educators with the program options that most closely approximate their preferences. This option contains a considerably stronger central role for district administrators than the one envisioned by the regulated market model, but a considerably less centralized one than the nested hierarchy.

Another possible option might be called "cooperative contracting." This model combines a contracting model of finance, in which funding is delivered to schools by contracts with consumer or producer cooperatives, based on per capita reimbursements for services. As in the regulated voucher model, schools are free-standing organizations, run by their owners, that select staff and students themselves within a structure of public regulations designed to provide protection against monopoly and discriminatory practices. The main difference between the cooperative contracting model and the regulated voucher model, at the provider level, is that the form of organization allowed to participate in public financing would be restricted to consumer or producer cooperatives. This mechanism would be much like the preferential financing currently offered by the federal government for health maintenance organizations, which are consumer- or producer-owned providers offering health care on a flat-fee, rather than a fee-for-service, basis. Content could be centrally influenced in this model by a centrally administered examination system, which would provide direction for curriculum content without prescribing the actual subjects and materials to be taught.

There are many other possibilities. The important point is not to present an exhaustive analysis of options, but to illustrate the way in which alterations of policies affecting finance, attendance, staffing, and content change the form of organization and the relationship between clients and providers of education. With the movement of finance from individual consumers, to consumer cooperatives, to producer cooperatives, to schools in a decentralized system, to school districts, the locus of fiscal leverage shifts among key actors. The conditions of affiliation between educators and their clients change with the movement of attendance and staffing decisions from individual clients, to cooperatives, to matching systems, to centralized bureaucracy. With the shifting of content decisions from consumer-driven, to exam-driven, to school site planning, to central rule making, the locus of decisions about what is taught also shifts. Each shift has large implications for the distribution of power and authority in the provision of public schooling.

SHOULD POLICYMAKERS EXPERIMENT WITH CHOICE?

Another consequence of this analysis is to array a range of options for enhancing and constraining client and provider choices on several dimensions, and hence to break the large, dichotomous choices proposed by voucher and tax credit advocates down into smaller, bite-sized pieces that policymakers can digest and experiment with on a smaller scale. One of the chief complaints by critics of the existing system, as we saw, was that its structure imposes prohibitively large and unequal costs on clients who are dissatisfied with the quality of the schooling they were dealt. Changes of residence and enrollment in private schools, we saw, were extraordinarily "lumpy" choices, entailing large costs in money and time to make and reverse. The effect of breaking key dimensions of choice into smaller, more manageable pieces is to "smooth out" client choices, reducing costs and potentially making them more manageable for all consumers.

This analysis also underscores why it is important to frame experiments around the problem of choice in both supply-side and demand-side terms. (For another discussion of the argument for joining supply-side and demand-side changes, see Nathan, 1983.) Loosening up choice on the consumer side, through changes in attendance policies, for example, while leaving constraints on the provider side, in the form of limits on staff assignment and content decisions, results in increasingly diverse client demands being placed on a narrow and rigid structure. Loosening up choice on the producer side, in the form of increased school-level responsibility for staffing and content, while leaving constraints on the consumer side, in the form of centralized attendance policies, results in more school-level control, but not necessarily more responsiveness to client demand. Whatever the array of options, reducing central control on one side, without also reducing it on the other, will defeat the purpose of enhanced choice by putting one or the other side at a disadvantage.

Is there any firm evidence on which to base a judgment that these structural options, or any others we might develop along similar lines, will improve the academic achievement of students? The short answer is no. The evidence suggests that there is no simple causal relationship between choice, as we have discussed it here, and students' academic performance (Rutter et al., 1980; Lightfoot, 1983; Purkey and Smith, 1983; Rowan, Bossert, and Dwyer, 1983). Saying there is no direct causal relationship, however, is not the same as saying that there are no grounds for experimentation with choice.

In the absence of such evidence, there are many reasons why it might be useful to experiment deliberately with options of the sort just outlined. Among the major reasons are, first, that the limits of local centralization have been clearly established. The centralization of finance, attendance, staffing, and content exact a relatively high cost in administrative overhead, and in the diversion of energy and commitment from the central tasks of teaching and learning. Even the greatest alleged strength of the system—its ability to deliver a relatively standard product to a relatively broad clientele—is undermined by the facts, first, that it is hemorrhaging one-fifth to one-half of its clientele during their adolescent years, and, second, that the education of those who remain is at best, highly variable in quality, and at worst, dismal.

Second, consumer and producer choice may be values worth recognizing in their own right, regardless of their instrumental relationship to student performance. A basic philosophical premise of democratic thought is that government derives its authority from the people, rather than possessing inherent authority. When nominally democratic institutions such as the public schools become bureaucracies with interests of their own, serious questions arise about their relationship to those they are supposed to serve. Loosening up the structure of schools, providing more influence for citizen consumers and professional providers, is one way of signaling the bureaucracy that its interests are not paramount.

A third rationale for experimenting with new forms of consumer and provider choice is that it may be a way of engaging the creative energy of parents and educators in solving serious educational problems, independent of whether choice by itself is a good or effective thing to do. Hierarchies of the type represented by local centralization condition clients and providers to look up for solutions, to higher-level administrators and policymakers, rather than inward at themselves or outward toward their peers. Pushing decisions on finance, staffing, attendance, content, and organization out into the schools may result in more attention at that level to the deliberate design of teaching and learning, rather than to implementing plans formulated elsewhere.

Against these arguments in favor of experimentation with policies directed at educational choice, we should array several cautions. The first and most obvious is that the existing system has proven extraordinarily resilient in the face of attempts to change it. In the Alum Rock (California) voucher experiment, for example, the information educators made available to parents on their educational options was not useful in helping parents discern differences among programs, and there is substantial evidence that the programs themselves did not represent carefully thought-out and implemented options. Teachers and administrators fought and defeated proposals to publicize achievement test scores across programs, on the grounds that they did not provide fair comparisons. And teachers and administrators opposed the introduction of a third-party organization to act as an "impartial" arbiter on questions of information and administration (Cohen and Farrar, 1977).

In other experiments with choice, the results are not much more encouraging. Teachers and administrators tend to adapt client choice systems to ease their effects on established patterns, rather than adapting their behavior to the new incentives introduced by client choice. Small-scale, within-district experiments create divisions between participants and nonparticipants—parents, teachers, and students alike. These divisions result in charges of inequity that create political problems for school administrators and local board members. Alternative programs tend to lose their distinctiveness and their support among teachers and clients over time (Raywid, 1985; Cohen and Farrar, 1977; Nault and Uchitelle, 1982; Rand Corporation, 1981; Murnane, 1986; Metz, 1986).

Second, recent studies of public secondary schools show that students are already presented with a considerable array of choices among courses and alternative programs within schools, but that the typical student either chooses a program that lacks coherence or defers to a standard program specified by another adult, typically a counselor, which also lacks focus. Only in exceptional instances do highly motivated students choose academically challenging programs. The typical teacher accepts this state of affairs as inevitable, although he or she may find it objectionable in principle (Powell, Farrar, and Cohen, 1985; Boyer, 1985; Sizer, 1984). The picture presented by this research is one in which student choice functions to reinforce a mediocre, substandard level of academic content and performance, rather than higher expectations.

On the other hand, some evidence shows that a few public schools are successful at creating environments in which academic learning occurs among students from a variety of backgrounds. These settings are usually described as ones in which educators have clear expectations for academic success, educators provide reinforcement for student achievement, students operate under clear guidelines for behavior and discipline, educators agree on academic objectives, and school leadership supports teachers in instructional and discipline decisions (Rutter et al., 1980; Lightfoot, 1983; Purkey and Smith, 1983; Rowan, Bossert, and Dwyer, 1983). Conspicuously absent from this research, however, is any evidence about the influence of parent, student, or teacher choice in those settings on student achievement.

Third, any experiment with educational choice must come to terms with the problem of active versus inactive choosers. Some evidence shows that parents differ by race and social class in the amount of information they have about available options and in their preferences for academic content, discipline, and instructional style (see Nault and Uchitelle, 1982). One possible consequence of experiments with increased choice for clients and providers is a situation in which nominally neutral mechanisms produce highly segregated school populations. Another possible consequence is one in which active choosers congregate in one set of schools and inactive choosers end up by default in other schools, creating a stratified system that is responsive to the former and ignores the latter. (See Hirschman, 1969.)

Finally, there is no guarantee that enhancing client or provider choice will increase the quality of education provided to the average student. Most, if not all, of the power of client choice to improve schooling rests on the ability of clients to make informed choices. High-quality information about the content and performance of schools is difficult and costly to get, must be collected with care, and must be interpreted with detachment and skepticism after it is collected because it presents a limited picture of what schools are about. Supply-side competition introduces strong incentives for providers to present superficial or inaccurate information on effectiveness, to package information to promote their product, and to protect certain types of information that would be useful in making client choices as proprietary. Because providers control the "technology" of schooling, they have a significant advantage over consumers in the control of useful information. Demand-side competition introduces strong incentives for active choosers to use their market power (money, time, influence, access) to gather and use information that improves their relative position in the market. In other words, one effect of introducing greater choice may simply be to increase competitiveness without increasing quality, because quality is an ambiguous commodity in education.

In summary, the major argument in favor of experiments with increased choice is that they provide a much needed prod to a system that is increasingly top-heavy, complacent, clumsy, and ineffective in its relations with its clients. The major problems associated with such experiments are either that they will be coopted by the system they seek to change or that, if they succeed, they will impose the risks of mindless and destructive competitiveness without the benefits of greater attention to quality.

NOTES

1. States have, of course, made major inroads into local authority over finance, personnel, and content, through tax and revenue equalization, labor relations laws, certification requirements, and content mandates. In this sense, there is a significant degree of state centralization in certain key areas. But at the level of what might be called "allocation decisions"—that is, deciding who will do what in which setting—local boards and administrators still play the dominant role. When I speak of finance, staffing, attendance, and content, I mean allocation decisions in these areas.

2. Evidence on this point is scanty, but suggestive. Surveys suggest that something like one-third of urban districts have schools that are specifically identified as "magnet" or "alternative" schools, but the designers of these surveys suggest that they seriously underestimate the proportion of programs offering choice to parents or students. The surveys do not include within-school alternatives, district-wide transfer schemes, or education and employment-training programs outside the public school system. Nor do they attempt to measure the frequency of active parental or student choice in absence of specific programs designed to offer choice. See Raywid (1984, 1985).

3. In a 1982 survey, about 12 percent of parents said they had chosen to send at least one child to a private school and about 20 percent of parents whose children were enrolled in public schools said they had actively considered private schools. About 53 percent of public school parents said they considered the quality of the public schools in making residential choices. Significantly larger proportions of minority and low-income people than in the general population said they had exercised active choice by these criteria. Overall, though, the private school population is more likely to be white, affluent, and well-educated than is the general population (Williams, Hancher, and Hutner, 1983).

4. I am indebted to Mary Metz and Mary Anne Raywid for assistance in framing this distinction, though neither is responsible for the use I have made of it.

REFERENCES

Boyer, Ernest. *High School: A Report on Secondary Education in America.* New York: Harper and Row, 1985.

Cohen, David, and Farrar, Eleanor. "Power to the Parents? The Story of Educational Vouchers," *Public Interest,* No. 48 (1977): 72–97.

Coleman, James. "Schools, Families, and Children." Ryerson Lecture, University of Chicago, 1985.

Coons, John, and Sugarman, Stephen. *Education by Choice: The Case for Family Control.* Berkeley: University of California Press, 1978.

Hirschman, Albert. *Exit, Voice, and Loyalty: Responses to Decline in Firms and Organizations.* Cambridge, MA: Harvard University Press, 1969.

Lightfoot, Sara Lawrence. *The Good School.* New York: Harper & Row, 1983.

May, Peter. "Hints for Crafting Alternative Policies," *Policy Analysis* 7 (1981): 227–244.

Metz, Mary. *Different by Design: The Context and Character of Three Magnet Schools.* New York: Routledge & Kegan Paul, 1986.

Michaelson, Jacob. "A Theory of Decision Making in the Public Schools: A Public Choice Approach." In *Organizational Behavior in Schools and School Districts,* ed. Samuel Bacharach. New York: Praeger, 1981.

Murnane, Richard. "Family Choice in Public Education: The Roles of Students, Teachers, and System Designers," *Teachers College Record* 88, No. 2 (1986): 169–189.

Nathan, Joe. *Free to Teach: Achieving Equity and Excellence in Schools.* New York: Pilgrim Press, 1983.

Nault, Richard, and Uchitelle, Susan. "School Choice in the Public Sector: A Case Study of Parental Decision Making," in *Family Choice in Schooling: Issues and Dilemmas,* ed. Michael Manley-Casimir. Lexington, MA: Lexington Books, 1982.

Powell, Arthur, Farrar, Eleanor, and Cohen, David. *The Shopping Mall High School: Winners and Losers in the Educational Marketplace.* Boston: Houghton Mifflin, 1985.

Purkey, Stewart, and Smith, Marshall. "Effective Schools: A Review," *Elementary School Journal* 83, No. 4 (1983): 427–451.

Rand Corporation. *A Study of Alternatives in American Education,* Vol. 7: *Conclusions and Policy Implications.* Santa Monica, CA: Rand Corporation, 1981.

Raywid, Mary Anne. "Synthesis of Research on Schools of Choice," *Educational Leadership* 41 (April 1984): 70–78.

Raywid, Mary Anne. "Family Choice Arrangements in Public Schools," *Review of Educational Research* 55 (Winter 1985): 435–467.

Rowan, Brian, Bossert, Stephen, and Dwyer, David C. "Research on Effective Schools: A Cautionary Note," *Educational Researcher* 12, No. 4 (1983): 24–31.

Rutter, Michael, Maughan, Barbara, Mortimore, Peter, Ouston, Janet, and Smith, Alan. *Fifteen Thousand Hours: Secondary Schools and Their Effects on Children.* Cambridge, MA: Harvard University Press, 1980.

Sizer, Theodore. *Horace's Compromise: The Dilemma of the American High School.* Boston: Houghton Mifflin, 1984.

Spring, Joel. "Dare Educators Build a New System?" In *Family Choice in Schooling: Issues and Dilemmas,* ed. Michael Manley-Casimir. Lexington, MA: Lexington Books, 1982.

Tyack, David. *The One Best System: A History of American Urban Education.* Cambridge, MA: Harvard University Press, 1974.

Tyack, David, and Hansot, Elisabeth. *Managers of Virtue: Public School Leadership in America, 1820–1980.* New York: Basic Books, 1982.

U.S. Department of Education. "Justice and Excellence: The Case for Choice in Chapter I." Washington, DC: U.S. Department of Education, November 15, 1985.

Williams, Mary Frase, Hancher, Kimberly Small, and Hutner, Amy. "Parents and School Choice: A Household Survey." School Finance Project Working Paper. Washington, DC: U.S. Department of Education, December 1983.

CHAPTER 3

Choice and the Restructuring of American Education

James G. Cibulka

Choice is a latecomer to the educational reform movement of the 1980s. It received endorsement from the National Governors' Association in 1986 with the publication of its influential monograph *Time for Results*.

Of course, proposals to improve choice in one form or another have been around for a very long time, preceding the recent reform movement. Milton Friedman (1955) called for educational vouchers decades ago, and there have been unsuccessful efforts at the state level (such as John Coons's California initiative in the late 1970s) as well as at the federal level (the Reagan administration's proposal to voucherize, the Elementary and Secondary Education Act, Chapter 1). Policy efforts to improve public education in central cities through magnet and specialty schools date back to the 1960s.

Yet it is fair to say that these various past efforts were disjointed and had no unifying theme such as "choice." Nor did they enjoy broadly based support cutting across ideological differences and partisan group interests. Vouchers and tax credits raised time-worn debates that long have surrounded aid to private schools—whether such aid is constitutional, whether it will harm the nation, and in particular whether it will erode public school support and quality. Magnet and specialty schools initially were associated with racial desegregation; while they were efforts to avoid controversial "forced busing" (as critics were wont to label such policies), these schools generated new controversies about "creaming" that sustained criticism of desegregation.

By contrast, choice has become appealing in recent years for at least two reasons. First, its link to private school aid (objectionable to the political left) and to desegregation (resisted by the political right) has been blurred. Now "choice" frequently refers to reform within the public school sector. It may have little to do with racial desegregation, as exemplified by some magnet schools and by cross-district open-enrollment plans. This reformulation of choice permitted it to be defended on terms appealing to a wide (although by no means universal) spectrum of ideologies and a broad range of public opinion; it became an egalitarian extension of the principle of local control—itself tainted by income inequality because access to good schools depends on resources for housing—devolved to the level of the family. To be sure, the political left still is wary of choice as possibly leading to inequality, but thus far its reservations have not coalesced into open hostility to the concept.

A second reason why choice is more popular than in the past is that this reformulation has been executed within the context of the public school reform movement. This movement has lent more urgency to the proposals, and, indeed, has given them more legitimacy, as they have come from powerful organizations such as the National Governors' Association. The Reagan administration in its second term of office turned away from aid to private schools as a principal advocacy and endorsed public school reform. By its end and the advent of the Bush administration, choice had re-emerged as a major strategy for public school reform, devoid of the private school aid issue. It has been labeled "restructuring" by the Bush administration.

Yet if choice is restructuring, what about earlier efforts to define restructuring as teacher professionalization and teacher empowerment, associated with the so-called second wave of educational reform? The National Governors' Association clearly advanced choice as part of this second wave, conceiving of it as a complement to other restructuring efforts.

On their side, the actual producers of public schools, represented by professional associations, school boards, and the like, have learned to accommodate and in some instances endorse teacher professionalism and school empowerment but remain cautious in their reaction to choice as a restructuring goal. Concerns over equity often are mentioned. Less frequently admitted is that choice would challenge the quasi-monopoly structure of present schooling arrangements. So while choice has enjoyed growing popularity, and has few ardent opponents, it has yet to win support from all educational interests.

The belated inclusion of choice proposals on the platter of educational reform raises an important problem that is the central focus of this chapter. From a social planning as well as political perspective, how does choice fit within this larger reform agenda? Will the addition of choice as still another course on an already quite full reform menu prove incompatible with other reforms or, on the contrary, will it complement and even strengthen restructuring efforts?

Thus, while choice has emerged as an appealing reform platform because of a vagueness of conception, it is far from evident that the current political success of choice, even if the concept persists, will lead to genuine reform of U.S. schools. In order to understand both the opportunities and the limits operative here, we must begin by more clearly defining both choice and restructuring.

THE PARAMETERS OF RESTRUCTURING

The reform movement has evolved through a number of phases. Initially it focused on improving the quality of the teaching force and raising educational standards. Many states passed comprehensive, omnibus legislation to address the many facets of these two dimensions, and numerous states also have passed a second round of legislation to strengthen (and occasionally repeal) these provisions affecting such diverse matters as teacher certification, salaries, class size, course and graduation standards, student testing, and the minutes, hours, and days of instruction.

Although attention to these aspects of reform is by no means exhausted, or their goals wholly achieved, recently a new focus has emerged, somewhat ambiguously labeled "restructuring." The term appears to have been borrowed from business (hardly an unprecedented development), which has been much preoccupied in the last decade with how to restructure U.S. industry to make it more competitive in the global economy, as well as with mergers, leveraged buyouts, and related processes for restructuring ownership. The language of restructuring also applies to nation-states, principally *perestroika* and *glasnost* in the Soviet Union. Thus, restructuring is applied widely to mean different things in diverse contexts.

Elements of restructuring have been present in the educational reform movement from the start, to be sure. Numerous states passed legislation experimenting with or mandating restructuring of the teaching profession through such devices as career ladders and merit pay. A small number at first (more now) offered encouragement for experimentation with site-based management, or as it is sometimes referred to, "collaborative school management" (Caldwell and Spinks, 1988). Now, however, these devices are being advocated as the necessary path of educational reform.

Precisely what restructuring consists of no one seems to know, or at least a consensus definition has not emerged. Yet its starting premise is that the entire delivery system for U.S. elementary and secondary education must be redesigned. This premise represents a departure from the assumptions undergirding the first wave of reforms, where incremental (although multifaceted) reforms were sought. For a decade or more, U.S. educators have focused on school improvement efforts, aided in many states by funds and technical assistance. Yet restructuring moves beyond improvement. As David (1987) puts it, structural change is a puzzle with interlocking parts. Operating on isolated pieces is not sufficient, because the parts of a social system are interdependent.

This revelation is hardly new, having been well established in change theory for decades and, in fact, having influenced educational reform efforts of the 1960s. Why do Americans find it necessary to relearn what they already knew? There seem to be three answers to this question. First, the powerful are telling the educational establishment that incremental change is not sufficient. Restructuring has been advocated by progressive elements in the nation's business and political establishment, such as the Carnegie Forum on Education and the

Economy, the Committee for Economic Development, and the National Governors' Association. Some elements of the educational establishment—particularly the American Federation of Teachers, led by Albert Shanker—also advocate restructuring.

The second reason is the evidence concerning the relatively poor performance of U.S. youth. Such evidence indicates that neither the best pupils in the United States nor the average ones perform well in international math and science comparisons. Employers continue to complain about poorly prepared youth lacking basic literacy skills. Also, concern has mounted about the estimated 29 percent dropout rate in the United States, which poses a problem for employers already facing labor shortages in coming years due to the nation's aging population. Indeed, this evidence provides the basis for the arguments advanced by such groups as the Carnegie Forum and the nation's governors that the first wave of reforms so far has produced inadequate fruits. It animates their conviction that a more radical approach is required.

A third reason for the interest in restructuring is that the educational establishment, both practitioners and researchers, obviously has been unable to offer conventional solutions that are convincing to the business and political establishment or to the concerned public more generally. Educators turned their backs on radical reform in the 1970s and early 1980s, repudiating the advocacies of the 1960s as too extreme. Even black educators such as Ronald Edmonds asserted that we know what needs to be done to educate poor children successfully, and offered straightforward prescriptions that launched the school effectiveness efforts that spread across the nation's landscape. Some educators, such as the controversial former Secretary of Education William Bennett, argued that the solutions to U.S. education are simple.

Most advocates of restructuring, by contrast, while not repudiating all the lessons of recent decades (for example, the importance of focusing reform at the school level), are no longer convinced that the answers are reducible to a uniform response such as the school effectiveness movement embodies, or to piecemeal change such as school improvement programs have typified. Thus, the lessons learned two decades ago about the need for a systemic perspective when advancing educational reform enjoy renewed currency today.

Those who advocate restructuring fall into four somewhat overlapping groups. First, individual school systems are experimenting. This development is still very scattered, but significant innovations are underway, and some of these self-initiated efforts are being studied closely as possible prototypes. Second, foundations, businesses, or universities are working with some school systems or with other organizations such as the Education Commission of the States and the National Governors' Association to sponsor restructured schools projects. Some of these groups, such as Carl Marburger's National Committee of Citizens in Education, have specific advocacies, such as the inclusion of parents in restructuring. Third, individual unions or professional associations such as the American Federation of Teachers and the National Education Association are sponsoring restructuring projects. Finally, states themselves are encouraging such efforts. And although the direct efforts of the U.S. Department of Education in restructuring have been somewhat peripheral, it too has been somewhat involved.

RESTRUCTURING STRATEGIES

Restructuring is likely to be an evolving concept, and it is likely to continue to mean many different things, depending on state and local contexts and values. I distinguish between *core strategies* and *ancillary strategies* for restructuring. Core strategies are almost universally accepted as key elements by restructuring advocates (but are obviously less accepted by critics). Ancillary strategies are those that are advocated by some restructuring proponents, but opposed or simply ignored by many others.

CORE RESTRUCTURING STRATEGIES

Let us first turn to the core strategies.

Core Strategy 1: Teacher Professionalization. Restructuring advocates argue that until teaching becomes more of a profession, it will not attract or retain a highly qualified teaching force. Professionalization requires improved salaries, more opportunities for advancement within the teaching ranks, and improved working conditions.

Core Strategy 2: School Empowerment. A process of empowerment at the school level is linked to Strategy 1 because it is arguably one way to improve working conditions for teachers. Accordingly, school empowerment must reach beyond the principal to include teachers. Some reform advocates wish to empower other stakeholders at the school level, such as parents, students, and interested community members. Consequently, the concept of school empowerment leaves open the question of precisely who at the school level is to be empowered. Models of school-based management sometimes emphasize teacher control, others stress client control, while still others are hybrids. Further, some school empowerment plans look a great deal like administrative decentralizaton or regional decentralization, as these reforms were attempted twenty years ago in America's larger, urban school systems, now with the added emphasis of school-level accountability.

Core Strategy 3: Higher-Order Thinking Skills. Restructuring advocates argue that the curriculum and teaching in schools must be radically redirected to emphasize higher-order thinking skills. The details of this agenda are only now being worked out, as is evidenced by the recent revamping of the Scholastic Aptitude Test (SAT).

Initially, higher-order thinking skills were thought to apply to the intellectually most able youth. The concept has evolved, however, in a more inclusive direction; the targets of restructuring increasingly are defined as the whole spectrum of students—the underachievers, the average, and the intellectually able.

Core Strategy 4: Dropout Prevention. As public attention has focused on the high rate of failure and dropping out in inner-city public schools, abetted by the concern of business over an impending labor shortage, reformers have extended restructuring goals to this problem. The range of solutions explored move beyond higher-order thinking skills to include preschool education, early remediation, parent education, and other strategies. Many of these are not new, but they are being examined within a context of changing roles, rules, and responsibilities.

Restructuring is a process, in other words, that is intended to lead to important improvement in the outcomes of the educational system through dramatic changes in instruction as well as in management and governance. The concept leaves unspecified which elements of the delivery system must be altered, but they could include the length of time students are in school, the content of the curriculum, the nature of student-teacher interaction, and a veritable host of other possibilities. These strategies are presumed to be interlocking. Strategies 3 (higher-order thinking skills) and 4 (dropout prevention), for instance, are said to require successful implementation of Strategies 1 (teacher professionalization) and 2 (school empowerment). One example frequently offered is that teachers cannot be expected to convey higher-order thinking skills to their charges if the conditions of work in schools neither provide nor reward opportunities for teachers themselves to model these skills.

ANCILLARY RESTRUCTURING STRATEGIES

The ancillary strategies are as follows.

Ancillary Strategy 1: Performance Incentives. Some reformers argue that any reward that is extrinsic to individuals or organizations—such as money or even praise—cannot be restructuring, since restructured systems are supposedly self-motivating. Yet performance incentives do represent an alternative to state mandates that rely solely on regulatory authority. As motivational tools, incentives shift attention from negative to positive inducements. They may be used as an adjunct to mandates or as a purely voluntary device. Many educators have associated incentives with employee reward systems such as merit pay. Partly because of their unpopularity, other approaches to performance incentives emphasize rewards to entire organizational units such as schools (Cibulka, 1989). Thus, the merit schools concept was a major centerpiece in George Bush's promise to be the "education President."

Ancillary Strategy 2: Deregulation. Recently there has been a growing interest in removing state and federal regulations from schools, either as a reward for being meritorious or as an incentive to become so. This is an analogue at the intergovernmental level to school empowerment within local educational authorities; school-based management sometimes requires waivers of school board policies and union-management contracts. State and federal waivers follow the same principle. Some reform proposals merely would deregulate schools that already are performing well by testing or accreditation standards.

Ancillary Strategy 3: Accountability Reporting. A policy development that preceded the recent language about restructuring is the increasing use of standardized tests by states and the federal government to make comparisons among schools and school districts. It is possible to argue that this approach seeks explicitly or implicitly to standardize content and routinize teaching, and therefore runs counter to restructuring aims. Yet the opposite argument can be made as well. Test comparisons may reduce regulation of schools around process goals and free them to compete around comparable outcomes. Without accountability reporting, consumer information on which to make school comparisons may be limited and anecdotal.

CHOICE: A CORE OR ANCILLARY REFORM STRATEGY?

As I stated earlier, choice has emerged as a popular reform strategy. Whether it will become a central element of reform (a core strategy) or will be at the periphery of reform (an ancillary strategy winning only partial acceptance) is a matter that has yet to unfold. The outcome depends principally on the willingness of the producers of public education as well as the political left (whose interests on this matter hardly are identical) to accommodate this concept. The many possible configurations that choice arrangements can take make it a potentially adaptable concept capable of incorporating diverse interests. In this section, I review some of the variations available within choice as a reform strategy, returning in a later section to its link to restructuring.

The core of any choice arrangement is to assure that consumers will be able to exercise a preference for a type of school. Institutional arrangements that constrain this goal are many. Highly centralized educational systems may offer a uniform diet for all patrons, while decentralized systems such as that in the United States may have many choices that are not equally available to all consumers. These different national contexts mean that the goal of improving consumer choice will require quite different reform strategies. In the United

States, for example, the central problem of any choice plan is to decouple consumer demand for schools from housing demand. At present the consumers with choice are those who can move among jurisdictions until they can find a school system, and even a particular school within that system, that matches their preferences. In practice, moving requires resources that are not evenly distributed by social class and race. Further, the transaction costs of residential relocation may be too high even for those with resources. Thus, U.S. choice proposals are intended to reduce these barriers by allowing consumers more easily to demand schools independent of their residential choice. There are a variety of ways to accomplish this goal, as illustrated by the various choice plans discussed later. Regardless of the plan, however, it must alter one or more of a limited set of parameters. Governments can control, or at least influence, the degree of choice available to citizens by controlling or regulating the supply of schools, pricing arrangements, variations in services and quality available at these schools, and access to quality schools. Restructuring efforts to expand choice potentially address all these dimensions, although as we shall see, most current restructuring proposals are sharply confined.

The Supply of Schools

If all schools are owned and operated by a central government, it will control supply, and standardization normally follows. The existence of multiple governments that are planning for and operating schools, as in federal systems, introduces a bit more consumer choice, because supply decisions will be made in a more decentralized manner than the first example. The availability of private schools opens still a different avenue for choice, because some supply decisions will be made by private (or nonprofit) providers in response to market demand. Along this dimension, it is possible to envision a system in which governments have no role in owning schools or regulating private ones such that suppliers respond to demand entirely through market arrangements. Thus, governments can influence the supply of schools, and hence consumer choice, in two ways: first, by the degree of centralization of the system, and, second, through the government's regulatory policies toward public and private school suppliers. In this second area of regulation, government either can attempt to reduce barriers for entry into the market by private schools, or it can constrain the ability of government schools to ignore consumer demand by limiting supply of schools. (School officials typically do this by rationing the number of schools in high demand and forcing consumers to "choose" underused [unpopular] schools.)

Pricing Arrangements

As governments have taken over ownership and operation of schools, typically they finance them through tax revenues rather than user fees, on the theory that education is a public good. Tax support, however, removes a degree of control from the consumer. Although as a taxpayer the consumer may influence the cost of supplying education, as an individual consumer there is no longer an opportunity to use money to purchase a particular bundle of services at the school level. With respect to costs, schools are responsible to the collectivity of taxpayers, not to individual consumers. Where consumers have direct control over pricing, they can more effectively influence the cost as well as the quality of education.

Variations in Service and Quality

Most economists view variety in the supply of private goods as the advantage of market arrangements, because consumer preferences are assumed to vary, both with respect to quantity and quality desired. Many economists view it as desirable that quality gradations are permitted, arguing that this favors efficiency for the individual consumer and for society.

Government laws and regulations, legal decisions, and labor-management agreements all have the effect of introducing greater uniformity in cost and quality, normally in order to remedy a perceived inequity associated with variation. The cost of these efforts, it is argued, has been to reduce experimentation and responsiveness to consumer needs. The purpose of choice plans is to expand consumer access to the variety that already exists among schools and districts and to encourage the development of more variation where it is demanded by consumers.

Consumer Access to Quality Schools

In its narrow confines, microeconomic theory does not concern itself with inequitable purchasing power by consumers. Another branch of economic theory addresses the issue of income distribution. Yet these two concerns cannot be so easily separated in the case of education, which is in some respects a public good benefiting the entire society and which is a constitutional guarantee in American states. Thus, a truly comprehensive strategy to improve consumer choice would begin with the recognition that existing differences in quality do not necessarily reflect consumer preferences but instead lack of options, and that consumers begin with unequal resources (such as time, information, and communication skills). Choice schemes that ignore these initial differences in the consumption process (even where purchasing power is equalized) may merely exacerbate existing inequities as efforts are made to introduce some market elements into traditionally government-provided services. A variety of approaches can be taken to address this problem—income redistribution, fiscal policy (particularly revenue distribution schemes), tax policy, regulatory approaches directed at school officials, or technical assistance approaches addressed to helping consumers, such as parent information and education.

A Brief Taxonomy of Choice Arrangements

In practice, the current interest in improving consumer choice has not drawn fully on the policy options available to governments, as just described. A somewhat narrower range of options has been under discussion. Figure 3-1 distinguishes among various kinds of choice arrangements that have been proposed.

We exclude from our concern totally private schooling arrangements with all-private funding—a pattern that once existed in many countries but that is nearly, if not totally, extinct throughout the world today. If governments choose to create some arrangement of state support for schools, they need not create and operate such schools, merely fund them in part or full. For purposes of building this taxonomy, we will maintain the distinction between public support and government operation, because it has implications for the amount of choice available to consumers under particular institutional arrangements. Therefore, the reader will note on the far right side of

Public Only	Public-Private	Private Only
Intradistrict	Vouchers	
Interdistrict	Opting out	
	New management of existing schools	
	Forming new schools	

Figure 3-1
Choice Arrangements Under Public Funding

Figure 3-1 that "Private Only" is meant to designate a publicly subsidized yet privately operated system.

On the left side of Figure 3-1, we note that one type of choice is "Public Only." Two variations exist. Intradistrict plans create magnet or specialty schools available as an alternative to traditional neighborhood attendance area schools. Where these schools have racial quotas to achieve desegregation, they frequently are referred to as "controlled choice" plans (Alves and Willie, 1987). Interdistrict plans, such as Minnesota's open-enrollment plan, give consumers access to schools outside their school district; these cross-district plans may include access to traditional attendance area or specialty schools.

Some choice plans can be labeled "Public-Private" because they give consumers access to private schools. Voucher plans would permit consumers to select from a range of government-owned as well as private schools. Opportunities to "opt out" of the locally available public school are a kind of public-private arrangement. In Denmark, if a majority of parents is dissatisfied with the local school, those parents can form a new one with government funding. In Great Britain, under the Educational Reform Act of 1988, a majority of the parents can vote to opt out of the existing local educational authority and receive central government funding as a grant-maintained school.

To understand how these reforms would improve consumer choice, see Table 3-1. It indicates how, if at all, each reform would affect the four parameters introduced earlier—supply of schools, pricing, variation in services, and equitable access for consumers.

All the plans attempt to give the consumer greater variation in services (although not necessarily quality). Some choice proposals

Table 3-1
How Reform Proposals Improve Consumer Choice

Reform	Supply	Parameter Altered Pricing	Variation	Equal Access
Intradistrict specialty and magnet schools			x	(x)
Interdistrict			x	
Vouchers	x	x	x	(x)
Opting out	x	x	x	
Private only	x	x	x	

Note: Parentheses (x) indicate that this parameter may be addressed in some plans.

would address the supply aspect of the arrangements. Vouchers presumably would increase the supply of private schools due to the new subsidy they would bring, and possibly vouchers would change the supply of government schools as they attempt to compete with private schools and with one another. Opting out is a direct way to increase supply by allowing consumers to form or maintain a school independent of traditional government controls. The Thatcher government in England hopes that new opportunities for opting out, combined with a system of enrollment caps and funding, may lead to the closing of underused schools, thus decreasing total supply while also improving consumer choice as new schools are demanded. Finally, a publicly funded, privately run system would aim to allow fluctuation of supply to correspond to demand. There are other devices for attempting to introduce choice through a "supply-side" strategy. One not mentioned specifically in Figure 3-1—because it is not commonly proposed—is reduced government regulation of private schools. This policy reform would tend to reduce barriers for suppliers, and most likely would increase the supply of schools.

The more "radical" choice plans in the bottom half of Figure 3-1, when compared with the intradistrict and interdistrict plans, also would reform pricing decisions by decentralizing them at least partly to the consumer level.

It is less clear how any of these plans incorporate guarantees for equity in the consumption process. Magnet and specialty school plans sometimes provide parent information about the choices available, although not typically intensive education on how to make an intelligent choice of a school and how to be an effective consumer once the choice is made. Some voucher proposals, for example, address this problem while others ignore it.

RESTRUCTURING FOR WHAT PURPOSE?

I turn now to a crucial issue in discussions of choice plans and restructuring in general. What are the legitimating principles used by proponents of restructuring to defend their reforms?

Choice advocates speak of "liberty" and "responsiveness." It is inferred that greater responsiveness will improve the system. There are several possibilities. The system may become more technically efficient; that is, productive. It may become more allocatively efficient with respect to costs. It may become more equitable. Productivity and, more recently, equity have been the principal rationales used in the core restructuring proposals discussed earlier.

On reflection, it is clear that various choice proposals do not uniformly maximize responsiveness, technical efficiency (productivity), allocative efficiency (cost), and equity. Plans with pricing arrangements are intended to make the educational system more cost-efficient. The extent to which any of the plans would improve productivity is unclear, but we can speculate, based on information about current intradistrict and interdistrict plans. There is little evidence that these existing plans have created dramatic improvement in student achievement. In the case of magnet and specialty programs in urban schools, the principal reason seems to be that these programs affect only a small portion of the student population. Where many other schools remain "poor," the improvements are not available to all youngsters. This situation complicates the task of improving magnet schools themselves, because under such conditions there is a greater tendency for some parents to choose the schools for custodial reasons (safety) rather than for reasons relating to the quality of the academic program. We need not elaborate on the fact that choice plans that limit the supply of good schools also aggravate already existing quality gradations among the schools. This development runs directly counter to the equity goals of controlled-choice plans with desegregation goals.

Interdistrict plans are likely to have limited impact on improving productivity because of the limited numbers of consumers who thus far have chosen to participate (Bennett, 1989). Opting-out plans, however, eliminate entire schools from the control of school officials. Therefore, they create an incentive for these officials to become more responsive in order to preserve resources, jobs, and respectability. Whether those schools that opt out will become more productive and cost-efficient depends on the goals of patrons who opt out, unless government officials hold them accountable through regulatory or fiscal means.

More dramatic choice plans, such as vouchers, strive to place control over choice in the hands of all consumers, not merely those who are dissatisfied. Therefore, they represent a more systematic attempt to improve productivity through competitive market devices. Yet the greater are the opportunities for improved productivity, the more the potential sacrifice to equity goals—since improvement of equity for some consumers could well be obtained only at a net cost to other consumers. This is a balancing act, to be sure.

In short, choice proposals, like other restructuring plans, often beg the question of what purpose they serve. The perfect choice proposal—responsive, productive, cost-efficient, and equitable—has yet to be designed. Better (even if not perfect) proposals undoubtedly can be developed, but they will require careful thought about how they will advance or impede these values.

RECONCILING CHOICE WITH OTHER RESTRUCTURING STRATEGIES

If a particular choice plan is likely to be a compromise among different legitimating principles, the same tradeoffs may well operate with respect to the relation between choice and other restructuring strategies.

Consider the potential compatibility between choice and teacher professionalization (Core Strategy 1). Choice cuts both ways with respect to this goal. Strong market competition among schools— particularly in plans that give more decision-making power over price to consumers, and where certification standards are loosened to create hiring flexibility for school officials and to alleviate teacher supply shortages—would tend to drive down teachers' salaries. Pushing in the opposite direction would be the incentives a market system would create to find more cost-effective instruction, through such devices as career ladders. Such incentives could improve the status and salaries of teachers who attain "master" rank or some equivalent. Thus, your conclusions about whether choice favors teacher professionalization depend on your assumptions about what changes (salaries, roles, or both) will foster professionalization. It should be pointed out, of course, that bland choice plans that avoid creating competition over price among schools are unlikely to have any impact on teacher professionalization.

The relation between school empowerment (Core Strategy 2) and choice is less equivocal. There are different ways to define the concept of site-based management, but in any case choice seems to complement this strategy. Some site-based management plans enhance the authority of school principals and staffs but not parents. In that case, choice offers the consumer some additional influence—a market veto, so to speak. A different approach to site-based management gives power to parents and community members, in collaboration with the principal and staff. Hirschman (1970) observed that consumer voice works best where there are ways for the dissatisfied consumer to leave; the two are not so much alternatives as they are complementary strategies in this second approach to site-based management. Hence, choice would seem to strengthen school empowerment restructuring strategies.

Will choice abet the teaching of higher-order thinking skills and dropout prevention goals (Core Strategies 3 and 4)? The outcome would seem to depend very much on the nature of the choice plan in question. Without greatly improved accountability reporting (Ancillary Strategy 3), consumers would have difficulty evaluating whether higher-order thinking skills were being taught in their school of choice. Little evidence suggests that choice plans in operation today—or hypothetical ones, either—would unlock the arcane mysteries of the curriculum and instructional process to most parents. A strategy of parent education, alongside more sophisticated accountability reporting, would be necessary before choice truly could generate pressure for improved teaching of higher-order thinking skills.

Whether choice would reduce the nation's appalling dropout rate seems a more straightforward matter in one respect—it is quite easy to identify school failure in the form of dropping out, easier than it is to know whether higher-order thinking skills are being taught well.

Yet the question arising here is whether the parents of potential dropouts can be induced to use choice arrangements to demand better schools. Skeptics argue that they will not, causing the least able and motivated to be congregated in the worst schools to an extent even greater than today. Whether this dire scenario would actually develop depends first, on how equitably a particular choice plan is designed, and second, on how much faith one has in the educability of the poor.

Choice is potentially very compatible with two ancillary strategies: performance incentives and deregulation. (Accountability reporting already has been discussed briefly.) A choice plan that works well will bring status and resources to schools that prove successful; this reward is a performance incentive *par excellence*. Indeed, a choice arrangement might eliminate any need for monetary incentives, which are bureaucratic substitutes for market incentives.

Deregulation is quite consistent with choice plans, as has already been implied. Choice requires greater school autonomy. Yet some degree of regulation in the interests of equity and, arguably, quality would continue to be called for. Constraints on admissions decisions and pricing would be two obvious places where some degree of government regulation in a choice plan could be defended, even as other aspects of school operations, such as curriculum and staffing, were deregulated from bureaucratic oversight. Deregulation, in other words, probably never would be absolute, but if it were applied selectively, it would be quite complementary to choice as a reform strategy.

CONCLUSION

This analysis has demonstrated that choice and restructuring take many forms. When choice is addressed as a restructuring strategy, the degree to which it would accomplish some legitimating goals, such as greater productivity, cost-efficiency, or equity, depends on specific parameters in the plans themselves. Whichever plan is singled out, though, it can be seen readily that some of the legitimating goals, not surprisingly, are in tension if not conflict. Some choice arrangements have great potential for improving productivity and cost-efficiency, but at an inequity cost that many Americans find unacceptably high.

Choice has been tacked on to a pre-existing reform agenda, most notably recent efforts to restructure U.S. schools. This incremental approach to policymaking is nothing new in the United States. Problems of logical consistency among the elements of restructuring abound; we identified no fewer that seven core and ancillary restructuring strategies, and choice adds an eighth. If we ask how these all fit together, the answer is that they do not. At best they are loosely coupled; at worst, sometimes contradictory. On the positive side, choice extends the emphasis on school empowerment and deregulation already in restructuring efforts. Yet choice *may* prove problematic for teacher professionalization. Further, choice may do little to assist programmatic reforms such as teaching higher-order thinking as well as reducing the number of dropouts; indeed, some fear exists that choice may aggravate the latter goal. Whether this fear is exaggerated is not easily resolved. So far the reform movement has not increased the dropout rate and has even reduced it marginally for some at-risk groups such as Hispanics.

What this analysis suggests is that a shotgun approach to reform, so characteristic of Americans in the past and once again being played out, is very risky indeed. If we want to succeed in our current reforms, we must think more carefully about how to maximize the interdependent elements in these educational reform strategies rather than approaching them piecemeal.

Restructuring is an encouraging step beyond our nation's previous preoccupation with incremental educational reform. Yet if restructuring suggests the need for a comprehensive intervention, it is also true that the task of defining how its parameters interlock and reinforce one another has barely begun. Recent discussions of choice show some danger signals that we have stepped on still another bandwagon. There is much potential in this newest addition to the reform agenda, but choice will accomplish little without very careful planning.

The stakes are very high this time if we fail to reform our schools effectively, both for our children's future well-being and that of our nation.

REFERENCES

Alves, Michael J., and Willie, Charles V. "Controlled Choice Assignments: A New Approach to Desegregation," *Urban Review* 19 (1987): 67–86.

Bennett, David A. "Choice and Desegregation." Paper presented at the Conference on Choice and Control in American Education, Madison, Wisconsin, 1989.

Caldwell, Brian J., and Spinks, J. M. *The Self-managing School.* New York: Falmer Press, 1988.

Cibulka, James G. "State Performance Incentives for Restructuring: Can They Work?" *Education and Urban Society* 21 (August 1989): 417–435.

David, Jane L. "The Puzzle of Structural Change." Paper presented at the Symposium on Structural Change in Secondary Education, National Center on Effective Secondary Schools, Palo Alto, California, 1987.

Friedman, Milton. "The Role of Government in Education." In *Economics and the Public Interest,* ed. Robert A. Solo. New Brunswick, NJ: Rutgers University Press, 1955.

Hirschman, A. L. *Exit, Loyalty, and Voice.* Cambridge, MA: Harvard University Press, 1970.

CHAPTER 4

Parent Choice in Four Nations

Charles L. Glenn

This brief overview—based on a much more extensive series of papers prepared for the Office for Educational Research and Improvement—considers parent choice of schools in four nations of special interest for U.S. policymakers.

It is to France that we owe the "myth of the common school," the school sponsored and controlled by the nation in order to shape future citizens to a single set of political loyalties, and it was in the Netherlands that this program was most successfully challenged in the name of parent choice of schools for their children (see Glenn, 1988). Recent controversy in both countries has brought parent choice back into the political agenda.

Great Britain has been, of all Western democracies, least concerned to use government-operated schooling to achieve national unity, though in the postwar period British education was profoundly reshaped in the interest of reducing social inequalities. The Thatcher government has made a strong effort to promote more parent choice, in the name of promoting efficiency through competition. In Canada, by contrast, the extension of parent choice has been in response to religious and language diversity.

FRANCE

Conflict over the control of education, and over its content, has surfaced in ever new forms in France for the past two hundred years. It was in France that the Jacobins—the party that gained control of the French Revolution in 1792 and unleashed the Terror—enacted the first educational legislation of modern times based on radical principles: that the child belonged to the state, that parents were if anything a hindrance to the state's mission of shaping its future citizens, and that the Church was a bitter enemy of the state because of its rival claim to educate. In the 1880s the French government, calling directly on the Jacobin precedent, carried out an aggressive program of penetrating every village to undermine the influence of parish priests (seen as antirepublican and a hindrance to progress) with that of schoolteachers, those "Jesuits in short coats."

When French president François Mitterand met, in 1977, with representatives of those elements in the Catholic Church anxious to achieve a breakthrough in their relationship with the Socialists, he was told that

> the education question is carved into this country as the last symbol of the confrontation between two Frances; it remains the irritating obstacle that prevents the resolution of the last differences between the Left and the Church. (Leclerc, 1985, p. 15)

Mitterand had no olive branch to offer; he considered the supporters of Catholic education to be stubborn adversaries. The policy of the Socialist Party was and would continue to be that France needed a single system of education, expressing a secular world view. True to his word, Mitterand's government moved, in the early 1980s, to extend its control over publicly funded private schooling and so precipitated a political crisis that contributed to the Socialist defeat in the 1986 elections.

The special resonance of controversies over education and parent choice in France—and, from France, to much of the world—can be understood only from a historical perspective. The successive French republics, often facing an internal opposition and lacking the easy legitimacy of a monarchy, made claims on the minds and hearts of "their" children that could accept no rival claims by the Church. In the 1880s and subsequently, the Third Republic made a concerted effort to gain a monopoly of popular schooling. The Church it faced made far more absolute claims than did the established Protestant churches of England or the German states. Conflict was inevitable.

The basis for the present system of public funding in France was created by the *Loi Debré*, adopted at the start of the Fifth Republic in 1959, while the *Loi Guérmeur* of 1977 extended it further. These were perceived as "so many defeats for the secular camp." A further blow to opponents of support for private schools in 1977 was a ruling that there was no constitutional barrier to a secular government funding confessional education.

The *Loi Debré* created a number of alternatives for nonpublic schools: (1) to continue completely independent of government intervention, subject to employing qualified teachers; (2) to be absorbed into the national public education system; (3) to accept government requirements as to curriculum and testing in exchange for staff salaries (*contrat simple*); and (4) to accept, in addition, some government control over pedagogy and the selection of teachers, in exchange for operating expenses as well as salaries (*contrat d'association*). (See Savary, 1985, pp. 35–38.)

The *Loi Guérmeur* strengthened the independence of private schools under contract by giving the principal the power to initiate the hiring of staff who would be paid with public funds, subject to government confirmation. This power makes it possible to refuse to consider teachers whose convictions do not correspond to the school's identity. Private schools are in a sense placed in a more favorable position than public schools, which are subject to a highly centralized and bureaucratic process of assigning staff. The largest (and politically potent) national federation of forty-nine teaching unions, the Federation de l'Education Nationale (FEN), has been strongly opposed to this provision, since it has far more opportunity to exercise its influence in a centralized personnel system. The requirement that teachers agree with the purposes of a private school limits the job opportunities for its 400,000 members, three-quarters of all French teachers.

On the Catholic side, there has been a persistent suspicion that government funding would lead to increasing government control, with private schools carried irresistibly into the public system by a sort of escalator effect. This suspicion was stated as a demand by the secular forces in 1959: "If the private sector is destined to receive State aid, it is appropriate that it be subjected to the financial, administrative, and pedagogical control" of the national Ministry of Education (Leclerc, 1985, pp. 72–73). This expectation forms a continuing theme and is the background of the crisis in the early 1980s.

The political compromises enacted in these statutes were threatened in 1981 with the election of Socialist François Mitterand as president. In his campaign, Mitterand had called for "a great national public education service, unified and secular," including "all establishments and all staff."

The victories for confessional schooling had been bitterly opposed. The secular teacher unions and other powerful groups formed, in 1953, the National Committee for Anticlerical Action (CNAL), an umbrella organization that has continued to be closely associated with the parties of the Left; their petition against the *Loi Debré* collected ten million signatures. The goal of the CNAL has continued to be "to bring together in a common school, in the name of science and of brotherhood, all the children of the one Fatherland, thus cementing French unity and preparing that of humanity." Thus their program was not simply to prevent funding to private schools but indeed their nationalization into a single state-controlled system (Leclerc, 1985, p. 63).

Typical of attitudes in the anticlerical camp toward confessional schooling is the statement of Jean Cornec—long-time leader of a parent organization dedicated to secular education—to an applauding rally in 1977 that "the Catholic hierarchy has never ceased to reduce mankind to a state of slavery, to oppress ideas, to limit freedom" (Leclerc, 1985, p. 27). Thus appeals to "educational freedom" on behalf of Catholic schooling were dismissed as antithetical to the true freedom that could be assured only by government-operated schooling. The laws providing public funding to private schools should be repealed immediately (Savary, 1985, p. 206).

The initial proposals of the new government, advanced by Minister of National Education Alain Savary, aroused tremendous resistance from those committed to Catholic education. These proposals included the appointment of principals and of teachers by the government, the training of teachers exclusively in public institutions, and the strict application of attendance zones to private (as to public) schools. These changes would mean the end of the Christian character of private schools, charged the supporters of Catholic schools.

French public opinion was favorable to the continued independence of private schools, and less than one voter in four wanted to see state financial aid discontinued. The organization of parents of students in private schools, the National Union of Parent Associations for Free Education (UNAPEL), had nearly a million members, easily mobilized in defense of continued subsidies and against any intrusions on the prized independence of its schools. Its anticlerical counterpart, the CNAL, made its own efforts to mobilize supporters, but was not able to bring out more than some three hundred thousand—itself no mean number for an essentially negative position.

A survey in 1983 found that 51 percent of those questioned were prepared to sign a petition in support of private education, compared with 28 percent who would sign in support of a single unified system. Curiously, 30 percent of the Communist supporters and 35 percent of the Socialists indicated support for private education. Two years earlier, 81 percent of the French people surveyed supported free choice of schools, with 30 percent in favor of making the government funding even more generous to make private education completely cost-free (Leclerc, 1985, pp. 196, 103).

The supporters of Catholic education were alarmed by Savary's proposals. Once their schools were absorbed into a vast system of state education, how could they preserve their identity and thus their purpose? They were not opposed to national unity, of course, but as Fr. Guiberteau pointed out, "this unity is fashioned from diversity and not from the totalitarianism of a public system in which we would not be able to express ourselves." After all, a Catholic school is not simply like any other, with a chaplain added; it involves a "global choice, a will to transmit everything that is specific to Christianity through a climate of Gospel values" (Leclerc, 1985, p. 107).

Selection of school directors and staff by the public education authorities and the training of all teachers in public institutions would surely destroy the Christian character of Catholic schools. It was certainly true that the principals of public schools could not select their teaching staff, but it was difficult to see how the distinctive identity of a private school could be maintained without that right.

The specific identity (*caractère propre*) of Catholic schools was clearly at the heart of the issue. The National Committee for Catholic Education (CNEC) insisted that this identity must mark all aspects of the life of the school, including the development of skills and knowledge. This insistence required free choice for families, real autonomy for each school, collaboration by the staff of the school in a common educational enterprise (thus implying that they could not be transferred around individually, like public school teachers), choice of the principal and staff, and special training for teachers. For the National Union of Parent Associations for Free Education (UNAPEL), the specific identity of each school represented a sort of moral contract between the staff and the parents who had chosen that school (Savary, 1985, pp. 190–191).

Parent involvement was the key to the eventual defeat of the government's proposals. Private education was well situated in this respect because (unlike, for example, in the Netherlands or Belgium) each private school is dependent on the parents of its students to provide funding for facilities. The 1983 survey just cited found that 62 percent of the private school parents were prepared to demonstrate in support of educational freedom, while only 11 percent of the public school parents felt equally strongly about a unified secular system (Leclerc, 1985, p. 196, note).

Gigantic demonstrations—the last of them bringing more than a million supporters of private schools to the streets of Paris in June 1984 (including 570,000 clocked through the railway stations and others who arrived on nearly six thousand chartered buses)—showed how strongly parents felt about retaining an alternative to the state system of schooling. Although Catholic school supporters formed the backbone of the demonstrations, there was strong representation of Jewish schools as well, together with a hundred thousand students and parents from nonconfessional private schools. The CNAL organized its own massive though rather smaller demonstrations to show the continuing strength of anticlerical sentiment, but nothing could match the outpouring of support for parent choice.

The upshot, in July 1984, was the resignation of Savary and the abandonment of any efforts by the Socialists to change the ground rules for education. For the anticlericals, Leclerc (1985) notes, this was a disaster: "The integration [of private schools into the public system] of which they had always dreamed, even a government of the Left with an abolute majority in the legislature could not implement."

The subsequent defeat of the Socialists in the 1986 elections was attributed, by many observers, to this debacle. One suggested that the orderly river of parents on the pavements of Paris in June 1984 had not sought to overthrow the government but had done something much more damaging: they had simply ignored it (Dutourd, 1985, p. 164).

With two million students and some 150,000 staff, Catholic education in France is not likely to disappear, especially in view of the tremendous show of support in 1984. The question remains, whether or not there is more demand for parent choice and for alternatives to the common public school than there is for explicitly Catholic education as such. To a substantial extent, sophisticated parents exercise choice within a public system that, in the name of unity and equality, has refused to acknowledge its legitimacy. Faced with this reality, the teacher unions have admitted that more flexibility is needed, and the government set in motion a certain number of experiments with the system of attendance zones (Savary, 1985, pp. 32, 55). The question arises, why the concept of distinctive identity (*caractère propre*) could not be applied to public as it is to private schools. To do so would be truly revolutionary, as Leclerc observes, because it would take decentralization to its logical conclusion "in turning our backs once and for all on the old monolithism" of the public education system (1985, p. 161). It would be the ultimate renunciation of the Jacobin dream of molding citizens in a single pattern and to the same set of loyalties and attitudes.

THE NETHERLANDS

Dutch education is generally considered the most highly evolved system of parent choice in the world. It serves as a reference point for both positive and negative arguments about choice in the United States—often with little factual basis.

Educational freedom is written into the Dutch Constitution. Article 208, adopted in 1917, guarantees the freedom to provide education, and explicitly to appoint teachers and select curriculum, with government oversight only with respect to quality and the moral character of the teachers (Akkermans, 1980, p. 9).

A high proportion of students—approximately 70 percent at the elementary level—attend schools operated by nongovernment organizations. In 1980, there were 546,918 (31.4 percent) students in public kindergarten and elementary schools, 492,541 (28.3 percent) in Protestant, 644,684 (37 percent) in Catholic, and 58,775 (3.4 percent) in "neutral" (nonconfessional) private schools.

Under the elementary education law, most recently revised in 1983, schools may receive public subsidy of all operating costs with enrollment levels that, in most nations, would ensure their closing or consolidation. The "average" elementary school has 159 students, with a capacity of 199 and thus a 20 percent excess capacity (James, 1982, p. 24). This is considered a fundamental protection of the right of access to a school with the desired *richting* (denominational or pedagogical character).

In theory, at least, it is simple to start and obtain funding for a new elementary school. Each community (or several together) must develop a plan each year specifying which public and private schools will be funded for the following three years. A private school must be included in the funding plan if its responsible authority can show that it will be attended by a sufficient number of students; this varies according to the size of the community, from 200 students for a community with more than 100,000 inhabitants to 80 students for a community with fewer than 25,000 inhabitants. If no other school is available that provides an education of the same *richting*, these numbers are lower: from 150 down to 60 for the smaller communities, with the national government reserving the right to set the number still lower in special circumstances.

Once approved, a private school must be maintained in the municipal funding plan if it continues to meet minimum enrollment standards. In a community with less than 25,000 inhabitants, a school is threatened with closing if for three years it enrolls fewer than 50 students, but this critical number drops to 30 students if there is no school of the same type within 3 kilometers. In the largest communities, over 100,000, a school will be closed only if its enrollment drops for three years below 80 students, provided that there is no school of the same type within 3 kilometers (Ministerie van Onderwijs en Wetenschappen, 1984: Articles 54–56, 107 of the Elementary Education Law effective August 1985).

In a period of declining enrollments and school closings, it is of considerable importance to determine what in practice is meant by "the same *richting*." The availability of a nearby Catholic school, for example, would permit the closing of another that is underenrolled; no issues seem to have arisen over whether a Catholic school whose religious instruction is based on liberation theology—and there are many in the Netherlands—is equivalent for parents to another that stresses the traditional catechism, or vice versa.

This question of equivalence has arisen repeatedly with respect to Protestant schools, because some 5 percent of them are religiously conservative "Reformational" schools founded in conscious opposition to the perceived laxness of the Protestant-Christian schools (see the section, later, on "distinctiveness"). As early as 1933, the government decided that these groups of schools were in fact not equivalent and that the former had all the rights of a distinct *richting*, but the issue continues to arise as local government seeks to consolidate schools (Koppejan, 1985, p. 96).

More recently the question has arisen, whether a "neutral" private school, one that reflects no single belief or world view but is distinctive only in terms of pedagogy, may be considered equivalent to a public school offering the same program and (by law) committed to the same neutrality. Is there, in other words, a right to such a private school distinct from any issue of conscience? An advisory opinion of the Education Council in May 1985 found that there is such a right, since even the deliberate lack of common convictions can be seen as a "philosophical foundation."

The right also exists to choose among public schools, although local government is permitted by law to establish school attendance districts for public schools in order to promote their efficient use. The law provides that admission to public schools under such circumstances shall be on the basis of the attendance district, unless the parents have given written notice to the municipal authorities that they wish admission to a school in another attendance district (Elementary Education Law, Article 44). In a 1986 judgment based on statements made when the law was adopted, the Council of State found that a municipality had to grant this request (Vroon, 1986).

Some recent proposals have been made to enforce attendance districts in the interest of containing "white flight" in racially changing urban areas, but these have run up against constitutional objections.

Although the freedom to establish (*stichting*) and to give a distinctive character to a school (*richting*) are well protected by law, that of managing instruction (*inrichting*) is more limited by government requirements. The responsible authority manages the financial and personnel affairs of the school, appoints teachers, selects the curriculum and materials, and determines the disciplinary code as well as the role of religious instruction and other optional courses, but it must do so within the framework of extensive government regulation. Some private school advocates feel that this restriction threatens to make the freedom of *richting* meaningless (Jong Ozn., 1984).

The responsibility of government to assure the competence of every school has led to detailed prescription in such areas as the minimum and maximum number of lesson periods a week and their length, the class size norms, the required competence of teachers, their salaries and rights, and the ways in which student achievement is measured at key transition points. Because the government pays all teacher salaries directly and supplements from the responsible authority are not permitted, there is no way of rewarding effort or competence (James, 1982, p. 15).

The consensus among the major political parties in support of school choice has been disturbed by the increasing militancy of the Association for Public Education (VOO), a "propaganda organization for public education" (Leune, 1983, p. 409) representing some four thousand public school associations and parent councils. The VOO has called for a new "school struggle" to sweep away what it considers the outmoded and counterproductive relics of *verzuiling*. In alliance with the union representing educators employed in government-operated schools (ABOP), the VOO has argued that confessional education is neither demanded by parents nor provided by most Catholic and Protestant schools, and presents an obstacle to the "constructive educational policy" that national and local government should be free to pursue in the interest of social justice and equality (Schoten and Wansink, 1984). The VOO argues that a loss of distinctive identity on the part of confessional schools calls into question their claim on public support as an alternative to public and nonsectarian private schools. In contrast with the pattern of recent decades, in which private schooling has been the rule and the government has "filled in" where that failed to meet the needs of particular groups or areas, these advocates of public schooling argue that the government-operated school should become the norm for Dutch education.

An extensive study of the reasons for parent choice has been made in the Utrecht area. Parents were asked about their primary reason for selecting an elementary school. Of 666 sets of parents who responded to the written inquiry, the researchers reported, 70 percent stated that school quality was the most important consideration, and only 22 percent said *richting* was most important. This response seems to suggest that there is an oversupply of religious schooling in the Netherlands (Eck, Groot Antink, and Veraart, 1986). However, this conclusion would be misleading. Many parents who value schooling shaped by a particular religious tradition would nevertheless put quality even higher; indeed, it is striking that as many as 30 percent of the parents were willing to give quality the second place to another school characteristic. A more satisfactory analysis of the strength of motivation would ask what proportion of parents would accept a school at some distance from their home. Considered in this way, the figures suggest a rather different picture: 54 percent of the parents regarded the *richting* of the school as more important than the distance from home to school. It is fair to conclude, then, that for something more than half of the parents the religious or ideological characteristics of the school were important considerations in making a selection. For 27 percent of the parents, *richting* was more important than quality, while for 44 percent *richting* was the least important consideration.

Such surveys do not discredit the present system of parent choice in the Netherlands; on the contrary, the fact that parents differ significantly on what they want suggests that diversity in schooling meets a real need. The mistake is to interpret the data in terms of either-or, as though schools can vary only in *richting* or in pedagogy, not in both. The fact is that the constitutional guarantees of educational freedom, though intended primarily to protect liberty of conscience, have the effect of providing space for pedagogical diversity as well. There is no single model of Catholic or of Protestant schooling in the Netherlands, but at least as much diversity among schools in each group as there is among public schools in the United States.

Dutch parents who want schooling for their children that is strongly marked with religious perspectives may be disappointed, however, despite their constitutional guarantees of choice. This desire of parents has less to do with issues of funding or of government interference than with the difficulty that many Catholic and Protestant schools experience in maintaining their distinctive identity.

Despite the right of parent choice, controversy also exists over the extent to which individual public schools may become distinctive in an effort to attract students; from a legal perspective, the Education Council found, freedom of *richting* applies only to private schools. All public schools represent the same *richting* and should implicitly have no distinct flavor.

Some public school advocates are eager to define a positive rather than a negative character, in order to stress the distinctive mission of public schooling in relation to social renewal. They are concerned about research indicating that most municipalities make little effort to translate a "public school identity" into concrete pedagogy and school climate (Detering and Kalkman, 1986). On the other hand, others argue, the unique role of the public school is to be acceptable to everyone, particularly by showing respect for individual religious convictions, and thus it should not become the confessional school of nonsectarianism, even though this character might express the preference of most parents who choose public education (Graaf, 1983, p. 43).

There have been recurrent calls for privatizing public education, or at least for placing individual public schools under "responsible authorities" that are closer to the school than is municipal government, in the interest of effectiveness and coherence (Wallage, 1983). Surveys indicate that, for most parents, the distinguishing characteristic of public schools is their neutrality, not their public governance. Social Democrats in particular are divided between a belief that education should be carried out by government in the interest of broad social goals, and a commitment to parent involvement and responsiveness to the desires of those most directly affected by schooling. (See Leune, 1983.)

In a discussion paper issued at the end of 1987, the conservative Liberal Party (VVD) called repeatedly for giving public schools the legal status of neutral private schools, while their coalition partners, the Christian Democrats (CDA), urged that public schools be privatized (*School en Besturen*, April 1988, pp. 4–5). In budget debates in March 1988, the Cabinet suggested that savings could be made in the education budget by abolishing municipal education departments altogether. Minister of Education Deetman pointed out, however, that some parents choose as a matter of principle for schools operated directly by government and committed (by the constitution) to respect for all beliefs and convictions, and such choices must be respected as well as those for confessional schooling. If there were no public schools, he added, there might have to be more government interference with private schools to protect the right of every parent to an inoffensive education; thus the result of eliminating public schools might be to reduce rather than to increase diversity (*Schoolbestuur*, April 1988, pp. 4–5).

The autonomy of the Dutch elementary school—with respect to curriculum, pedagogy, and hiring staff, though not to budget, schedule, or firing staff—may not be as great as that of the private school in the United States, but it is considerably greater than that of most U.S. public schools. Not every Dutch school uses its autonomy to good effect, but the opportunity is there, and many—particularly at the elementary level—continue to justify French visitor Georges Cuvier's comment in 1811 and English visitor (and poet) Matthew Arnold's in 1861, that they are the best in the world.

Certainly the opportunity for parents to make educational choices is more elaborately protected in the Netherlands than anywhere else. Not every parent makes wise choices, of course, and many simply select the nearest school, but the research on the process of choice suggests a balancing of considerations that cannot fail to encourage subsequent involvement in the educational process.

U.S. economist Estelle James gives a balanced view of the "preconditions, costs and benefits of privatized public services" in the Netherlands:

> [My] discussions with Dutch parents and educators indicate that the preference for private schools stems from the belief that they are more personal and responsive to parental wishes, that they spend their funds more effectively and use their fees to secure better facilities. Also, private schools, in effect, label their ideology ahead of time, so parents know what they will be getting, in contrast to public schools which ostensibly have no ideology, except that which the individual teacher adopts (James, 1982, pp. 18–19).

My own impression from visits to Dutch schools and discussions with a wide range of policymakers is that the Dutch have scarcely begun to appreciate the power of choice for school improvement. The constitutional guarantees of educational freedom have been understood as a defense against encroachment by the state rather than as a framework for true diversity and school-level decision making.

The answer, surely, is not to restrict choice and diversity, but to open the system up through continued efforts to profile the identity of individual schools more sharply, and through greatly improved parent information efforts as a basis for sound choices. There are encouraging signs that the necessary discussions are well under way in hundreds of schools and parent councils. In this respect, and in the care with which freedom and fairness are administratively protected, U.S. educational reform can learn a great deal from the Dutch experience.

GREAT BRITAIN

Expansion of parent choice of schools is currently one of the most controversial issues in British politics, despite a system that provides, by U.S. standards, a very substantial amount of choice already. Some of the existing choice has—as in the United States—been available in private and often elite schools that serve about 6 percent of total elementary and secondary enrollment at present. Within publicly managed schooling other kinds of choice exist, mostly based on the denominational association—which may, in practice, be greatly attenuated—of schools.

Popular schooling developed in the nineteenth century primarily by voluntary initiative, and government leadership developed relatively late. When it did, the intervention was motivated far less than on the continent or in the United States by a concern to implement a state pedagogy in a common school for the sake of national unity.

As a result, private schools have been taken into the public system under arrangements that permitted them to retain their denominational identity, and parents continue to be able to choose, for example, a Church of England or a Roman Catholic school that is public in most respects by U.S. standards. The proportion of students attending "independent" private schools is lower than in any nation of the European Community except West Germany and Luxembourg. Religious diversity is largely though not entirely accommodated through such government-supported schooling.

In recent years, legislation has extended parent choice in England and Wales and in Scotland.

ENGLAND AND WALES

The Education Act of 1944, adopted in the wartime spirit of unity and social reconstruction, provided for two types of publicly supported schools in England and Wales: county schools, established and operated by local education authorities, and voluntary schools, established by churches or benevolent individuals (generally some generations ago) and financially supported by the local education authorities. County schools presently represent more than two-thirds of publicly supported elementary schools and four-fifths of secondary schools.

There are three types of "voluntary" schools. The local authority pays all of the costs of "controlled" schools, and appoints the teachers; "aided" schools and "special agreement" schools receive operating costs from the authority but their sponsors must pay 15 percent of the capital (facilities) costs in exchange for the right to appoint teachers. Around 20 percent of British children attend "voluntary aided" schools.

Despite this extensive accommodation of confessional diversity within publicly funded education, it is not clear that it has continued to offer sharply profiled choices. The effect of supervision by local education authorities has led to a great deal of uniformity between council and voluntary schools, while secularization has weakened the confessional identity of many of the latter:

> Denominational bodies, though they have won the right to receive considerable public aid whilst retaining the power to appoint teachers of a particular faith, now in practice often consider themselves fortunate to obtain a teacher or lecturer of any religion or of none (Murphy, 1971, pp. 123–124).

Extension of parent choice became a basic element of Conservative education policy with the Charter of Parents Rights included in the party's platform for the October 1974 elections. Over the following years, it was put forward as a cornerstone of educational reform:

> While the rationale for parental choice had initially emphasized freedom from state control and the assumption of parental responsibilities for their children, it was now presented as a means of improving educational standards—the introduction of market forces would force unpopular (poor) schools to close and enable popular (good) schools to expand (Adler, Petch, and Tweedie, 1987, p. 296).

The Conservatives' 1979 platform promised that

> Our PARENTS' CHARTER will place a clear duty on government and local authorities to take account of parents' wishes when allocating children to schools, with a local appeals system for those dissatisfied. Schools will be required to publish prospectuses giving details of their examination and other results.

Soon after taking office in 1979, the Conservatives filed legislation to implement their educational program, including parent choice, and it was enacted as the Education Act of 1980. An official explanation of the legislation informed local authorities that they were required to

> make arrangements for enabling parents of children who are in their area to express a preference as to the school they wish their children to attend, and for the parents to give reasons for their preference. . . . They may fulfil their duty in a variety of ways. Some may invite parents to express a series of preferences in priority order, others may propose a school at which a place is available but provide for parents who wish their child to attend a different school to express their preference in response (Department of Education and Science, 1981).

The legislation also required the local authority to pay tuition and other costs for children who gained admission to a school operated by another authority or to a "voluntary" school, with parents paying for transportation.

This sweeping requirement to honor parent choices was restricted significantly by a provision that admission could be denied if it would "prejudice the provision of efficient education or the efficient use of resources." With such broad language, an authority determined to discourage choices could turn down many requests. Thus the negative impact used as a justification could be on any school in the system, not just on the school a student was seeking to leave or to attend. Parent choice is rarely convenient to education authorities for whom stability and predictability are primary virtues of sound management. If, for example, the movement of children out of an unpopular school will cause it to operate at less than optimal student-teacher ratios, and thus impose additional costs, it could be refused under the provisions of the 1980 act.

Another feature of the 1980 legislation was the Assisted Places Scheme, under which "bright children from less affluent homes" may be admitted to the independent (private) schools, with the government paying part or all of the costs. In 1986, some 22,000 students were supported in this way in 226 independent schools, in some cases on a boarding basis.

These measures did not satisfy a group of hard-line Tories who asserted, in a 1986 "Radical Manifesto,"

> There is no longer a consensus about education in Britain. Doubts about education are now so deep-rooted that people cannot readily agree on educational policy. The country stands in need of a period of open debate, during which new and freer institutions of education will be able to flourish and to win the support of the public (Hillgate Group, 1986, p. 1).

The lack of effective parent choice, they argued, had helped to debase the quality of education:

> Like every monopolized industry, the educational system has begun to ignore the demands of the consumers—parents and children—and to respond instead to the requirements of the producers—LEAs [local education authorities] and teachers. [Thus] the first and most important step in any comprehensive reform of the state educational system is to give more power to the parents. We believe this should be done by giving all parents a right which the rich have always enjoyed—the right to choose and to obtain the most suitable education for their children. Parents should be free to withdraw their children from schools that are unsatisfactory, and to place them in the schools of their choice. They should not be compelled to see their children subjected to lessons which they regard as morally or religiously offensive, nor should they be forced to stand helplessly by, while their children are subjected to grotesque social or political experiments in the name of education (Hillgate Group, 1986, p. 1).

In order to implement the Conservative program, Education Minister Kenneth Baker proposed legislation in mid-1987, adopted largely unchanged in mid-1988, to extend both parent choice and the autonomy of individual schools. The "open enrollment" provision requires local education authorities to admit the greatest possible number of students to popular schools rather than to protect less popular schools by imposing artificially low limits at the schools to which their students might transfer. (See Department of Education and Science, 1987.)

One effect of this legislation, critics warned, would be racial segregation, as white parents took advantage of the opportunity to flee schools that had many Asian or West Indian students (in inner London alone, there are twenty secondary schools with over 60 percent minority enrollment). White parents of twenty-six children in Dewsbury in West Yorkshire protested this fall because they were blocked from doing exactly that: their local school (Church of England) is 85 percent Asian, while a nearby school, also Church of England and officially "full," is 90 percent white (*Times Education Supplement*, September 11, 18, 1987). One commentator noted that "by promising 'consumer choice' to parents, Mr. Baker has unleashed powerful forces that could lead to conflict" (*Economist*, September 12, 1987).

The Social Democrats sought to make their own mark as supporters of parent choice, on the basis of the conviction that Britain is becoming a

> society in which a considerable proportion of what used to be called the proletariat believe their interests to be inextricably bound up with those of the traditional middle class. It is sometimes clumsily called "embourgeoisification" and it is what the Prime Minister is hell-bent on doing to the inner cities. . . . [V]oters are opting for the Tories because they believe in the values espoused by them—and if that is what the customers want, then is it not what a democratic political party should give them? Parents . . . want more choice and vouchers is the way to give it to them. But in order to protect the weak, the vouchers system should only be "cashable" at schools which did not impose selection tests, did not charge additional fees, and were recognized as efficient by HM Inspectorate (Hugill, 1987).

Social Democrat education specialist Anne Sofer proposed to provide vouchers to all parents, redeemable at both publicly funded and private ("independent") schools (*Times Education Supplement*, August 28, September 4, 1987).

It is curious, given the interest of Baker and his allies in the U.S. experience with magnet schools as a model for what increased parent choice could mean for British education, that so little attention has been given to an essential element of magnet schools: controls to assure that they promote racial (and thus social) integration. U.S. policies to promote parent choice, unlike those in place and proposed in Britain, are by no means willing to accept segregation as a necessary cost. On the contrary, choice has emerged, in the United States, as a more effective means than mandatory assignments ("busing") to achieve integrated schools.

There are signs that the Conservative program to promote parent choice—although opposed by most educators and only moderately supported by parents—has managed to change the terms of education reform efforts, and more so than has yet occurred in the United States. The National Union of Teachers (NUT), for example, has begun to commission opinion polls to determine what parents are looking for in schools, and how satisfied they are with what is now provided. Shifting power from local education authorities to schools and parents, one NUT spokesman conceded, "could lead to higher standards and an improvement in the education service" (*Times Education Supplement*, January 29, 1988).

SCOTLAND

The Education (Scotland) Act of 1946 required education authorities to

have regard to the general principle that, so far as is compatible with the provision of suitable instruction and training and the avoidance of unreasonable public expenditure, pupils are to be educated in accordance with the wishes of their parents (Adler, Petch, and Tweedie, 1987, p. 290).

This provision was part of the compromise that brought most confessional schools into the public education system, with parents having a right to select such schools unless it would create too great a burden on the local authority. Essentially what it protected was the right of government to continue to operate confessional schools, not the right of individual parents to control the education of their children (Raab and Adler, 1987, p. 158).

This requirement meant less than appears on the surface, since it set no requirements as to how assignments would be made. A broad area of discretion was left for education authorities to decide that efficiency required that students attend their local school on the basis of attendance zones. The tradition of the "common school" is rooted as deeply in Scotland as anywhere else in the world. This was reinforced by the growing interest, after World War II, in the "omnibus school" providing a comprehensive secondary program to all students in a residential area. In 1977, the proportion of students for whom nonroutine assignments were sought was less than 1 percent in most of Scotland, and far less in rural areas.

Parent choice, although implicit in the 1946 legislation, was given a strong boost by the Education (Scotland) Act of 1981. Under this act, pushed through by the Conservative majority in Parliament over the resistance of the Labor-dominated local education authorities and professional associations in Scotland,

> parents were given the right to request that their children [be] admitted to a particular school or schools; education authorities are required to comply with parental requests unless a statutory exception to this general duty applies; dissatisfied parents have the right to appeal to a statutory appeal committee and, if the latter finds in favor of the parent, its decision is binding on the authority; and education authorities are required to provide parents with information about the school to which their child has been allocated and about any other school if the parents ask for it (Adler, Petch, and Tweedie, 1987, p. 303).

Although these provisions are parallel to those in England and Wales, in several respects the Scottish legislation provides even more rights to parents. The grounds on which parent choice may be denied are much more narrowly stated: only when approving the request would require employing an additional teacher or significant extensions or alterations to the school facility or would "be likely to be seriously detrimental to order and discipline at the school or the educational well-being of the pupils there" (Adler, Petch, and Tweedie, 1987, pp. 303–304).

The number of requests for out-of-district assignments doubled from 10,456 in 1981–82 to 20,795 in 1984–85, more than half of them for elementary schools. School requests were made by parents of all social classes. In one sample,

> even in the suburban area manual workers were relatively more represented among those making placing requests (37 percent) than their presence in the population (20 percent) would lead us to expect (Adler, Petch, and Tweedie, 1987, pp. 302, 304).

The primary reason (60 percent) given by parents requesting an elementary-level assignment was avoidance of their local school, often because of the perceived roughness of its students, and preference of another for safety and school climate reasons. The educational program offered was to some extent a secondary consideration (Adler, Petch, and Tweedie, 1987, p. 299).

According to another study,

the majority of parents have in mind a broad general agenda in selecting a secondary school for their child and are as much if not more concerned with social considerations than with educational ones (Adler, Petch, and Tweedie, 1987, pp. 309–310).

This emphasis on issues of school climate rather than of pedagogy does not mean, according to the researchers, that those head teachers are correct who asserted that parents were not well enough informed to make sound choices among schools. Indeed,

> many parents seemed to have quite clear pictures of the working ethos of a school. Parents repeatedly saw both the happiness and the educational success of the child as being related to the stability and atmosphere of the school, though they varied in the extent to which they saw the nature of the school's intake [of students] or the actions taken by staff to be the main determinant of that working environment. In some instances parents had access to information (e.g., about bullying and attitudes of local peer groups) which may have led some parents to have been *better* informed than some teachers (Macbeth, Strachan, and Macaulay, 1986, p. 124).

It might be expected from this analysis that most of the movement in urban areas would be from schools in lower-income areas to schools in adjacent middle-income areas. This pattern did show itself to some extent in Edinburgh, though in Dundee "the pattern of movements is almost entirely within areas that are homogeneous with respect to housing tenure and social class." The exception that conforms to the original expectation are those transfers between noncontiguous schools. In Edinburgh, 83 percent of the requests and in Dundee 85 percent were to contiguous schools (Raab and Adler, 1987, pp. 164–171).

In Dundee and Edinburgh, certain schools experienced sharp gains or losses in enrollment. Two out of thirty-eight elementary schools in Dundee lost more than half their attendance area population, while seven gained more than half of their entering class from outside their attendance areas. There were very few pairs of schools between which students moved in both directions. The viability of some schools with heavy losses is now in question:

> Overall, the advantages for some children of attending larger secondary schools with more balanced intakes and higher staying-on rates appear to have imposed substantial costs on other children whose curricular choices and wider educational opportunities have been further restricted (Adler, Petch, and Tweedie, 1987, p. 312).

In other words, an unrestricted system of choice provides advantages to those who make choices and disadvantages to those who do not. It is difficult to judge this situation from an equity perspective. One line of argument would stress that at least some students are saved from a bad education by the opportunity to choose a school in a middle-class area. As Scottish Education Minister Alex Fletcher argued in launching the choice program in Scotland,

> Some schools in deprived areas are battling against the odds despite all the public money that was poured into their area, and the effect on the children is that it locks them into the one social strata.

Meanwhile, mandatory assignment based on strict attendance districts "effectively confines disadvantaged children to the deprived areas in which they live" (quoted in Macbeth, Strachan, and Macaulay, 1986, pp. 31–32).

The argument on the other side, of course, is that only children of the more ambitious and upwardly mobile working-class parents are likely to benefit from a choice program, and that the result is to leave the education for those students who remain behind even more dismal.

Does parent choice in Scotland actually promote social integration (as the Conservatives claimed that it would) by allowing poor children to escape their inner-city schools? In the case of one school studied, it did appear that the

> influx of [urban] pupils was seen as being "responsible" for the changing ethos of the school providing it with a more comprehensive spread in terms of socio-economic status and ability, and thus more like the other comprehensive schools in the city, that these parents were to some extent seeking to avoid (Macbeth, Strachan, and Macaulay, 1986, p. 286).

The overall study found that those living in public housing did receive some benefits from the new system of choice:

> our evidence does seem to support the argument that the legislation has had an egalitarian effect by providing for council tenants that element of school choice which had largely been the preserve of house-buyers (Macbeth, Strachan, and Macaulay, 1986, p. 302).

Indeed, "for those who cannot choose [a] school through house purchase or private schooling the legislation does seem to have provided an attainable mode of choice" (Macbeth, Strachan, and Macaulay, p. 334). Even though only a minority may take advantage of this opportunity, it reflects a significant reconceptualization of the relationship of parents and government in education:

> From 1945 onwards, it has been assumed that the interests of the individual coincided with those of the [local education] authority, thus the best way of promoting an individual's rights was to improve the provision of education. Now, for the first time, the interests of the individual and the concerns of the authority were seen, at least in some respects, to conflict and the individual was seen to be in need of protection from the authority (Adler, Petch, and Tweedie, 1987, p. 305).

On the other hand, the same researchers conclude, consistently with my earlier comments about the U.S. experience with parent choice of schools, that the 1981 act

> has not achieved the right balance between the rights of individual parents and the collective duties of education authorities. . . . [They should be] given more powers to control admissions to school, subject to effective safeguards, which would ensure that these powers are used responsibly to prevent parental choice from prejudicing equality of educational opportunity or the duty placed on education authorities to promote "adequate and efficient education" for all (Adler, Petch, and Tweedie, 1987, p. 322).

CANADA

The cultural similarities between Canada and the United States can conceal significant differences. One of these has to do with the scope permitted, in Canada, for parent choice of schools. Although the curricular content of Canadian education is in many respects similar to that of education in the United States, differences in structure and governance lead to far greater diversity and parent choice in Canada.

In the United States, efforts to give a religious flavor to a public school or to extend public funding to schools not operated by government are, in most cases, struck down on the basis of the federal Constitution or of even stricter state constitutions. The fundamental national laws in Canada, by contrast, give many parents a right to denominational public schools and pose no impediment to funding of private schools. Indeed, one of the few constitutional responsibilities of the federal government in education is to assure that this right is respected by the provinces.

It is difficult to give a synopsis of parent choice of schools in Canada because the situation and policies differ widely among provinces and are the result of political compromises at the provincial level rather than of the application of nationwide legal principles, as in the United States.

The first, and historically most significant, group of parents seeking an alternative to the common public school are Roman Catholics. To a substantial extent, the desire for a Catholic education has been accommodated within the structure of public education. This is undoubtedly the major reason that the proportion of Canadian students in private schools (around 4 percent) is low in comparison with the United States (around 10 percent) and other democracies.

In 1867 the British Parliament enacted the British North America Act of 1867, uniting the four colonies of Upper Canada (Ontario), Lower Canada (Quebec), New Brunswick, and Nova Scotia in a Confederation. This "Constitution Act" gave the provinces exclusive authority to make laws about education, but guaranteed the continuation of denominational schools in Quebec and Ontario, then as now the two largest provinces, and applied to other provinces where such schools already existed at the time they entered the Confederation. This legislation had the effect of protecting the schools of religious minorities, Protestants in Quebec and Catholics in much of Canada, since Alberta and Saskatchewan adopted the provision for separate Catholic schools when they joined the Confederation in 1905. Over time the Protestant separate schools have lost their denominational character, outside Quebec, and are simply the public schools of the majority, while separate Catholic schools continue in Ontario, Alberta, and Saskatchewan.

The educational concerns of religious groups other than Catholics (and mainstream Protestants) have been met largely through their own efforts until recent years, when there has been some movement toward providing public support for schools established by them. Although there are (loosely) Protestant public schools in Quebec, and the public schools in several other provinces have a Protestant heritage, there is no recognized right for individual denominations to receive public support for "separate" public schools.

Despite the lack of guarantees in constitutional law, the number of private schools increased rapidly in Ontario and British Columbia during the postwar decades. Bergen (1981) suggests that this increase was related to developments in the wider society. As they have become secularized, public schools

> no longer reflect a "Christian" or "Christian Protestant" ethos. Those members of society who found the public schools of three or four decades ago sufficiently "Christian" to provide the kind of educational environment they wanted for their children, no longer find such to be the case. Consequently, in recent years there has been a stronger interest in private schools among more conservative denominations (Bergen, 1981, p. 3).

The postwar immigrants from the Netherlands, in particular, brought with them a tradition of denominational schooling that led to the founding of the first "Christian Reformed" school in 1945. By 1985–86, more than 19,000 students were attending schools in the Reformed tradition.

Another group with a strong commitment to schooling informed by their religious views are the Hutterites, an extremely conservative Anabaptist church related to the Mennonites. Because they live in homogeneous farming colonies, the Hutterites have been able to make use of their local public schools, supplemented by language and religion instruction before or after school. Local authorities have been willing to accommodate the Hutterite practice of recognizing 15-year-olds as members of the adult community; they are excused from school on the basis of receiving training as apprentices through their responsibilities in the Hutterite community.

The group around which there has been the most controversy recently is the Holdeman group of Mennonites, who came into conflict with provincial authorities in Alberta in the 1970s when they withdrew their children from the public schools and began to educate them in unauthorized schools of their own. One leader of this group wrote to the Premier of Alberta,

> We definitely feel that we have a culture and a way of life to preserve for our children and that the trends in our greater society are not conducive for this. We plan to give our children a curriculum that will foster self-discipline rather than permissiveness; respect for authority rather than disrespect; interdependence rather than independence; consideration for the rights of others rather than "I'll do my own thing"; and respect for God, his creation, and his institutions (Quoted in Bergen, 1978, p. 14).

The growth of demand for private schooling in Canada (and in the United States) is surely related to such concerns to shield children from what are seen as the destructive aspects of modernity. Altogether there were at least 234,260 students attending 1,300 private schools in Canada in 1985–86, up from 188,350 attending 800 schools a decade earlier. Some 40,000, or 17 percent, of these students attend Catholic schools, a very low proportion by the standard of other countries and to be explained by the ample provision for "public" Catholic schools in Canada.

Religion is not the only basis for seeking such alternatives. Stamp notes that

> the private school sector in post-1960 Ontario also witnessed a rapid rise of schools founded for nonreligious, purely educational, or philosophical reasons. . . . Such schools began to proliferate in the mid-to-late-1960s, often as radical alternatives to the perceived inflexible, all-too-structured nature of the public school. In time the more radical or "free" schools moderated or died, and were replaced by more middle-of-the-road and eventually right-wing alternatives. Their growth challenged the public school sector to confront the concept of secular or philosophic pluralism in addition to religious and cultural pluralism (Stamp, 1985, p. 202).

Parents supported these very diverse private schools, according to the president of the Ontario Alliance of Alternative and Independent Schools, because of their "belief that the public education system lacks some kind of fundamental moral content" (Robert Routledge, 1976, quoted in Stamp 1985, p. 204). Stamp concludes that

> Whatever the motives in their founding, whatever influences they had on public education, Ontario's private schools had assumed a significance in the early 1980s that could not have been predicted a generation earlier. Their religious diversity reflected the multicultural nature of the province; their philosophic diversity mirrored Ontario's secular pluralism. Proponents of public education had long hoped to accommodate such diversity within the state-supported school system. But an increasing minority of students and parents had chosen the private sector (p. 205).

These private schools did not receive public funding as did Catholic schools, and this lack clearly raised questions of equity. There is increasing pressure to make equal provision for all schools chosen by parents, provided that they meet government standards, as has been the case since 1977 in British Columbia. The government of Ontario appointed a commission in 1984 to study this issue and the arguments made on both sides. Those opposed to further funding for private and confessional education relied essentially on two lines of argument.

The first, going back a hundred years and more, describes the public school as the "common school" of the nation, the crucible of national identity. Already in 1972 the Commission on Educational Planning for Alberta warned that the increasing number of private schools "might lead to an unsustainable degree of educational and social fragmentation." Similarly, the Ontario Commission on Private Schools asserted that

the values reflected by the boards of education are seen as the shared values of almost all Canadians, irrespective of their religious background. That is, the relatively secular, humanistic nature of the public schools is seen by some to truly reflect the current societal conditions in Ontario and Canada (Shapiro, 1985, p. 25).

In answer to the argument that public schools, by seeking neutrality, are based on values that are acceptable to the majority of Ontario residents, Olthuis—writing from a Calvinist perspective and the Dutch tradition of educational pluralism—pointed out that

the number of persons embracing the educational philosophy of a particular educational system does not determine the public or private status of that system. Surely in a free society the majority would not wish to foist its value judgments on minorities under the guise that minority beliefs are private and majority beliefs are public. . . . However desirable some may consider the existence of a public educational philosophy, and however vigorously they may contend that secular humanism or nonsectarianism is such a public value, the truth is that all educational philosophies are as private or as public as one another. . . . Attempts to erase fundamental differences in the name of a superficial uniformity are not conducive for true unity. The claim that the differences between Roman Catholics, Jews, Protestants and Secularists do not affect education, results from failure to take these various faiths seriously. . . . The recognition of fundamental differences is a mark of true tolerance and not a sign of bigotry. One of the characteristics of genuine freedom is that people of different beliefs can live together peacefully in a nation and enjoy equal rights and privileges. The freedom to differ and the right to act accordingly constitutes the basic difference between a free and a totalitarian society (Olthuis, 1970, pp. 7–8).

The Ontario Commission itself came down, in its report, on the side of those who believe that it is important for Canadian society that the public schools "seek a common unifying core":

Schools are better able to teach common understanding and shared values if they are less homogeneous and can, at least potentially, bring children of different backgrounds together (Shapiro, 1985, p. 39).

Supporters of Jewish or Catholic or Calvinist schools countered that "schools are better able to teach common understanding and shared values" if they themselves reflect such a common understanding and shared values, and that this is more likely in a school chosen by teachers and parents on the basis of their convictions about education and character. As the commission conceded,

Public schools too often easily assumed that the mere physical presence of various groups within their student bodies somehow, of its own accord, bred tolerance and understanding. . . . It must be admitted that no one knows just which schooling experiences are most likely to produce understanding and tolerant adult citizens and, from the point of view of minority groups, large-scale common settings are often repressive settings (Shapiro, 1985, p. 50).

The argument is made that government has a right to educate its citizens on the basis of values that it believes will serve the common good, but Holmes (1985, p. 124) pointed out in a paper included in the commission's report that

Those who believe in the state's right to impose an education on every child are not normally willing to embrace any education that any state may actually choose to promulgate. Liberal rationalists objected to the Catholic hegemony of French education in the Province of Quebec. They, in turn, now that education in that province has been largely secularized de facto (but not yet de jure), are loth to consider the objections of those who, in turn, reject secular humanism.

The argument for a public school monopoly in order to shape students on the basis of common values has lost much of its force as society—in Canada as in the United States—has lost confidence that there are indeed such shared values. In place of that argument public school advocates now more commonly stress the need to assure educational equity and fair chances in life through diminishing the effect of elite private education.

The commission was told that "support for private schools will erode the financial and ideological support for public schooling which in turn will deny equality of educational opportunity . . . by fostering a two-tier system of schooling inimical to the democratic traditions that public schools are intended to serve" (Shapiro, 1985, p. 47). After all,

> if such funding should result in any large transfer of either the higher achieving or the more affluent students from the public to the independent schools, the ability of the public schools (as the schools of "second choice") to offer equal educational opportunity will have been destroyed (Shapiro, 1985, p. 51).

On the other hand, there is a real question whether public schools in fact promote equal opportunity through bringing together heterogeneous groups of students. In Canada as in the United States, students from affluent families, from poor families, and from those in between tend to attend schools—whether public or private—with students of similar social class. As Holmes (1985, p. 127) notes,

> It appears inconsistent to endorse education as a public good, but then demand that a certain class of citizens (those with money) be excluded from involvement in the public operation.

The logic of the equal opportunity argument—if applied consistently—would require banning of private schools altogether, as well as mandating school assignments on a metropolitan basis, designed for social class as well as racial integration. There are certainly some elite private schools in Canada, but many other private schools are anything but elite, and, indeed, less so than public schools in affluent communities. A policy seeking equal opportunity must logically concern itself with how children whose parents (for whatever reason) do not wish to enroll them in the available public schools can be assured of an adequate education. It must seek to achieve this end while respecting the parental rights that all modern democracies acknowledge.

REFERENCES

France

Dutourd, Jean. *La gauche la plus bête du monde*. Paris: Flammarion, 1985.
Glenn, Charles L. *The Myth of the Common School*. Amherst: University of Massachusetts Press, 1988.

Leclerc, Gérard. *La bataille de l'école: 15 siècles d'histoire, 3 ans de combat.* Paris: Denoel, 1985.

Savary, Alain, with Catherine Arditti. *En toute liberté.* Paris: Hachette, 1985.

Netherlands

Akkermans, P. W. C. *Onderwijs als constitutioneel probleem.* Alphen aan den Rijn: Samsom, 1980.

Detering, Paul, and Kalkman, Wim. "Bestuur en identiteit van de openbare school," *Inzicht: Vereniging voor Openbaar Onderwijs,* 120, 1 (February 1986).

Eck, M. van, Groot Antink, W. M. J. M., and Veraart, P. W. V. *Gewenst basisonderwijs in de tweede helft van de jaren 80 in de provincie Utrecht.* Utrecht: Tangram, 1986.

Graaf, F. Th. de. "Een nieuse bestuursvorm voor het openbaar onderwijs?" In *Het bestuur van het openbaar onderwijs,* ed. P. W. C. Akkermans and J. M. G. Leune. Den Bosch: Malmberg, 1983.

James, Estelle. *The Private Provision of Public Services: A Comparison of Sweden and Holland.* New Haven: Institution for Social and Policy Studies, Yale University, 1982.

Jong Ozn., Klaas de. "Ruimte voor christelijk onderwijs," *Bulletin: Unie "School en Evangelie,"* 12, 6, June 1984.

Koppejan, J. "Ontstaan en groei van het reformatorisch onderwijs." In *Belijden en opvoeden: Gedachten over de christelijke school vanuit een reformatorische visie,* ed. M. Golverdingen and others. Houten: Hertog, 1985.

Leune, J. M. G. "De bestuursvorm voor het openbaar onderwijs ter discussie." In *Het bestuur van het openbaar onderwijs,* ed. P. W. C. Akkermans and J. M. G. heune Den Bosch: Malmberg, 1983.

Ministerie van Onderwijs en Wetenschappen. *Wetten voor de basisschool.* The Hague, 1984.

Schoolbestuur, 8, 4 (April 1988).

School en Besturen, 8, 2 (April 1988).

Schoten, A. P. M. van, and Wansink, Hans. *De nieuwe schoolstrijd: Knelpunten en conflicten in de hedendaagse onderwijspolitiek.* Utrecht: Bohn, Scheltema, and Holkema, 1984.

Vroon, Bas. "Doorbraak in strijd tegen schoolgrenzen," *Inzicht: Vereniging voor Openbaar Onderwijs,* 120, 5, September 1986.

Wallage, Jacques. "Naar een Raad voor het openbaar onderwijs." In *Het bestuur van het openbaar onderwijs,* ed. P. W. C. Akkermans and J. M. G. Leune. Den Bosch: Malmberg, 1983.

Great Britain

Adler, Michael, Petch, Alison, and Tweedie, Jack. "The Origin and Impact of the Parents' Charter." In *Scottish Government Yearbook.* Edinburgh: Government of Scotland, 1987.

Department of Education and Science. *Circular No. 1/81: Education Act 1980: Admission to Schools, Appeals, Publication of Information and School Attendance Orders.* London: Department of Education and Science, 1981.

Department of Education and Science. "Admission of Pupils to Maintained Schools." London: Department of Education and Science, 1987. (mimeographed).

Hillgate Group. *Whose Schools? A Radical Manifesto.* London: Hillgate Group, 1986.

Hugill, Barry. "How Vouchers Fit into Sofer's Battle Scheme," *Times Educational Supplement,* 4 September 1987.

Macbeth, Alastair, Strachan, David; and Macaulay, Caithlin. *Parental Choice of School in Scotland.* Glasgow: Department of Education, University of Glasgow, 1986.

Murphy, James. *Church, State, and Schools in Britain, 1800–1970.* London: Routledge & Kegan Paul, 1971.

Raab, Gillian M., and Adler, Michael. "A Tale of Two Cities: The Impact of Parental Choice on Admissions to Primary Schools in Edinburgh and Dundee." In *Research Papers in Education* 2, 3, 1987.

Canada

Bergen, John J. "The Alberta Mennonite Holdeman Private School Controversy: A Case Study in Minority Group Maintenance." Unpublished paper, University of Alberta, 1978.

Bergen, John J. "The Private School Alternative," *Canadian Administrator* 20, No. 5 (1981): 3.

Holmes, Mark. "The Funding of Private Schools in Ontario: Philosophy, Values, and Implications for Funding." In *Report of the Commission on Private Schools in Ontario,* ed. Bernard J. Shapiro. Toronto: Provincial Government of Ontario, 1985.

Olthuis, John A. *A Place to Stand: A Case for Public Funds for ALL Public Schools.* Sarnia: Ontario Alliance of Christian Schools, 1970.

Shapiro, Bernard J. *Report of the Commission on Private Schools in Ontario.* Toronto: Provincial Government of Ontario, 1985.

Stamp, Robert, "A History of Private Schools in Ontario." In *Report of the Commission on Private Schools in Ontario,* ed. Bernard J. Shapiro. Toronto: Provincial Government of Ontario, 1985.

CHAPTER 5

Teacher Choice: Does It Have a Future?

Denis P. Doyle

The concept of choice is deeply embedded in the U.S. social and political fabric. That this is so is hardly surprising. Our twin traditions of political liberty and equality mean that each American is expected both to choose and to be competent to choose.

In most dimensions of U.S. life, choice is a reality. It is central to our political and economic system. Democracy institutionalizes choice; capitalism is based on it. Since the advent of the New Deal, "consumer" choice has become a hallmark of our domestic social programs. Social Security, for example, provides intergenerational transfer payments that may be disposed of in any manner the beneficiary deems fit. So too may Medicaid and Medicare recipients use

This chapter was originally prepared for the Task Force on Teaching as a Profession of the Carnegie Forum on Education and the Economy, and is published here with permission from the Carnegie Foundation of New York.

their benefits to choose among providers. Food stamps need not be redeemed in government commissaries, and welfare recipients may spend their meager allowance as they like. Indeed, choice in domestic social programs is viewed by most people as a triumph of human dignity. No longer do the elderly face the ignominy of the poorhouse, nor do the indigent ill find themselves assigned to the county hospital.

The concept of consumer choice within the public sector has emerged in the last fifteen years as an important conceptual and philosophical issue, one that crosses traditional political and ideological lines. The most noteworthy books on the subject make the point. First, at least in point of time, is *Exit, Voice, and Loyalty*, Albert O. Hirschman's (1970) intellectual *tour de force*. In this elegant short book, Hirschman makes the point that loyalty to institutions is a principal source of institutional vitality, that institutions freely chosen are energetic and vigorous, and that institutions that fail to respond to the legitimate claims of their members forfeit their loyalty and eventually lose them through "negative choice," or exit.

Second, there is *To Empower People*, by Peter Berger and Richard Neuhaus (1970). This short but powerful book makes the point that mediating structures—churches, unions, fraternal associations, neighborhoods, schools, and the like—stand between the megastructures of the modern corporate state and the individual. They provide a refuge from the intrusions of giant, impersonal bureaucracies; they buffer individuals and groups by protecting them. The power of mediating structures is that they are freely chosen; they are communities of shared intellectual and moral values. Their importance is revealed in the fact that they are the organizational forms first chosen by people in distress. When problems occur, people turn first to family and friends, then to mediating structures. Only when other recourse is exhausted do they turn to government. Recognizing this, democratic governments provide a legal framework for mediating structures, guaranteeing the right to worship as we choose, to form and join unions, and to participate in other forms of voluntary association such as scouting and fraternal and benevolent groups. Only in totalitarian societies are these activities proscribed.

Third, there is Charles Schultze's book *The Public Use of Private Interest* (1977). In this provocative and closely reasoned work, Schultze argues that the public sector must harness private interest to public purpose. In so doing, the commonweal will increase as private satisfactions are increased.

Each of these books owes a major debt to the nation's founders, who knew that private interest, including private passions, must be modulated by the state, with a formal constitution, one that both limits the powers of government by making the people sovereign, *and* pits interest against interest. In such a regime, no one interest triumphs. Political decisions are by their nature transitory and provisional; each actor and set of actors has a fair and open opportunity to influence the course of public debate and decision. The key to choice—whether through public elections or private decisions—is legitimacy. If authority—political or moral—is legitimate, choice is fair and necessary. Democratic capitalism and choice are indivisible. Without choice, neither democracy nor capitalism is conceivable.

CONSUMER CHOICE IN EDUCATION[1]

If consumer choice abounds in most areas of life, what of education? There the picture is mixed. In higher education, the idea of choice is enshrined in federal policy and most state policies. Public colleges and universities compete for students with each other and also with private institutions. Enrollments are not guaranteed. And much public financial aid for higher education is student centered, not institution centered.

For the well-to-do and upper-middle class, of course, choice is a matter of course at all levels of education. Consumers may buy what they prefer. For the lower-middle class and working class, however, choice at the elementary and secondary level is severely limited. For the poor, it is chimerical. Indeed, the simple fact is that administrative habits—geographic assignment of students to neighborhood schools—together with compulsory attendance consigns most children to public schools they did not actively choose.

As with all generalizations, there are important exceptions: an ambitious, not just well-to-do, parent may select a neighborhood and thereby a school with some care. As well, in a small but growing number of cities the opportunity to choose an alternative public school is a real one. The most famous examples are New York's selective schools, Peter Stuyvesant, Brooklyn Tech, and Bronx Science (Doyle and Cooper, 1983). More recently, North Carolina has established the North Carolina School for Science and Mathematics (Doyle, 1983).

In addition to these well-known examples, the list of cities with magnet schools or magnet programs continues to grow. Originally a device to introduce "voluntarism" in cities facing court-ordered racial integration, magnet schools have become popular in their own right and may now be found in places as diverse as St. Paul, Minnesota; Houston, Texas; Albany, New York; Seattle, Washington; and Prince Georges County, Maryland (Doyle and Levine, 1984). A particularly interesting magnet variant has been put in place in Prince Georges County; "workplace assignment" schools give first priority to those parents who work near the school. They offer extended day care; parents may drop children off on the way to work and retrieve them on the way home. So far these schools have been enthusiastically received by minority parents.

These schools, as welcome as they are, are the exceptions that prove the rule. The vast majority of U.S. students—nearly 40 million of them—attend neighborhood schools, neither selective nor magnet schools. The reason is not hard to fathom. U.S. schools, to use David Tyack's (1974) riveting phrase, are the product of the "one best system." But the nation's 15,500 independent school districts look more alike than different because they emerge from a common culture, not because of centralized planning and management. This distinction has meaning. In Europe, a ministry of education makes sure that all schools are alike. In the United States, the force of shared educational values and attitudes leads to sameness.

TEACHING: BLUE OR WHITE COLLAR

With only a hint of exaggeration, U.S. schools are best described as a product of the industrial revolution, built on an explicit conception of the then modern firm. Thanks to the scientific management revolution in the factory, schools too began to approach the management of instruction using an industrial metaphor. The schools' objective was a uniform finished product, the graduate (Doyle, 1985). As students move down the assembly line, they are attended to by teachers (workers), who in turn are overseen by foremen (principals), who report to the area superintendent (plant managers), who in turn report to superintendents (CEOs), who are overseen by a school board (the corporate trustees). To complete the analogy, the taxpayer-citizen is the shareholder.

From this conceptualization, two points emerge. First, if the school is a factory, if the management of education can be understood as a uniform science, if there is "one best system," then choice is a null category. If all schools are the same—or at least earnestly striving to be the same—then choice has no meaning to parents, teachers, and children. Choice is an empty exercise if its object is undifferentiated. As Henry Ford is reported to have said, customers can have any color Model T they want so long as it is black.

Second, whatever nascent interest in choice exists in education has been consumer driven, not supplier driven. The reason "one best system" existed was not because it was forced on the schools by public clamor. The public did not march on state capitols demanding uniformity. But educators did. More to the point, a "culture" of education emerged as surely as a business culture did. And that culture of education led to a kind of national uniformity that no federal government program could have produced. As both cause and effect, there has been little interest in "choice" on the part of educators, although I believe that an all-public voucher system has as much to offer to teachers as to children and their families (Doyle and Finn, 1983). Insofar as education choice has been an issue, it has been fueled by parents who seek some diversity and variety, or by political actors who attempt to respond to constituents.

But if consumer interest in choice exists, it is by now clear that the capacity of consumers' demand—or interest—to generate choice in education is limited. It is limited in large part by the reality of the existing system. In the public sector, there is not much among which to choose; and if a family chooses a private alternative, it loses interest in the public sector. Ironically, the private schools act as a safety valve, depressurizing the public sector. When an unsatisfied constituent of the public sector "exits"—to use Hirschman's term—his or her loyalty shifts to the private sector. The public sector in the short run loses a thorn in its side; in the long run, it loses the very people who might help revitalize it.

Indeed, it is precisely the lack of substantive, educational distinctions among public schools that probably encourages so many middle-class families to choose among them on noneducational grounds. That is, they treat choice in education as an "amenity," the ambiance provided by attending schools peopled by fellow members of their social class. That, of course, is what the "good" suburban school is all about.

And it is this form of choice that alarms educators—for good reason. Choice as a device to secure an "amenity" is simply a popularity contest; it makes a mockery of education, confusing form with substance. Worse, choice as an amenity tends to exacerbate rather than moderate social class differences. A school chosen because of its grounds, or parking lot, or playing fields rather than its intellectual values has been chosen for the wrong reasons.

Substantive education choice is limited, then, to those consumers with highly inelastic demand for an education program not available in the public sector, and the resources to deliver on that demand. The facts speak for themselves. Forty million youngsters attend public school, while the parents of 5 million others choose to pay their own way in private school. The reasons for attending private school are numerous, but each is characterized by a strong preference for qualities not available in the public sector. As a consequence, it comes as no surprise to hear the frequently noted complaint that the quality-conscious consumer often leaves the public sector. But if this is true its reciprocal is also true—the less quality-conscious consumer stays behind. The effect is that the natural elites who would otherwise apply pressure to the public sector no longer have an interest in it. They are not only absent, but also silent.

Because of the ease of exit for the highly motivated and ambitious, trying to conceptualize a demand-driven choice system within the remaining public sector is analogous to trying to push a rope. It goes nowhere. This is so because the political and institutional competence necessary to successful choice systems resides in the school itself. Teachers and administrators are the actors with the institutional and intellectual resources at their disposal to make—or break—choice systems. This they have done. With the few exceptions already noted, consumer choice in elementary and secondary education cuts a pallid figure.

TEACHER ANTIPATHY TO CHOICE

Why have educators clung to the status quo? For the most obvious of reasons. In the original, unsullied sense of the word, they are conservative. They believe the most apt of conservative dicta: unless it is necessary to change, it is necessary not to change. Indeed, education is an inherently conservative enterprise. Its purpose is to conserve the best of the past and give it—intact—to the future.

At a less abstract level, there are other perfectly understandable reasons for educators' resisting consumer-driven choice schemes. What, after all, is in it for them? In the short run, choice systems offer very little to those on the "supply" side. Many politicians would just as soon stay in office without the expense and inconvenience of elections; so too many merchants and industrialists would just as soon have captive markets as compete for customers. Suppliers are not noted for voluntarily exposing themselves to risks and costs they would not otherwise have to bear. Teachers are no exception.

Teachers also resist consumer choice because of the factory model of schooling. Workers on an assembly line are not professionals. And for all the talk about teachers as professionals, there is the lurking fear—even conviction—among teachers, other educators, and the public at large that teachers are not professionals. How else explain the way teachers are treated and compensated? What other professional group has conditions of work so barren, is treated so shabbily? It is worth remembering that U.S. teachers labor under a heavy legacy, namely long-standing efforts to "teacher-proof" the school.

The idea was not always so outlandish as it now sounds. As management analyst Peter Drucker observes, in teaching we expect ordinary people to do extraordinary things. Indeed, the use of a common curriculum had as much to recommend it as a device to gloss over any teacher inadequacies as to provide student exposure to our cultural patrimony.

Given the exigencies of mass education, limited budgets, hordes of immigrants, and boundless faith in scientific management, moving Frederick Taylor and his stopwatch and clipboard from the factory floor to the schoolhouse door was a short step. And just as the genius of scientific management and the assembly line was to "dumb down" work, so too could the school be "teacher-proofed."

This, indeed, was the triumph of the industrial revolution. Skill and expertise were the province of the engineer and manager, and their insight was to disaggregate work into its individual parts. No longer was the skilled artisan and master craftsperson needed, except in design studios where the prototypes for mass production were created. Unlettered peasants, failed small farmers, the urban poor became—in a twinkling—assembly-line workers. As Charlie Chaplin showed us in *Modern Times*, anyone who could wield a wrench day in and day out was welcome in the factory.

Although teachers were not so obviously and dramatically demeaned, on a relative scale they were treated much the same. By and large they did not—indeed, to this day do not—choose their own books, or examinations, or curricula. They meet goals established by a bureaucracy to which they report. They are not expected to exercise independent judgment; they are not, in fact, in a position to do so. What would they judge?

If the commercial and industrial reality of the 1980s were the same as the 1920s, the present condition of teachers would be understandable if lamentable. But it is not. The reality of the knowledge-based society is not the reality Frederick Taylor knew. The modern firm looks not for mindless attention to endless detail but mindful attention to problem solving. Its stock in trade is applied human intelligence, employees who can analyze, synthesize, communicate, trouble-shoot, and make informed judgments (see Committee for Economic Development, 1985).

This is even more the case in the professions—medicine, law, accounting, architecture, dentistry, engineering, and the ministry. In these fields, practitioners are paid to make judgments, not suspend judgment. And make no mistake: the purpose of bureaucracy is to institutionalize the suspension of judgment. Any teacher who has ever worked in a large school district can offer eloquent testimony to this point.

PROFESSIONALS: WHO ARE THEY?

If teachers are not today treated as professionals, what might teacher professionalism involve? To answer the question, it is useful to look to the other professions: what is distinctive and characteristic about them? Seven broad aspects characterize professionalism.

First, there is the act of profession, which Webster's dictionary reminds us in its first definition is "the act of taking the vows of a religious community." Not until the fourth definition do we find the modern and secular meaning: "a calling requiring specialized knowledge and often long and intensive academic preparation." The body of expert knowledge that the professional commands is not known or accessible to the layperson. To be a professional is to be the master of a discipline and its interpreter; the discipline with the most intensive scientific grounding—medicine—provides the most vivid illustration. It requires the most arcane knowledge.

Second, disciplinary canons are established and enforced by fellow initiates, by peers. Webster also reminds us that a professional is "characterized by conforming to the technical or ethical standard of a profession." As a logical corollary, then, professionals are licensed by the state. It is worth remembering that this is an exercise of the state's police power: a license is permission to do something that is otherwise prohibited.

Third, and a reciprocal of both the first and second, professionals are exclusionary as they are inclusionary. They self-identify to promote their own interest while they distance themselves from nonprofessionals.

Fourth, professionals are typically self-employed, frequently in association with each other in partnership and limited corporations. Insofar as they rely on managers and administrators, professionals employ, and are not employed by such people. Webster, with no irony intended, notes that a characteristic of the professional is "participating for gain or livelihood in an activity or field of endeavor often engaged in by amateurs."

Fifth, and specially pertinent for this essay, professionals operate in a market of willing buyers and sellers: choice is the hallmark of professions, both as to suppliers and consumers.

Sixth, and little noted, despite the fact that most professionals practice in the private sector, they work in "public space." Their colleagues—their fellow professionals—are constantly looking over their shoulders, first in training, then in practice. There is continual peer review in terms of professional regard and status. Not to be confused with professional disciplinary proceedings, professional "regard" is central to professional accomplishment. It results in both referrals and accolades; it is the way in which professional status is rationed within the profession.

In addition, professionals practice in "public space" in that their results are there to see: their customers, real and potential, know—or can find out—what it is the professional has done. Indeed, the best professionals are not only well known, they are household names: Norman Shumway, Edward Bennett William, I. M. Pei, for example.

There is a seventh and decisive reason. The knowledge that professionals possess is not just technical and mechanistic, though in that it abounds. Architects must understand load-bearing capacities and know how various materials perform in different settings. Doctors must understand human physiology. And so on. But they are also involved in activities that are infused with value—while the value component may vary by profession, with architects concerned with esthetics and doctors with ethics, for example, they are nevertheless central to professionalism. This is nowhere more true than in the case of teaching. Indeed, of all the professions, values—moral as well as intellectual—are, if anything, most important in teaching.

EDUCATION AND VALUES

A principal part of the calling is to transmit values, for that is what education is all about. Ideas, concepts, and facts are not taught at random—they are organized into bodies of knowledge that are communicated for a purpose. And while it may sound old-fashioned, the purpose of education today is as it was in the time of classical Greece. It is to create virtuous men and women. What is a liberal education? It is education that prepares men and women to live lives of ordered liberty. Education is not simply recitation of facts; it is a discipline pursued for normative purposes.

If this is the case, then the claims about education's "knowledge base" must be considered with great care. That substantive knowledge is essential to education is beyond dispute; similarly, there is an emerging body of pedagogical knowledge that helps the teacher communicate what students are expected to master. But these two kinds of knowledge do not tell us "what," in the final analysis, should be taught. As a society we teach what we value, but those values are subject to interpretation and reinterpretation, to change and variation. And it is not simply a matter of some things being more important than others, or of reconciling conflicting claims. In a pluralistic society, many differing claims are legitimate. New York's Performing Arts High School is not better or worse than Bronx Science or Aviation, but it is certainly different. It is different for a reason; different people have different interests, capacities, and intellectual and esthetic interests. And it is desirable, reasonable, and proper to satisfy them.

The issue here is not educational relativism: "do whatever feels good." There is an abiding need for a core curriculum for all students, a commitment to our cultural and intellectual patrimony. But even this information can be communicated differently in different settings.

Finally, there is the question of status. It too is an important component of professionalism. Status, hard to define though it may be, describes the present and sets the tone for the future. High status attracts the best and brightest and confers psychic rewards to those already in the profession.

But status is not an attribute that can be conferred by edict; on the contrary, it is the product of a blend of attitudes related to performance. Jobs that are demanding and that require high levels of skill or qualities of mind that are in short supply enjoy high status. World-class athletes or musicians are few; they gain status the old-fashioned way—they earn it. Beyond the status enjoyed by high flyers is the status of a whole profession. It determines who will seek to enter it and who, having sought it out, will remain.

Not long ago—when few were educated as well as teachers— teaching was a relatively high status occupation. Parents, who were themselves not educated, held teachers, who were, in high regard. As American Federation of Teachers president Albert Shanker (1986) observes, teaching has become a victim of its own success. A more highly educated public is less respectful of today's teachers because the status gap is narrower. In many communities, in fact, the gap has been reversed. When large numbers of parents are better educated than the teachers in the schools their children attend, status erosion occurs. And it is not only a problem for teachers in service; it inhibits recruitment and severely limits self-selection into teaching. It is a classic double bind.

TEACHER CHOICE IN PRACTICE

Having said all this, what is the state of play in the teaching "profession" today? What is the range of choice teachers enjoy? Choice by teachers in the elementary and secondary world falls into four broad categories.

One, they may and do choose between public and private schools, and they may then choose within those broad categories once they have made their initial choice. If they choose private school teaching, the range of variation is enormous, from Quaker schools to military academies, from A. S. Neill "Summerhill" schools to classical academies, from storefront schools to boarding schools, from devout denominational schools to secular day schools.

Teachers who choose the public sector find the range of substantive variation small, but there are still important differences among schools: teachers may choose among pastoral rural schools, wealthy suburban bedroom communities, fast-paced urban schools. They may choose among heterogeneous and homogeneous, wealthy and poor, progressive and regressive states and districts. And they may choose between large and small districts: the nation's 15,500 districts include New York City with nearly one million students, and 304 districts of fewer than 299 students (National Center for Education Statistics, 1983).

Two, once having chosen a system, a teacher with seniority may have some choice of buildings and within the building some choice of courses or classrooms or building duties.

Three, teachers may have a choice of building in those districts that support specialty and magnet schools. In districts where they exist, teachers may express a preference for teaching in such a school.

But in all these examples the administrator is still king; the only institutional protection the teacher enjoys is seniority. Final decisions about teacher assignment are made for administrative reasons by administrators. Union contracts may soften and humanize the relationship, but they have not reversed the polarity. True, administrators work within broad policy guidelines set down by lay school boards, and they should be at least dimly aware of the realities of interpersonal relations, but they still call the shots.

There is a final form of "choice" that deserves brief comment. It is do-it-yourself "choice" exercised by the "canny outlaw" (Doyle and Finn, 1984). This is the creative and constructive rule bender, the principled teacher who will not bow to the bureaucracy, the teacher who chooses to be his own man or her own woman. This is the teacher who makes Horace's compromise, the fictional teacher Sizer (1984) so eloquently describes.

Once having chosen, however, most teachers find themselves fixed in place unless they resign and begin again. Many teachers, of course, find themselves involuntarily in the labor market. "RIFed" (laid off) or married to a spouse who relocates, such a teacher must perforce choose again. And so it goes.

TEACHER CHOICE IN THEORY

Is there any reason to think that provider choice might make a difference to teachers, that it might improve on the status quo? From a conceptual standpoint, the answer must be yes. Choice is a defining characteristic of the true professional, and even if teachers are not now treated as professionals, they should be. This is because the best teachers fit the other criteria used to identify professionals generally. In this regard, experience and history are the best guides. From time immemorial, the best teachers have been professionals: by example and practice, they demonstrate their commitment to their calling. They are competent, exacting, caring; they exercise disciplined judgment; they are moral men and women who have made a lasting impression precisely because they are professionals.

If teaching is—or should be—a profession, the role and scope of teacher choice should be enlarged. Teachers should have the opportunity to maximize their own professional choices—where they teach, what they teach, and under what circumstances. (At a macro level, this means rethinking such issues as the portability of teacher pensions between districts and between states, and meaningful reciprocity in teacher licensing and credentialing. Although these two subjects are important, they are beyond the scope of this essay, except to observe that the other professions have made substantial headway in this area, and teachers would do well to emulate the behavior of their fellows.)

One development on the horizon, however, deserves special note: the moves now under way to explore board certification of teachers. Advanced by Albert Shanker, here is a reform proposal that could make a difference. No other single reform is potentially more important. First, it would signal teacher determination to assume responsibility for the future of the profession. No longer would teachers be passive objects subject to the tender mercies of administrators.

In addition, it would strengthen teachers' ties to their disciplinary traditions as it identified and rewarded demonstrated levels of high accomplishment; both these developments would set the stage for significantly increased professionalism. It would lend much needed status to the beleaguered and would permit a rational examination of pay differentials that are consistent with professional standards. It would set the stage for meaningful peer review and should lead to increasing teacher involvement and participation in such important areas as textbook selection and the identification of appropriate tests and measures for both teachers and students. In sum, it would be a giant step toward teacher professionalism.

If board certification were a reality, professional reluctance to engage in choice systems should evaporate. No longer pawns in a system run by administrators, board-certified teachers and their colleagues in education would enjoy greater autonomy and independence. At the same time, they would bear heavier burdens of accountability. Expected to exercise judgment, they would be held responsible for results. If the results are good, so much the better; if not, so much the worse. In either case, the chain of accountability would be shortened. In this setting, choice is inescapable: professionals cannot pass the buck. It stops with them.

Until such time as board certification becomes a reality, however, a number of other steps should be considered in the arena of teacher choice. As it happens, the literature on teacher choice is sparse, in large measure because, until recently, to think of it at all was merely an academic exercise. Although this is in part a commentary on the power of the status quo, its practical significance is that teacher choice proposals must of necessity be cut of whole cloth. To think about it, we must turn to the other professions as models.

PRIVATE PRACTICE OPTION

The most obvious option is the private practice option now the norm in other professions. In this model, the professional may be an independent practitioner or, as is more commonly the case today, may voluntarily join a partnership or professional corporation. In either case, services are offered to the public at large. It is noteworthy that joint practice, long the habit of attorneys, is relatively new in medicine. Although the reasons are not altogether clear, they are related at least in part to increasing specialization. Specialization is, of course, related to the knowledge and practice base of the profession. General practice law and general practice medicine were more common in a less complex society, just as one-room schools were. For the same reason, it is reasonable to expect that the private option most attractive to teachers would be some form of joint practice, not the fee of solo practice.

Although a private practice option, in which teachers would offer their services to a client group in much the same way a group of physicians offer their services in an HMO, may seem alien to public education, it is worth exploring as a conceptual exercise. For a fixed fee, an agreed-to level of service is provided: the terms and conditions of service provision are established by the professionals. And just as physicians rely on allied health service providers to rationalize their work—using nurse practitioners, for example—so too might teachers use paraprofessionals and aides to rationalize their roles. One particularly intriguing dimension of this idea is the "teaching partnership" (Shaten and Kolderie, 1984).

Although examples of this approach in the public sector are not numerous, neither are they unknown. For example, ARA Services, the nation's largest provider of food and transportation services, also makes available comprehensive health care services. For a fixed fee, ARA can offer complete emergency room and shock trauma services for a community, including physicians, nurses, ambulance, pharmaceuticals, and necessary equipment. There is no conceptual barrier to doing the same thing in education.

In fact, in many areas of education, contracting for professional services is the norm. Legal and medical services are frequently purchased privately. And when large government entities—such as the U.S. government—directly employ professionals, they are typically brought on under terms of separate salaries and hiring authority wholly outside the civil service system's general schedule.

The implications of a private practice option are far-reaching and run counter to the U.S. public school experience, however. First, in education in particular, it would create a dramatic break with precedent: professionals do not work for administrators, administrators work for professionals. Paraprofessionals, aides, and the like also work for professionals. This reversal is not to be confused with supervising the aide the school district hires; the aide really works for the professional. Nor should this arrangement be confused with career ladders, which are managed by administrators. A historic analogue is the medieval guilds, which were self-regulating. The contemporary analogue is the law firm that employs a wide range of people, some of whom—associates and junior partners, for example—are serving a probationary period as they are judged by their peers.

Second, professional income is dependent on professional performance. An efficient and effective law partnership or HMO has profit to share at year's end; so too could an education private practice arrangement. Such profit sharing should not be confused with merit pay; professional profits are generated by and then shared by the professionals themselves, not distributed by paternalistic administrators.

The practical limitation of the "private practice option" is that it is essentially a private sector response; teachers would organize themselves in the private sector and offer their services on a contract basis. There is so little public school precedent for it that it is truly radical. Imagine this: once in place teachers would contract with a school district or school committee, or they might also contract with individual families. It is a genuinely startling idea, and whatever conceptual interest it offers must be tempered with political reality. It is not likely to happen without major changes in attitudes and the structure of schooling.

Doubters need only look at existing private schools where such arrangements are already possible; few exist. On the contrary, the prototypical private school is organized in much the same way the public school is. Boards oversee them and administrators run them; curriculum and textbook decisions are made by third parties; so too tests and measures are adopted and interpreted by third parties. Private school teachers work for administrators, not themselves. If private practice options are rare in the private sector, where we expect entrepreneurship, risk taking, and innovation, it is not likely to emerge on a large scale in the public sector. (For an interesting discussion of issues related to private practice options from a union perspective, see Shanker, 1985).

PUBLIC PRACTICE OPTION

If a private practice option is not likely to occur in the near-term future, what kinds of teacher choice systems are more realistic? The most obvious is a "public practice option," to permit or encourage choice by teachers of substantively different teaching environments. There already exist selective speciality schools and magnet schools that offer some opportunity for teacher choice, and there is every reason to believe that this is an expanding part of U.S. education.

The role of magnet schools from the consumer's standpoint is by now widely known; they are open-enrollment schools, organized thematically to present a program of special emphasis and shared intellectual or vocational values. Some are highly selective, the most extreme case being the Hunter College schools, which require very high scores on intelligence tests as a condition of admission. Others are highly selective but deliberately representative, such as the North Carolina School of Science and Mathematics (NCSSM). In this case selectivity is balanced by—or includes—attention to race, ethnicity, character, motivation, gender, and geography.

In addition to schools of great distinction, there are the more typical magnet schools in which selectivity is limited to questions of racial or gender balance and demonstrated ability to do the work. The power of these schools is their ability to create voluntary communities of scholarship. They work because they represent some of the intellectual, pedagogical, and organizational diversity found in mediating structures. Students and teachers want to be there. They are institutional embodiments of what economist Charles Schultze describes as public uses of private interest. They harness the larger purpose of the public school—education for democracy—to private needs for community.

Conceptually, as it is, it is not difficult to imagine teacher-designed and -run magnet schools, and successful ones grow out of active teacher participation in the design and implementation stages; without such teacher involvement, they would founder. But only rarely do magnet schools have the same organizational autonomy as private schools of comparable stature. Bronx Science, Boston Latin, and NCSSM do have substantial autonomy, but they are unusual. Both as a formal matter of law and actual matter of practice, teachers do not "control" the school.

Greater autonomy and professional independence, then, could be accorded magnet schools to give teacher choice more meaning. For this to occur on a wide scale, magnet schools would have to become the norm, not the exception. One way for them to become the norm is to convert whole districts or even regions to magnet programs, in which all schools would be magnets. So far no school district has converted its entire system to magnet schools. The reasons for this are obscure, but a powerful reluctance to convert apparently grips all the nation's school districts. Eventually, however, one district, then two, then many might convert, and teacher choice on a wide scale could become a reality because it would then be a necessity. Arbitrary assignment of teachers to magnet schools by the central office simply makes no sense.

Even absent magnet schools, it is possible to imagine teachers running their own schools within the public sector; a single building in a large system could be given the professional autonomy to manage itself, both administratively and substantively. Teachers could select their own administrator—who would work for them or be one of them—and by so doing restore the original meaning of the term *principal*: "principal teacher." In some Catholic schools to this day, administrative responsibility is rotated among teachers, just as deanships in some universities are.

In a public practice option, teachers would be required to set their own standards and establish conditions of work and performance. To make such a system work, an old idea would have to be revised, namely school site budgeting. The school's budget could be derived from enrollment, as it is at least on paper in many schools today. Income would depend on the number of children enrolled. But in a teacher-run school, expenditure decisions would be made by teachers. For example, in a teacher-run school the opportunity to decide how to staff and organize a ninety-student third grade would not axiomatically lead to hiring three teachers: one or two teachers might decide to serve ninety children more effectively by selective reliance on different instructional technologies and techniques. The teachers might decide to substitute capital for labor (computers) or one kind of labor for another (two aides for one teacher).

This is, of course, precisely what other professions do: today practitioners perform functions physicians used to do. Computer-assisted drafting frees the architect to concentrate on design considerations. But this is precisely what scandalizes unions. Substitute capital for labor? Low-priced labor for higher-priced labor?

No wonder this issue is sensitive. It is an easy call for management, a tough call for labor. Historically unions have been concerned with job security and the absolute number of union members employed, rather than with floating selected salaries higher for a narrower band of employees. Unions took the realities of the Industrial Revolution as a given; they reacted to and did not create the industrial, commercial, and bureaucratic enterprises for which they labored. In this dimension, unions differ most sharply from both guilds and professions, for in these the impulse had been to strengthen the hand of the individual guild member or professional.

However, if teachers take the issue of professionalism seriously, they have it within their power to forge a new institution and a new set of relationships to make it work, for both consumers and providers. They could design the school to fit the knowledge-based society of which it is a part. Schools can emerge from their historic foundations, laid in the industrial revolution, to new foundations laid in the modern, postindustrial society (Shanker, 1985).

Such a shift in attitude by teachers and their unions will not be caused by exercises in pure thought, however; they will be fueled by necessity. In this case, necessity is the teaching market in the late twentieth century. Is there any reason to think that the United States as a nation will provide the pay and status appropriate to a true profession if that profession numbers well over two million people? Not likely; the arithmetic of a $10,000 raise for *all* the nation's teachers is too dramatic. However, substantial raises for half that number are plausible. But it is plausible politically only if teachers themselves embrace it as an idea that serves their long-term professional interests.

There remains the most important and pressing question: having presented a conceptual framework to begin thinking about teacher choice, what are its political and practical limits? Those limits are obviously set by teachers and their unions: if school managers and trustees have their wits about them, they will realize that teachers cannot be forced to participate in choice systems. If not, they will be like the U.S. commander in *Teahouse of the August Moon*, who was determined to push democracy down the throats of his charges whether they wanted it or not.

Teacher choice systems self-evidently rise or fall on what teachers think of them. This in turn will be strongly influenced by what teacher union leaders think of choice systems: Will they strengthen or weaken collective bargaining? Will they encourage or discourage teacher commitment to the modern union movement? Will they accelerate or retard recruitment of new union members? These are hardly idle questions (Doyle, 1984).

The role and place of teachers' unions still perplex many members of the public, in some measure because the unions are a relatively new phenomenon. But they are clearly a necessary and appropriate part of modern schools. The question is not whether teacher unions should play a strong role, but the nature of the role they play. Does a skilled trade and craft union model fit the modern school? Unhappily, the preliminary answer is yes, so long as schools are organized like factories along lines laid down by the scientific management movement. The answer is no if schools emerge as institutions staffed and managed by autonomous professionals. Then the union model is not the factory worker but the guild artisan, who is a member of a voluntary and self-regulating association of independent and equal individuals who share a commitment to and mastery of specialized knowledge. And while the guild member is a craftsperson rather than an assembly-line worker, he or she joins the guild because there is strength in union.

THE BACK OF THE BUS

Because unions are committed to democracy in the workplace, one of the most important questions raised by choice schemes has to do with queueing, or lining up: who is where in the queue, and what effect does that setup have? If "good" education and attractive schools are, by their nature, scarce, those people at the end of the queue will be irritable and cantankerous. Few people like the end of the line.

In private markets for goods and services, queueing does not usually raise ethical questions: people distribute themselves in queues by rationing their own resources: knowledge, time, and money. In the public sector, however, queueing as a form of rationing raises questions of access and equity. We assume, usually correctly, that people at the head of the queue are best off, that people at the end are most in need of the very services their position in the queue denies them.

Conceptually, at least, there are two answers to this problem. First, queueing for education is not like queueing for finished goods. There should be enough good schools to go around; students and teachers should not be playing educational musical chairs. When the choice music stops, all teachers and students should find themselves in desirable schools.

But if choice were simply imposed on the existing system, there would be large numbers of losers. This is because today's schools fall across a quality spectrum largely related to the social class of students. Conceptually, however, the opposite of a good school does not have to be a bad school. As the examples of Bronx Science and Performing Arts attest, the alternative to one good school can be another type of good school.

If teacher choice is tied to professional autonomy, including such prosaic matters as school site budgeting, the absolute number of "good" schools can be expected to increase. The end of the queue will be at least much smaller because there will be multiple small queues. A public sector market can bring together willing buyers and sellers just as a private sector market does.

But if professionalism and choice ameliorate the problem, it is not certain they will solve it altogether. Markets do have imperfections; the classic market imperfection, endemic to education, is lack of perfect knowledge. But in this case models are available to suggest remedies: assigned-risk pools, for example, can be used to temper modest queueing problems.

Students who for whatever reason do not choose a school or do not find space available in the school they choose, could be assigned to a school. Some comparative information has a bearing on the issue. Adelaide, Australia, for example, has had a comprehensive statewide, open-enrollment system in place for several years, and (in an interview with me) John Steinle, the superintendent, reported that 95 percent of the students get their first choice. Similarly, in the Netherlands places in graduate and professional schools are awarded by a weighted lottery because there are more qualified applicants than openings. In sum, there are technical solutions to queueing problems if there is the will to solve them.

The more important point is that teachers themselves, once they see choice systems as a set of challenges and opportunities, can make them work to their advantage and to the advantage of their students. No one prefers failure to success, and if teachers are in charge of their own destinies there is more reason to expect success than when they are not. Finally, improving the lot of most teachers—even if a small number are less than pleased—is not a trivial accomplishment. To create an atmosphere in which the circumstances of teaching are materially better for the majority would be an important advance.

Put baldly, then, the question is this: Do teacher choice proposals and union interests run at cross-purposes? If teacher choice increases professionalism, can unions organize professionals? Does the end of the factory model of education mean the end of education unions? Only if the union refuses to change. As the school is changed, so too must the union change. Old attitudes and habits will no longer suffice.

Greater teacher professionalism must occur or the enterprise of public education will falter. The modern postindustrial society must have schools that reflect the economic and social realities of the present. The factory model of the school simply will not work.

GOING PUBLIC

Choice in and of itself is a category without meaning—choice for what purpose, we must ask. Its purpose is to secure a higher good, which by its nature is both indeterminant and provisional. It is for this reason that we choose our leaders: hereditary ascent—or descent, as the case may be—does not serve the interests of a free and equal people. But if people are free, they may choose unwisely as well as wisely and we have ample evidence of poor choices. *The Shopping Mall High School*, for example, describes choice run amok (Powell, Farrar, and Cohen, 1985). Free to choose courses from the boutiques and miniboutiques that make up the prosperous comprehensive high school, students too often take the path of least resistance: they seek and find the lowest common denominator.

Teachers are not children, and they have the maturity and wisdom to resist temptations to which younger people may yield. But adults too are subject to temptation: the attractions of a beautiful physical plant or the relative ease of teaching pliant students can distract from a sense of higher purpose. But in reality, this is as much a description of the present as a future of teacher choice.

An environment of teacher choice is less likely to sink to the lowest common denominator. Teachers who choose are collaborators, they invest in the system of which they are a part. Instead of incentives that reward passivity and encourage "getting ahead" by "getting along," teacher choice restores proper incentives. Teachers become stakeholders, and they care what their colleagues do and think. As educator Phillip Schlechty (1986) points out, medicine came of age when it "went public." It did so because of the hospital and the emergence of clinical experience. So long as doctors worked in isolation, not just in "solo" practice limited to house calls and office visits, they were truly private practitioners. They *did* bury their mistakes. In the glare of the clinic, however, doctors were subject not just to peer review but instant peer feedback. So too, we could expect teacher choice and its greater professionalism to take the teaching enterprise "public."

WHO WILL TEACH?

We are left then with the single most important aspect of teacher choice, the aspect that simply sweeps aside all other issues: who chooses to teach? That is the future of our public schools.

We have learned to our chagrin over the past two decades that the best and brightest are not choosing to teach. And we have a fairly clear understanding of what is going on. We know that low pay is a barrier to entry, we know that women and members of minorities are no longer limited to teaching as their only career option, we know that the Depression and draft deferments no longer point able people into teaching.

But if we know that these negative factors are no longer at work, we also know that positive factors that might work are also absent. We now expect our teachers to be college graduates with a substantive major, and in many states expect them to earn a fifth year either before or directly after becoming teachers. No longer will a two-year degree from a normal school suffice.

The difference is not just quantitative, time served; there is a qualitative difference. College graduates with substantive degrees expect to be treated like competent adults. The factory model school does not attract them; the professional model may. Bright young people do not find bureaucratic environments appealing; to the extent that they are well educated, they find bureaucratic environments hostile to their own professional ideas about autonomy, independence, and personal satisfaction. As noted by the report of the AFL-CIO Committee on the Evolution of Work (1985), known popularly as the Donahue report, "It is increasingly true that the measure of a good job is high discretion as much as high pay." It goes on to say that "Americans are less likely to see work as a straight economic transaction providing a means of survival and more likely to see it as a means of self-expression and self-development." Although the Donahue report does not disaggregate its data by teachers, what is true of the workforce generally must be true of teachers in particular.

Teacher choice, then, includes who chooses to teach, and those we hope will choose to teach are a different lot from the present teaching force. To be successful, unions must recognize this new reality and tailor their activities and purposes to reflect it. What do good teachers want that unions can provide? Bread and butter issues, of course—salaries and benefits. But they also want what economists call "psychic" income, nonfinancial sources of satisfaction. This has always included conditions of work; professionals, however, think of conditions of work more broadly than factory workers. They are not limited to safety and physical comfort. First and foremost, it includes the opportunity to find professional satisfaction.

NOTE

1. An enormous literature on choice has arisen over the past two decades, almost exclusively directed at questions of student choice. The most well-known choice ideas have to do with education vouchers and tuition tax credits; more recently, magnet schools have attracted substantial attention.

The standard contemporary literature on education vouchers begins with Milton Friedman (1962). See also, Jencks et al. (1970) and Coons and Sugarman (1982). Most analysts cite Adam Smith's *Wealth of Nations* (1776) as the first modern source of the voucher idea, with John Stuart Mill's *On Liberty* (1859) as its most persuasive spokesman. The occasional literature on vouchers is very extensive. One bibliography runs to seven pages, with dozens of entries. For a general description, see Doyle (1981). More recent contributions of note include Glenn (1986), Murnane (1984), Raywid (1984), and Nathan (1984).

REFERENCES

AFL-CIO Committee on the Evolution of Work. *The Changing Situation of Workers and Their Unions.* Washington, DC: AFL-CIO, 1985.
Berger, Peter L., and Neuhaus, Richard John. *To Empower People.* Washington, DC: American Enterprise Institute, 1970.
Committee for Economic Development. *Investing in Our Children: Business and the Schools.* New York: Committee for Economic Development, 1985.

Teacher Choice: Does It Have a Future?   119

Coons, John, and Sugarman, Stephen. *Family Choice in Education*. Berkeley: University of California Press, 1982.

Doyle, Denis P. *Debating National Education Policy: The Question of Standards*. Washington, DC: American Enterprise Institute, 1981.

Doyle, Denis P. "Public School Masters Its Private Lessons," *Wall Street Journal*, 7 December 1983.

Doyle, Denis P. "Window of Opportunity," *Wilson Quarterly* 8, No. 1 (1984): 91–101.

Doyle, Denis P. "Business and Schools: An Evolving Partnership," *Washington Post*, 17 November 1985.

Doyle, Denis P., and Cooper, Bruce. "Is Excellence Possible in Urban Public Schools?" *American Education* 19 (1983): 16–26.

Doyle, Denis P., and Finn, Chester E., Jr. *Educational Quality and Family Choice*. Washington, DC: American Enterprise Institute, 1983.

Doyle, Denis P., and Finn, Chester E., Jr. "American Education and the Future of Local Control," *Public Interest*, No. 77 (1984): 77–95.

Doyle, Denis P., and Levine, Marsha. "Magnet Schools: Choice and Quality in Public Education," *Phi Delta Kappan* 66 (1984): 265–271.

Friedman, Milton. *Capitalism and Freedom*. Chicago: University of Chicago Press, 1962, Chapter 6.

Glenn, Charles L. *Family Choice and Public Schools: A Report to the State Board of Education*. Boston: Bureau of Equal Opportunity, Massachusetts Department of Education, 1986.

Hirschman, Albert O. *Exit, Voice, and Loyalty: Response to Decline in Firms, Organizations, and States*. Cambridge, MA: Harvard University Press, 1970.

Jencks, Christopher, et al. *Educational Vouchers*. Cambridge, MA: Center for the Study of Public Policy, 1970.

Murnane, Richard J. *Family Choice in Public Education: Possibilities and Limitations*. Washington, DC: American Enterprise Institute, 1984.

Nathan, Joe. *Increasing Families' Educational Choices: Need, Mechanics, and Impact*. St. Paul, MN: Public School Incentives, 1984.

National Center for Education Statistics. *Digest of Education Statistics 1983–84*, Table 50, p. 62. Washington, DC: National Center for Education Statistics, 1983.

Powell, Arthur G., Farrar, Eleanor, and Cohen, David K. *The Shopping Mall High School: Winners and Losers in the Education Marketplace*. Boston: Houghton Mifflin, 1985.

Raywid, Mary Anne. *Family Choice Arrangements in Public Schools: A Review of the Literature*. Hempstead, NY: Center for the Study of Educational Alternatives, Hofstra University, 1984.

Schlechty, Phillip. Presentation at the joint AFT-NEA seminar on Board Certification of Teachers, Washington, DC, February 3, 1986.

Schultze, Charles L. *The Public Use of Private Interest*. Washington, DC: Brookings Institute, 1977.

Shanker, Albert. "The Making of a Profession," *American Educator* 9, No. 3 (1985): 10–17, 46, 48.

Shanker, Albert, et al. "How Not to Fix the Schools: Grading the Education Reformers," *Harper's* 272 (February 1986): 39–51.

Shaten, Jessica, and Kolderie, Ted. *Contracting with Teacher Partnerships*. Sacramento, CA: Sequoia Institute, 1984.

Sizer, Theodore. *Horace's Compromise: The Dilemma of the American High School*. Boston: Houghton Mifflin, 1984.

Tyack, David. *The One Best System: A History of American Education*. Cambridge, MA: Harvard University Press, 1974.

Part II
Issues and
Controversies about
Choice

CHAPTER 6

Magnet Schools and the Reform of Public Schooling

Mary Haywood Metz

Magnet schools stand somewhere between bureaucratically controlled, standardized public schooling and models for voucher plans that allow parents to choose any school they like at public expense, including private schools. Magnet schools are public schools within traditional school districts. They differ from traditional schools in three ways, however. They were first established for the sake of racial desegregation. They consequently have firm quotas, or at least re-

Part of the research on which this chapter is based was supported by the National Institute of Education under Project 8–0640. Any opinions, findings, and conclusions expressed in this paper are those of the author and do not necessarily reflect the view of the National Institute of Education, Office of Educational Research and Improvement, or the U.S. Office of Education.

served seats, for students of different races; their student bodies are racially diverse. Students are recruited as volunteers rather than assigned by place of residence; they come, by choice, from a wider catchment area than do students in traditional public schools, often from throughout a district. Finally, in order to attract students to volunteer for these desegregated schools, each school offers a distinctive, often innovative, educational program to its students. Desegregation, parental choice, and innovation thus constitute the distinctive characteristics of magnet schools.

If magnet schools can combine all three of these characteristics in successful schools, one might expect them to be universally endorsed and to take the cities by storm. For just this reason, magnets are popular and their numbers are growing. But they are also resisted and resented—a subject of hot political debate in many communities. Furthermore, magnet schools' ability to deliver on their promises is fragile; it is often undercut by established, powerful organizational and political forces in public schooling. They also run afoul of a strong and pervasive societal myth, the idea that equal educational opportunity requires that the same education—a standardized education— be offered to all students.

THE POTENTIAL CONTRIBUTIONS OF MAGNET SCHOOLS

All three of the special contributions of magnet schools are potentially beneficial to students.

Desegregation

Although desegregation is currently out of fashion as a topic of policy discussion, the need for it grows with the growing proportion of children in the school population who are members of minorities. Soon that proportion will be one in three.

Despite continuing debate about the effects of desegregation on minority achievement, considerable evidence shows that desegregation bolsters minority academic learning—at least when minority students attend desegregated schools from the earliest grades (Mahard and Crain, 1983). White achievement in these schools, as measured by test scores, seems not to be affected by desegregation.

Less attention has been paid to the social effects of desegregation, especially to long-term effects. But some evidence shows that desegregation, again especially that starting in the earliest grades, leads minority children to be more likely to participate in mainstream institutions when they are older—to choose and be accepted in colleges, work settings, and neighborhoods where whites predominate and where greater rewards in money, status, and power are likely to be available (Crain, 1986).

But desegregation is not beneficial just for minority children who learn more and feel more at ease in predominantly white settings. Were the schoolchildren of the generation now entering school to be mixed up and seated in a single large room, every majority child would find a minority child sitting to his or her right or left. The one-third of the adults in the next generation who are now minority children must carry much of the weight of the civic and economic life of the society. Majority children cannot afford to grow up in ignorance of the minority children who will one day be the adults with whom they must cooperate to do society's work. Both majority and minority citizens will be ill served if members of both groups are not taught as children to regard one another as civic and personal equals, as well as to accept one another in such unequal relationships as supervisor and worker.

White students raised in the isolation of all-white or nearly all-white small towns and suburbs simply do not acquire the knowledge or attitudes that will allow them to participate constructively in the multiracial society in which they will live as adults. In short, for the good of the society, white children need to be in desegregated schools—or, better yet, desegregated neighborhoods—just as much as minority children do. Although the issues are slightly different, similar arguments can be made for schooling that brings together more fortunate children with the one-fourth of schoolchildren, a large proportion of them white, who live in official poverty.

Choice

Many analysts think that giving parents—and older children—some degree of choice in the schools they attend will make them more likely to support the school's program with enthusiasm. Because students and parents at magnet schools are volunteers, magnet schools are chosen in the same way that private schools are, although parents do not make a financial commitment to them. It is also possible for parents with similar ideas about education to form a community around schools offering distinctive types of education.

Innovation

Magnet schools' formal license to deviate from standard school practice provides them a key advantage in addressing current educational difficulties. Magnet schools are not only allowed, but expected, to offer different content or to teach in a different way from traditional schools. Such innovations can become natural experiments in which alternative ideas are tried out with interested parents and students, and can be adopted by other schools. Because magnet schools must be racially diverse, they are not subject to the objection that their innovations will work only with a very narrow band of students. Yet magnet schools can be intentionally designed for students with particular kinds of needs, interests, or talents; they need not always claim to be beneficial to all possible students.

Innovation in education is a necessity for the welfare of students in a rapidly changing industrial society. In our society, innovation seems especially important for students whose families are excluded from the mainstream because of minority racial or ethnic status, poverty, or both. These children generally achieve poorly in schools that follow current standard practice. By now a sizable literature in anthropology (Erickson, 1987; Heath, 1983) documents the cultural discontinuity between home and school that young children from such backgrounds often experience. Many such children feel forced to choose between the world of home and peers and that of the school. Not surprisingly, many choose their home worlds.

Older students, even those who have been reasonably successful in the early grades, may disengage from schooling as their peer group starts to question whether school will confer any real benefits on them (Ogbu, 1978). Minority students, especially, learn from the experience of older relatives who have found that education has little applicability on the job and does not bring steady employment or income.

Disengagement from secondary schooling is spreading far beyond minority young people, however. It is becoming evident that, as our economy contracts, more and more students who would once have been considered in the mainstream are coming to doubt the value of a high school education. Much of the reform literature suggests that the majority of students, those who are not heading for somewhat selective colleges, are growing restless with adults' claims that there will be rewards for more than minimal compliance with high schools' educational demands. Many are consequently distancing themselves from their schoolwork, especially at the high school level (Powell, Farrar, and Cohen, 1985; Sedlak, Wheeler, Pullin, and Cusick, 1986; Sizer, 1984). Both policymakers and parents are expressing increasing concerns about the level of engagement and of learning in schools for younger children as well. As the literature of the current reform movement repeatedly points out, U.S. children are not doing well on tests, especially tests of higher-order skills (National Commission on Excellence in Education, 1983).

From the progressive movement of the early 1900s through the local school initiatives of the 1960s, a countercurrent of varied innovative educational patterns has often successfully engaged culturally different or skeptical students in school learning. Magnet schools have the potential to institutionalize and legitimate some of these innovative patterns as *formally* acceptable alternatives to the "one best system."

SOME CONTRIBUTIONS OF MAGNET SCHOOLS

If you raise the topic of magnet schools in casual or general conversation, many people think of magnet schools as high schools and as designed for the most able students of a school system. This popular image reflects some of the problems of magnet schools discussed later. For the moment, let us underscore the fact that magnet schools in principle serve all ages and students of all abilities. Individual schools can be—and often are—designed to attract students whose abilities extend across the board or those who would not do well in traditional schools, as well as those who excel.

In the early 1980s, I studied magnet schools set up by one of the thirty-five largest districts in the country—to which I gave the pseudonym the Heartland School District. It used magnet schools to infuse a measure of voluntarism into a desegregation plan that responded to a federal court order. My study centered around in-depth observation of the interior lives of the three magnet schools established at the middle school level. I studied each for approximately one semester during its third or fourth year of existence. I also followed school district policies and politics over a seven-year period and interviewed several central office administrators and members of the school board. The study is reported at length in *Different by Design: The Context and Character of Three Magnet Schools* (Metz, 1986).

Two of the three magnet middle schools in Heartland were designed for nonelite students and served them well. Both created significant changes in the traditional forms of schooling. As a result, the teachers and students in these two schools were able to develop constructive social relationships in support of their academic work together that were much stronger than those I have seen in other schools I have studied—or most I have read about.

One of these magnet middle schools, Adams Avenue, had a student body that almost perfectly reflected that of the predominantly blue-collar Heartland district in the range of test scores of entering sixth-graders and in the number of students eligible for free lunch, except that it was somewhat poorer. Well over half the Adams Avenue students qualified for free lunch and half of those entering the sixth grade were reading at levels comparable to the bottom third of a national sample. At Jesse Owens, another of Heartland's magnet middle schools, more than two-thirds of the students were eligible for free lunch, and more than half were reading at a level comparable with the bottom third of a national sample. Indeed, almost half had reading scores comparable with the bottom quarter of such a sample—although math scores were somewhat stronger.

Both these magnet middle schools enrolled fewer than 400 students, and both modified traditional curriculum, grading practices, and classroom activities. Jesse Owens also had a modified daily schedule. Although they both altered traditional patterns in these common ways, their educational philosophies and curricular approaches were quite different.

Adams Avenue offered "individually guided education." In practice, this phrase meant that students progressed through a curriculum of carefully defined, skill-oriented objectives at their own pace, working in small groups with other children at the same level of skill. Students at all levels of accomplishment participated in the same classroom, but were divided into five or six skill-based groups. Teachers spent most of their time circulating among the groups. Grades reflected progress and effort, with separate notations of a student's absolute level of achievement. The skill-oriented curriculum was balanced with several projects that cut across subject areas, and with a rich extracurricular program in which the majority of students participated.

Jesse Owens offered open education. Students spent most of their day in self-contained multiaged classes; they kept the same teacher throughout their middle school careers. Together with this teacher, each student developed individual long-term and short-term goals and programs of activity to meet those goals. Activities sometimes included working with others in a group. Projects integrating subjects were encouraged. During much of the day, students could move about the school, using varied resource centers with staff available to help them. Grades were given in the form of narrative progress reports.

Both Adams Avenue and Jesse Owens enabled low-achieving students to make more sense of their education, and to demonstrate more involvement with academic activities than had similar students in other racially and socially diverse schools I had studied earlier (Metz, 1978a, 1978b). Teachers also felt more successful. They came to know their students better as people and were able to develop a more supportive, less discipline-oriented, relationship with them than had been possible in the other schools.

Students at Adams Avenue and Jesse Owens came from diverse social backgrounds. There were students at both schools who had solid histories of academic success, even though the majority at both schools scored below average. Both teachers and students felt, for the most part, that able students' needs could be met along with those of the low achievers because the curriculum and structure of teaching and learning activities were designed to accommodate students with diverse backgrounds, knowledge, and speeds or styles of learning. Furthermore, relations between children of different races were re-laxed and positive. At Adams, especially, there were many mixed-race groups in voluntary activities and many genuine friendships that crossed racial lines.

Adams Avenue and Jesse Owens strongly suggested that departure from traditional models of schooling can benefit children who have resisted school and done poorly. The schools also showed it is possible to educate such children together with children who have been more successful—with benefit to both groups. These schools demonstrate the positive potential of the innovative license that is given to magnet schools. They also show that such schools can desegregate across lines of social class, achievement, and race—and serve all their students well.

If we take these schools as indicative of the potential of magnet schools, we see that magnets are a policy instrument that can serve ends that are often seen in competition. They can, if carefully designed, meet ends of both equity and excellence. They can offer choice, voluntarism, and a match between a distinctive school program and children's distinctive needs that tailors education to the individual much more than the dominant approach offering standardized education. At the same time, through public control, requirements for racial diversity in recruitment, and rules for handling oversubscription that do not have class bias, they can recruit racially and socially diverse student bodies. Such student bodies serve the needs of the collective as well as the individual by enticing families to expose their children to racially and socially diverse peers. Magnet schools thus have the potential to create a better balance between individual and collective needs than either standard public schools or free market voucher programs. But one must stress the word *potential* here. Strong forces at work on magnet schools tend to undercut their realization of potential benefits.

PRESSURES UNDERCUTTING THE DISTINCTIVE QUALITIES OF MAGNET SCHOOLS

In having the potential to meet educational needs that stand in tension with one another, magnet schools become contested terrain. Interested parties—central office and building administrators, parents, community groups, teachers, and students—all may have different visions of the emphasis or interpretation magnet schools should place on varied aspects of their missions. As stakeholders' different perceptions are accommodated in practice, some aspects of magnet schools' missions may be compromised or transformed.

Racial desegregation, or at least racial integration—a social environment in which the races mix easily as social equals—seems to be the most easily compromised aim. Most of the rhetoric about magnet schools coming from current federal leaders and from advocates of choice is virtually silent about their potential for creating racially integrated environments. In the Heartland school district, while racial quotas were adhered to for the sake of compliance with the court order to desegregate, school district rhetoric included virtually no reference to the educative value of desegregation or the creation of social integration. At the two schools I have described, school-level administrators and teachers made interracial relationships and racial equity school priorities. The school district provided some human relations staff, but the central office thrust emphasized trouble-shooting at (nonmagnet) schools where racial tensions ran high, rather than building good relationships at any of the schools, magnets included.

There is little research to document how successfully magnet schools create physical mixing of students of different races within school walls, let alone constructive relationships among them. To know how well magnet schools create genuine racial integration, we need more ethnographic research based on prolonged participation in such schools. What research we do have, especially Janet Schofield's (1982) careful study of racial relations in one magnet middle school, suggests that interracial relationships often take low priority for both staff and parents. Adults find it difficult even to raise the topic for public discussion, and students come to see explicit discussion of race in public contexts as taboo. Rosenbaum and Presser (1978) also describe a school where the staff took the innovative mission of the school very seriously, but—except for one subunit—paid no attention to racial relations or to the differing needs of students from different home and school backgrounds. Research on desegregated schools that are not magnets finds it is common for the staff to place more emphasis on avoiding trouble than on building positive interracial relationships or even on meeting diverse student needs (for example, Cusick, 1983; Metz, 1978b; Rist, 1978, 1979). There are exceptions, however (Heath, 1983; Lipsitz, 1984).

Even meaningful parental choice is fragile in the real world of magnet schools. Magnet schools that develop positive reputations often attract more applicants than they can accommodate. Criteria for admission then limit parental choice and raise serious problems of equity. Admission by academic screening often seems inequitable in a public school, although when magnets are defined in terms that imply fostering academic excellence, staffs and families who are already admitted often favor it. First-come, first-serve admissions lead to long lines of parents, who sometimes camp out for several days in line. Single parents and parents with inflexible working hours are obviously disadvantaged by such a system. The student body of the school is slanted toward students from higher-income, better-educated families. Admission by lottery may be fairest and least likely to exclude students on social class criteria, but it undercuts the sense of parental control over children's fate that is one very significant benefit of choice.

Although magnet schools have the potential to be vehicles for innovations that can help alienated students, including poor and minority students, develop a more vital interest in school, they are subject to all the political pressures that also shape ordinary schools. That means they must win the support of the powerful members of a community. White school administrators often expect a magnet school's desegregated recruitment in itself to offer sufficient rewards to minority groups; they feel they must spend most of their efforts to design and nurture programs that will please and attract powerful, wealthy, well-educated white parents. Schools for the gifted and talented, or with emphasis on math, science, computers, or performing arts are likely to be more attractive to such parents than to those of ordinary lower-middle- and working-class students, let alone poor students. Such schools may have admissions criteria ranging from grades to teachers' recommendations or interviews—with all the potential for subjectivity and class bias, or even individual favoritism, these criteria can introduce.

Central administrators often say they need to attract the city's leaders in order to generate enthusiasm for voluntary enrollment and to get the ball rolling for community acceptance of an overall program of magnet schools. Well-educated, relatively affluent citizens have access to the media to get favorable publicity and they have good skills and connections to spread favorable accounts of the schools through the leadership groups in a community. These are also the families most likely to flee a city for the suburbs if they are displeased with the schools. Mindful of the tax base such citizens represent, as well as the influence they wield, administrators have pragmatic reasons to want to please them, to keep them both as city residents and in city public schools.

Magnet schools' ability to be genuinely innovative may also be inhibited by school districts' efforts to assist the very disadvantaged children that innovative education might help, but to do so through standardization of program. In Heartland, the school board instituted such programs as a single basal reader for all schools—to lessen problems experienced by children who move frequently—and a required supplemental course in reading for eighth-graders reading at below average levels. Such central decrees severely cramped the ability of magnet schools to offer genuinely distinctive or innovative education.

Linda McNeil (1985) describes in vivid detail ways in which steps taken by the Texas legislature and by one city to improve the character of teachers' performance through standardized teacher evaluation, curricula, and testing procedures, had the effect of undercutting not only the performance, but the morale, of the corps of teachers in magnet schools who had chosen these schools because they offered an opportunity to innovate. The reform movement, at least in the form taken by the first wave that emphasizes raising standards and centralizing the definition of good practice, flies in the face of the innovative thrust of magnet schools and is likely to have disabling effects on them.

Both school district staff and leading parents are frequently uncomfortable with schools that differ very much from traditional patterns in social structure or curriculum, even when they are magnet schools with a formal license to innovate. Often, magnet schools do not change the structure or basic curriculum of traditional schools but simply add an emphasis on a particular subject area, so that students may learn more about, or develop advanced skills in, performing arts or science while they otherwise receive a traditional school curriculum and experience. At some periods federal guidelines for funding magnet schools have stressed subject specialization as the heart of the definition of magnet schools. The Jesse Owens school in Heartland, which was an open education school, became ineligible for federal assistance during my study in 1980 because it did not fit federal definitions of a magnet school on these grounds.

Both high school staffs and the public in general seem to have well-formed and deeply rooted (Cohen, 1987) ideas of what constitutes good practice in schools. The powerful force of these traditional ideas should not be underestimated, particularly at the high school level (Metz, in press). Magnet schools, especially secondary schools, are subject to the pressures of tradition despite their license to innovate. The power of the image of traditional schooling goes deeper than a rational consideration of the needs of students and possible educational strategies to meet those needs. The third magnet middle school included in my study in Heartland was a school for the gifted and talented. It made no serious alterations in traditional school routines, curriculum, grading, or classroom activities. Teachers did not consider such changes part of their mission as a school for the gifted and talented, nor were they supposed to do so, according to the blueprint given the school by Heartland's central office. This school had more difficulty than Adams Avenue or Jesse Owens in reaching its low achievers (most of whom would have been average or above-average students in the other two schools) and in interracial relations. Teachers and administrators were frustrated by some students' lack of engagement and performance, but since they thought it inappropriate to alter the school's approach, they looked to the students to adjust to the school. It is relevant that this middle school differed from the other two in the study not only in its blueprint, but in its staff's orientation toward high school—as most had training and previous experience in grades 7 to 12, while most of the staff at both Adams Avenue and Jesse Owens had training and experience in grades 1 to 8.

The powerful hold of tradition suggests it will be an uphill battle for magnet schools to make meaningful use of their apparent license to innovate, especially at the secondary level. Magnet schools are the latest in a series of recurrent attempts to innovate and change U.S. schools, especially those serving the poor. Since well back into the nineteenth century, repeated imaginative efforts have been made to fit education to the background of the student, to give the student a more active role, and to allow for more diversity in the form and content of what is taught as local circumstances and students' curiosity dictate, especially at the elementary level. Many such attempts have produced enthusiastic learning, but have disappeared after perhaps slightly altering, but not removing, the restraining hand of standard practice. That there is such strong pressure toward making schools alike—despite the different perspectives, skills, and aspirations of their students and despite the recurrent appearance of new ideas—suggests that policy analysts should ask whether this similarity among schools is serving the needs or interests of society or of some powerful group within society.

CONTRADICTIONS IN THE SOCIAL
UNDERSTANDING OF EDUCATIONAL EQUITY

If it is true that culturally different children, children from low-income families—and, increasingly, even children from solid blue-collar families—do not prosper in traditional schools, why should there be social and even federal pressure to make magnet schools merely enriched in particular subjects, not genuinely distinctive in educational style? Why should educators and the public shrink from the thoroughgoing educational change that the magnet school idea can legitimate? Why should the potentialities for innovation that would help poorer urban children so often be ignored as magnet programs establish schools that are mere enriched traditional schools for the more privileged children of a city?

When educators discuss public schooling, they think of it as instilling the content of the curriculum and some of the social graces required to be a member in good standing of a school community. But education plays another very important role for society in preparing the young to enter into adult roles. Schooling sorts the group of babies born in any year into a set of eighteen-year-olds divided into groups labeled as suited for very different kinds of occupational futures.

Imagine what would happen if some year the goal that schools supposedly seek were actually accomplished. Imagine that suddenly all the graduates of all the high schools in the country were success-fully educated, so that all made perfect scores on the Scholastic Aptitude Test, not to mention having perfect A records throughout their schooling. Chaos would ensue. Colleges would not have room for all, but would have few grounds on which to accept some and reject others. Employers looking for secretaries, computer programmers, waiters, bus drivers, and factory workers would have jobs unfilled, as every student considered such work beneath his or her accomplishments.

Good education, or students' success at education, must remain a scarce commodity as long as education is used to rank young people and sort them into occupational futures that differ substantially in their attractiveness and intrinsic as well as monetary rewards. Society's recruitment of a workforce proceeds more smoothly if only a relatively few students excel while others have varied success in school. Those who perform well face less competition when large numbers of others do not.

In the United States, we say we do not believe in passing privilege from parent to child. We expect individuals to earn the favored slots in society through talent and hard work. We ask the schools to judge that talent and diligence. It is important to our national sense of a fairly ordered social system that all children have an equal opportunity through education. The poorest child must have access to as good an education as the richest, if we are to say that educational success is a just criterion by which to award young people a slot in the occupational hierarchy.

At the same time, education in this country is formally decentralized, officially the province of the states, and in many ways shaped by local school districts, numbering in the hundreds in each state. How then to guarantee an equal education? By guaranteeing the *same* education. Educators have built a social reality around the idea of progress through the grades as a standardized experience. It is supported by nationally distributed textbooks keyed to particular grades and nationally normed tests that report children's progress in grade equivalents.

We feel we are talking about something real when we say a child reads at the third-grade level. According to our formal expectations, a child who completes the fourth grade anywhere in the country should be able to move into the fifth grade in a different community without experiencing significant problems of adjustment because of the continuity or difficulty of academic work. High schools' remarkably similar curricula, requirements, and even textbooks are part of the same pattern.

The construction of standard curricula, standard academic requirements, standard expectations for performance in each grade, and standard activities to be pursued in the course of the school day is a way of assuring the public, the parents, and finally the students and the school staffs as well, that the schools do indeed offer every U.S. child equal educational opportunity. In such a setting, each student's success or failure in school can be interpreted as a reflection of individual merit. To deviate from this pattern to design an educational setting around children's needs, interests, prior knowledge, or special aspirations creates two problems for students. It risks offering the child less than full educational opportunity. To deviate also risks offering less than a satisfactory credential; employers or colleges will not know how to compare graduates to those from other schools. The result may disadvantage ambitious graduates—as well as confuse college admissions and industrial personnel departments.

At the same time that there is strong public consensus on the importance of offering a strong and standard curriculum to all U.S. children, there is unspoken but wide knowledge of an opposing principle. While schools are officially declared equal, middle-class parents and alert working-class parents work diligently to place their children in schools where they will receive an education that will be more than equal—that is superior. All across the country, such parents recognize that schools are far from the same, that children changing schools might find the next grade much more, or much less, demanding in a different community.

Parents usually regard schools that draw students from a higher social class as better. Peers are a crucial resource for each individual child, as teachers tend to teach to the general level of the class. Both research and conventional wisdom indicate that group levels of achievement rise as social class rises and fall as it falls. Schools with budgets sufficient to provide additional visible resources or activities, including smaller classes, are also attractive. These tend to be schools in communities with higher-income parents and so more generous tax support.

That schools are not the same, despite the appearance of standardization, is such an open secret that realtors advertise houses according to their school attendance area, where schools have a local reputation for high quality. Both particular neighborhood schools in larger communities and suburban systems will be mentioned in short real estate advertisements. Houses in such neighborhoods can cost thousands of dollars more than equivalent structures in neighborhoods where schools have a less sterling reputation.

Separate suburban school districts allow their residents far more control over the means to create superior schools. Ordinances requiring certain sizes for lots, or only single-occupancy housing, can keep out lower-income families. Fair housing groups across the country document the continued practice of racial steering by real estate agents and selective lending by banks. These policies can be used to keep many suburban communities all or mostly white. Suburban districts take advantage of their higher tax base to offer higher salaries for teachers, small class sizes, richer stores of materials, and special programs in their "standard" schools that are not available in the "standard" schools of nearby cities. The simple fact of being a suburb does not ensure wealth and luxury—some suburbs are predominantly working class. But suburban incorporation greatly assists relatively affluent communities in shaping their population and ensuring their tax base. It gives even communities where financial resources are modest more control over the population and policy of their schools than residents of large cities can hope to enjoy.

Differences between schools in communities of different social class are a reality that is widely recognized, but rarely mentioned in public discourse about education—except by those trying to get access to a better education for disenfranchised children. Americans are deeply attached to officially equal education based on standardization of curriculum and activities, but they also endorse, or at least accept, tremendous informal variety in the quality and content of education that is linked to the social class of segregated, socially homogeneous neighborhoods and suburbs. In a process that political scientist Murray Edelman (1977) argues is common in many areas of our political life, we rarely see—let alone openly acknowledge—the contradiction between these two principles.

Society's blindness to this contradiction serves the interests of the well-educated middle class. They can claim that the young are rewarded according to merit at the same time that they place their own individual children in contexts where merit is far more likely to blossom than in those to which poorer and minority children find themselves consigned. The "standard" education offered to others—ill suited to engage their commitment—ensures that the numbers of children with whom privileged students are genuinely competing on an equal level are substantially reduced.

MAGNET SCHOOLS' VIOLATION OF THE PUBLIC DEFINITION OF EQUITY IN SCHOOLING

Magnet schools draw political fire because they bring this tacit contradiction to consciousness. In order to draw volunteers, they must be *formally* nonstandard, different from other schools. They thus openly and officially violate the rule that schools should be alike in order to ensure a fair race. Worse, in order to induce volunteers to ride buses far from their homes and in order to induce whites voluntarily to participate in desegregation, these schools must be at least implicitly superior. They are sometimes explicitly so, with formal entrance criteria and notably richer resources than other schools.

Magnet schools thus do formally, openly, and with public flourish what affluent neighborhood and suburban schools do unofficially and inexplicitly. But because they do it formally, openly, and officially, magnet schools force communities to perceive and acknowledge these schools' departure from equality through sameness and standardization. They then come under attack for receiving extra resources and for "creaming" good students from a city's other schools.

Consequently, magnet schools are subject to a variety of pressures. They are criticized for being inequitable, even when they have few extra resources in the quality of students, teachers, or material objects, simply because they are symbolically superior. They often draw back—or are drawn back—from innovation because district staff or parents are disturbed by their departure from traditional patterns lest it endanger students' futures or undercut the image of fairness supported by standardization.

At the same time, they are subject to all the pressures to give political advantage to interest groups that are at work in U.S. education. Either through intentional design, or through patterns of choice by privileged parents in a city, certain magnet schools can draw selected student bodies reminiscent of suburban schools, even if more varied in color.

ATTACKS ON MAGNET SCHOOLS AS INEQUITABLE

Both in local districts and in some policy circles magnet schools are increasingly being perceived as instruments that create an inequitable hierarchy of schools within a district. Both school staffs and some policy analysts fear that as they attract selective student bodies they will not only provide an unfair standard of comparison for other city schools but will also draw the best students out of other schools in a district, leaving the weaker students in traditional schools without student leaders or the protection of active parents.

Where magnet schools have academic admissions criteria or where they are set up with programs such as gifted and talented education or math and science specialties, such "creaming" of good students from other schools in the district is likely to be a reality. Some districts seem to design magnet schools only of this kind, so that magnet schools do indeed become a separate track, bastions of privilege that attract middle-class, high-achieving children. Still, even in these districts, one must ask whether the number of spaces in these schools is sufficient to have a significant impact on other schools—aside from the symbolic impact of their consequent informal second-class status.

More important, not only is such a pattern of privilege and school-level tracking *not* inherent in the idea of magnet schools, it is often not the practical reality, either. In Heartland, only one school at each age level had admissions criteria. Many of the magnet schools, like Adams Avenue and Jesse Owens, attracted student bodies that were close to, or weaker than, a cross section of the district in terms of entering test scores. Although they drew some students with ambitious parents who had questions about traditional education, they also drew more than their share of especially difficult students who had been unable to learn or to cooperate successfully in traditional schools.

Even in Heartland, however, magnets had a symbolic demoralizing effect on "traditional" schools. Teachers and administrators in "traditional" schools, especially high schools, vastly exaggerated both the numbers of potential students they lost to magnet schools and the skills and other virtues of magnet school students. Wild rumors flew around in the traditional schools about the financial privileges of the magnet schools as well. For example, in one traditional middle school that I visited briefly for contrast, I was confidently told that every teacher in a magnet school had a classroom aide, something that did not even approach the truth.

Although magnet schools clearly are used in some districts in ways that create inequitable two-track or multitrack systems of schools, often the degree to which they do so is ambiguous and difficult to document. Since Heartland provided a case where such tracking was minimally present—with the exception of a very few highly visible magnet schools—the reaction of people there suggests that the symbolic issues of equity raised by the presence of magnet schools are at least as important as any real tracking that they can create.

The most interesting aspect of attacks on magnet schools as inequitable by parents, staff of other schools, and even many policymakers and educational researchers is the expression of outrage over magnet schools as inequitable *in the absence of parallel outrage at inequity in the privileges of suburban schools that have student bodies that are far more socioeconomically and academically selective than those at magnet schools.* Considering the furor of criticism for inequity that magnet schools have created in some cities and by some outside observers, there is surprisingly little criticism of the inequality of physical and human resources in suburban—especially affluent suburban—schools, as compared to those in cities. There is also apparently little conscious public awareness that suburbs use money earned by parents in the cities to support exclusive, highly funded schools that are inaccessible to city children.

There seem to be several reasons for blindness to the privileges of suburban schools among people who strongly object to magnet schools. Suburban schools are informally different, not formally so. They do not formally or openly violate the myth that all schools are alike and therefore equal. Furthermore, the incorporation of suburbs as separate communities with independent school districts blurs public awareness of the interdependence of social and educational processes in metropolitan areas as wholes. Teachers and principals do not expect their work to be directly compared to the work of suburban school staffs, but they do fear criticism if their test scores or the enthusiasm of their students do not equal those in magnet schools.

Even more important, separate incorporation makes suburbs inaccessible to traditional political pressures. Those who are aware of these inequities may also be aware that U.S. Supreme Court decisions on suburban desegregation in *Milliken v. Bradley* and on school finance in *San Antonio v. Rodriguez* have made suburban privileges difficult to attack through legal means. Magnet schools, in contrast, are creatures of school board policy and so subject to efforts to eliminate or transform them.

Given the striking inequities between suburban and city schools, there is enormous irony in the anger that magnet schools attract on the grounds of equity. Except where magnet schools have entrance examinations and are frankly schools for academic elites, it is likely that they are less different from the other schools of a city system in both composition of the student body and available resources than are the schools of many suburbs. Even traditional neighborhood schools in a city may differ more in the skills, attitudes, and home privileges of their student bodies than do magnet and nonmagnet schools. Schools in affluent city neighborhoods often have informal ways of obtaining superior resources in money and personnel despite standard funding formulas and hiring rules, through such channels as gifts and the choice of the school by senior teachers encouraged by colleagues or administrators to apply.

From the viewpoint of individual students, then, magnet schools are far more equitable than traditional schools. They allow more open access to students of all colors and economic backgrounds than do schools in middle-class white neighborhoods and suburbs—where admission requires money for expensive housing and white skin to get past housing gatekeepers. By uncoupling housing and school attendance and by reserving seats to create multiracial student bodies, magnet schools offer individual students more equitable access to excellent schooling than is otherwise available either within city limits or in metropolitan areas as wholes.

Magnets' openness to individual capable children without social resources is sometimes acknowledged by critics. They are more likely to question magnets' effect on schooling opportunities across the population, fearing that the presence of magnets leaves regular schools with the least able and ambitious students and teachers. It is not at all clear that this criticism is accurate in imputing losses in anything but symbolic status to regular schools with the introduction of magnet schools. The problem of able and ambitious teachers transferring out of schools serving poor children after a few years' service is a perennial one, though traditional neighborhood schools serving the middle class may experience some unaccustomed loss of teachers with the introduction of magnet schools. However, some excellent teachers who find the freedom to experiment and innovate in magnet schools essential to satisfaction in their work might leave teaching if they could not have the special freedom offered them in magnet schools (McNeil, 1987).

Furthermore, while magnet schools as a class tend to attract student bodies that are slightly more privileged in terms of both class background and prior educational achievement than the overall student population of their districts, an absence of magnet schools would not guarantee equitable distribution of these students through the ordinary schools of a city. In the absence of magnet schools, many of these students' families would move to neighborhoods where schools have good reputations, or to suburbs, or would send their children to private schools. Their moral support for schools would travel to these even more elitist settings, and often their tax dollars would leave central cities.

It is essential to contrast magnet schools to real patterns of schooling experienced in the recent past or likely to be experienced in the future, not to an idealized model in which families of differing backgrounds are equitably distributed across all schools. U.S. education currently has a system of choice in education based on residence and the availability of private education for the well-to-do. The broad costs and benefits of magnet schools, and their specific effects on equity, must be calculated within the context of the reality of constant migration to apparently superior neighborhood and suburban schools by those whose skin color and financial resources give them the most options. It is also crucial to these considerations that, unlike schools of choice supported by vouchers, magnet schools are public schools by definition. They are usually city schools or at least schools in racially mixed communities. As public schools, they can require residence (and thus responsibility to pay taxes) within the community from their students' families. As public schools, they can be subjected to political and legal pressure to set policies that dictate racially mixed student bodies and encourage socially diverse ones.

CONCLUSION

Magnet schools have the potential to be one of the most beneficial patterns emanating from the current wave of educational reform. They are one of the few changes in educational patterns that offer real promise of dislodging the hold of standardization on U.S. schooling. They do so by legitimating innovation that can be sweeping and genuinely experimental—since it is not proposed as a universal pattern and must be accepted only by volunteers. They are revolutionary in breaking the connection between student body composition and housing patterns, and in doing so in a context where genuine racial diversity is not only allowed but expected and even required. Not only are they racially diverse, but because recruitment is not linked to housing, they can also be socially diverse. Voluntarism and choice give parents a feeling of control over their children's fate in schools that are risky both because they are innovative and because they contain peers from dissimilar backgrounds.

Educational policymakers have made too little of the potential of magnet schools as exemplars. Because magnet schools have a license to innovate, they can be sites of natural experiments with varied approaches. Because they are voluntarily desegregated, socially diverse, and often also serve students with disparate abilities, they can be used to explore the most effective ways to work with such diverse groups. Voluntary parental enrollment in such schools may be the most forceful argument for their viability and even their superiority in the face of societal preferences for social and racial homogeneity. Their graduates of all races and classes are also likely to seek out diverse settings for college and for their own children's schooling.

Despite these potential benefits of magnet schools, their contributions are fragile and their promise easily squandered. Nothing exempts them from the ordinary political forces surrounding education. Powerful interest groups and parents with the obvious and subtle extra resources granted by good education, professional and managerial jobs, and superior financial resources will try to influence the design of magnet schools for their own ends and to shape admissions processes to the advantage of their own children. It is no accident that magnet schools are springing up and becoming visible as the upper middle class grows tired of commuting from exurbia and looks to gentrified city neighborhoods for new places of residence.

Yet, even when magnet schools in fact provide more open opportunity than other realistically available schooling patterns, they may be accused of inequity because of their symbolic violation of the appearance of equity through standardization. The simple presence of magnet schools symbolically demotes other schools in a district to a lesser status without any real change in their students, practice, or resources.

Magnet schools are also subject to pressure from the deep-seated social patterns that support standardized education. Both educators and parents often feel more comfortable if their genuinely innovative potential is ignored in favor of the establishment of schools that exemplify standard patterns with enrichment in one or another subject or accelerated work geared to gifted students.

Finally, while choice and voluntarism can support the distinctive patterns of magnet schools, they also jeopardize their security. Not only undersubscription, but oversubscription—with the jealousy and conflict it engenders—can make a magnet school's position precarious. Further, a really distinctive school faces an uphill task of parental education in order to get established.

For a program of magnet schools to succeed in realizing their potential, the people who design, advertise, and oversee them must be fully aware of the benefits such schools can confer and of the pitfalls they must avoid. Such people must be politically astute, firm, fair, and attuned to the welfare of all children and of the whole community. Still, they alone can not make magnet schools politically viable or educationally effective. Community leaders and parents who will spread enthusiasm must be recruited to support both the program as a whole and individual schools. Finally, each school can make good on what it promises only with teachers and administrators who are genuinely attached to all its relevant goals and practices.

Given the dominance of the self-interest of powerful groups that has shaped our current highly stratified system of schooling, it may seem unrealistic to hope that magnet schools can break out of this framework of political dominance except in short-term adjustments around federal desegregation orders. However, as business and civic leaders study current demographic patterns, it is possible they may reinterpret their self-interest. With one-fourth of current children growing up in poverty and one-third from minority groups, it is no longer in the self-interest of the powerful to consign such children to actually inferior, if supposedly standard, schools. Current poor and minority children must become the productive citizens who provide the labor force and the tax base on which depends the prosperity of the society. The children of the powerful will depend on their contributions and encounter them both directly and indirectly on a daily basis.

In that spirit, I dare to suggest what I think would be the optimal pattern of schooling, though it is not one that is likely to win political favor in 1989. If we want to make real the equity in schooling that we proclaim, and if we want to provide our children with a realistic preparation for the racially and socially diverse society in which they will live their adult lives, we need to make the schools racially and socially diverse now. Furthermore, we need to break up the student bodies of schools that are pockets of hopelessness, and to share the resources that the children who are best prepared for school can provide as peers for their age mates.

In most metropolitan areas, dissolving current school districts and creating districts shaped like pie slices would be the most effective way to create this kind of equity in most metropolitan areas. Such districts would serve students of varied races and classes. They should be small enough to maintain human scale and allow personal ties among personnel and between parents and staff. Establishing magnet schools in such districts could restore some sense of control to those parents who find such changes wrenching. Magnet schools could develop programs that break the lockstep of standardized schooling. They could try out patterns that show promise of being more effective with the diverse student bodies—patterns that would become the norm instead of the exception.

REFERENCES

Cohen, David. "Educational Technology: Policy and Practice," *Educational Evaluation and Policy Analysis* 9 (1987): 153–170.

Crain, Robert L. "The Long-term Effects of Desegregation: Results from a True Experiment." Paper presented to the National Conference on School Desegregation Research, University of Chicago, 1986.

Cusick, Philip A. *The Equalitarian Ideal and the American High School.* New York: Longman, 1983.

Edelman, Murray. *Political Language: Words That Succeed and Policies That Fail.* New York: Academic Press, 1977.

Erickson, Frederick. " Transformation and School Success: The Politics and Culture of Educational Achievement," *Anthropology and Education Quarterly* 18 (1987): 335–356.

Heath, Shirley Brice. *Ways with Words: Language, Work, and Life in Communities and Classrooms.* New York: Cambridge University Press, 1983.

Lipsitz, Joan. *Successful Schools for Young Adolescents.* New Brunswick, NJ: Transaction Books, 1984.

Mahard, Rita E., and Crain, Robert L. "Research on Minority Achievement in Desegregated Schools." In *The Consequences of School Desegregation,* ed. Christine H. Rossell and Willis D. Hawley. Philadelphia: Temple University Press, 1983.

McNeil, Linda M. "Teacher Culture and the Irony of School Reform." In *Excellence in Education: Perspectives on Policy and Practice,* ed. Philip G. Altbach, Gail P. Kelly, and Lois Weis. Buffalo, NY: Prometheus Press, 1985.

McNeil, Linda M. "Exit, Voice, and Community: Magnet Teachers' Response to Standardization," *Educational Policy* 1 (1987): 93–113.

Metz, Mary Haywood. "Clashes in the Classroom: The Importance of Norms for Authority," *Education and Urban Society* 11 (1978a): 13–47.

Metz, Mary Haywood. *Classrooms and Corridors: The Crisis of Authority in Desegregated Secondary Schools.* Berkeley: University of California Press, (1978b).

Metz, Mary Haywood. *Different by Design: The Context and Character of Three Magnet Schools.* New York: Routledge, 1986.

Metz, Mary Haywood. "Real School: A Universal Drama Amid Disparate Experience." In *Education Politics for the New Century,* ed. Douglas Mitchell and Margard E. Goertz. Philadelphia: Falmer Press, forthcoming.

National Commission on Excellence in Education. *A Nation at Risk: The Imperative for Educational Reform.* Washington, DC: U.S. Government Printing Office, 1983.

Ogbu, John U. *Minority Education and Caste: The American System in Cross-cultural Perspective.* New York: Academic Press, 1978.

Powell, Arthur, Farrar, Eleanor, and Cohen, David. *The Shopping Mall High School: Winners and Losers in the Academic Marketplace.* Boston: Houghton Mifflin, 1985.

Rist, Ray C. *The Invisible Children: School Integration in American Society.* Cambridge, MA: Harvard University Press, 1978.

Rist, Ray C. *Desegregated Schools: Appraisals of an American Experiment.* New York: Academic Press, 1979.

Rosenbaum, James, and Presser, Stefan. "Voluntary Racial Integration in a Magnet School," *School Review* 86 (1978): 156–186.

Schofield, Janet W. *Black and White in School: Trust, Tension, or Tolerance?* New York: Praeger, 1982.

Sedlak, Michael, Wheeler, Christopher, Pullin, Diana, and Cusick, Philip. *Selling Students Short: Classroom Bargains and Academic Reform in the American High School.* New York: Teachers College Press, 1986.

Sizer, Theodore. *Horace's Compromise: The Dilemma of the American High School.* Boston: Houghton Mifflin, 1984.

CHAPTER 7

Legislating Educational Choice in Minnesota: Politics and Prospects

Tim Mazzoni and Barry Sullivan

Public school choice has recently emerged as a central advocacy focus for those who would reform U.S. schools. Although much publicity has been given to President Bush's speech declaring choice to be "a national imperative" (Snider, 1989), the policy innovators on the choice issue are state lawmakers. More than twenty states have enacted or are considering legislation expanding educational choice for parents and students ("Half of States Show Interest," 1989). "Choice," according to Pipho (1989, p. 27), "could become the darling of new legislative ideas in 1989."

Nowhere has choice among public schools been more prominent as a policy issue than in Minnesota; nowhere have there been more choice statutes put on the books. Beginning in 1985 with Governor Rudy Perpich's bold proposal for interdistrict open enrollment and

149

ending in 1988 with the mandating of this idea by the legislature for all Minnesota school districts, the state has witnessed a series of enactments enlarging educational choice for parents and students. Among them are the following:

- *Postsecondary Enrollment Options Act* (1985). This act gives public school eleventh- and twelfth-graders the choice to seek to attend any public or eligible private postsecondary institution, part or full time, at state expense. The authority to exercise such an option is lodged with parents and students and not with the school district.
- *K–12 Enrollment Options Program* (1987). This program establishes and standardizes a *voluntary* open-enrollment program in which any of the state's school districts may participate.
- *High School Graduation Incentives Program* (1987). This program gives dropouts and at-risk students (ages 12 to 21) the right to seek enrollment in schools, postsecondary institutions (if eleventh or twelfth graders), or other alternative programs outside their resident district.
- *Area Learning Centers* (1987). Also aimed primarily toward at-risk youth and dropouts, the centers are required to serve secondary students (16 to 21) and eligible adults (21 and older) who want to finish high school in an alternative setting. Nonresidents of the school district where the center is located may attend without permission from local school boards.
- *K–12 Enrollment Options Program* (1988). This program *requires* that school districts permit their resident students to attend other districts. A district, however, may decide that nonresident students cannot enroll in its schools or programs. And participating districts may deny applications from nonresident students on the basis of capacity limits or desegregation regulations. (The program is to start in 1989–90 for districts with more than 1,000 pupil units; for all other districts, it starts in 1990–91.)

Although it is too early to judge the full impact of these innovations, the policymaking processes through which they were enacted have been the subject of case studies (Mazzoni and Sullivan, 1986; Mazzoni, 1986, 1988), studies that give rise to a number of political observations of interest, perhaps, to would-be reformers. The case studies all rest on multiple data sources: official documents, newspaper files, interest group publications, hearing tapes, observer notes, doctoral dissertations, and in-depth interviews. The interviews, numbering over 100 in total, were conducted with a cross section of participants and observers (that is, legislators and their staffers, executive agency officials, interest group representatives, and policy entrepreneurs) from 1984 through 1988. In addition to the two authors, interviews were conducted by DeeDee Carpenter, Clark Evans, Richard Clugston, Jr., and Lawrence Wells. Unless otherwise noted, quotations are from these interviews or from private sets of observer notes.

The primary purpose of this chapter is to discuss these observations, using findings from the Minnesota cases. A second purpose is to describe the current status of choice implementation in this pace-setting state.

POLITICS OF LEGISLATING CHOICE

Minnesota's experience in legislating choice can usefully be interpreted with respect to six general prescriptions. These goals are (1) to soften up the policy community to foster intellectual and political preconditions for change, (2) to get ready for a tough fight against established interests and ideals, (3) to combine insider power and finesse with outside pressure, (4) to protect the policy breakthrough from likely counterattack, (5) to bargain hard in existing or new arenas for incremental extensions of the new legislation, and (6) to encourage political champions, once committed, to work their policy systems to consolidate the innovation.

Soften up the Policy Community

In 1985 Governor Rudy Perpich made educational choice a front-burner issue in Minnesota. He redefined the choice issue so that the focal debate was not about "vouchers" but about "public school choice." He crusaded across the state trying to stir up grassroots sentiment. And it was he, a Democrat, who forged the bipartisan alliance with the House majority leader, a Republican, that led to the passage in the 1985 session of precedent-setting legislation: the

Postsecondary Enrollment Options Act. But to focus narrowly on enactment events is to miss the first major lesson of the Minnesota story, one that exemplified what Kingdon (1984, p. 134) aptly calls the "softening up" process: "Entrepreneurs attempt to 'soften up' both policy communities, which tend to be inertia-bound and resistant to major changes, and larger publics, getting them used to new ideas and building acceptance for their proposals."

Much softening up on the choice issue had taken place before Rudy Perpich launched his initiative. Individual policy entrepreneurs and a Twin Cities public interest group—the Citizens League—had been vigorously promoting the virtues of user options and market competition (for example, Citizens League, 1982; Brandl, 1983; Nathan, 1983; Kolderie, 1985). They had done the spadework that was essential to the flourishing of educational choice in the governor's office. Part of this work was analytic: exposing deficiencies in existing institutional arrangements; generating a vision of how the new K–12 system would look; formulating alternative proposals for restructuring schools; and identifying—or developing—research, rationales, and arguments to support student choice being the central dynamic in reforming education. Part of the spadework was political: disseminating the products of analysis; creating organizational networks to market policy alternatives; attracting financial resources from foundations to start and sustain promotional efforts; designing, introducing, and orchestrating testimony for voucher bills; and cultivating civic, business, minority, and other groups to become coalition allies. So diverse, omnipresent, and catalytic were these activities that they provided data for scholars to recast the very theory of policy entrepreneurs (Roberts and King, forthcoming).

During the early 1980s, the entrepreneurs and league elevated the saliency of the choice issue—defined at this time in voucher terms (that is, embracing private as well as public schools)—within the policy community. They set forth in detail and in countless forums an ideological alternative to the ideas underpinning the institutional structure of Minnesota public schools. Their analysis linked consumer choice and market competition to producer incentives for adopting reforms and to enhanced system performance. These ideas were old in that the general line of reasoning had been argued for centuries—and specific voucher proposals for U.S. schools had been propounded for decades—yet they were new in their formulation within the Minnesota context and in their being invoked as subjects of serious discussion. Although voucher bills remained a marginal concern for state lawmakers (hearings were held but no other legislative action was taken on these bills in 1983 and 1984), the choice idea had gained impetus and visibility in the reform debate. This was the advocacy climate when the California consulting firm of Berman-Weiler Associates decided on its recommendations (following an eighteen-month, $250,000 study) to the Minnesota Business Partnership.

The Berman-Weiler report, titled the "Minnesota Plan" and endorsed by the Business Partnership in late 1984, set forth a comprehensive plan for structural change (Berman, 1985). One of its recommendations, the one that served as the immediate stimulus for the subsequent Perpich initiative, proposed "stipends" for eleventh- and twelfth-grade students to choose from alternative programs offered by their district or by other state-approved public or private vendors. Although this provision might not have been the direct consequence of lobbying by the policy entrepreneurs, it certainly reflected—and reinforced—the climate they had shaped. The entrepreneurs, working with and through the league, were a necessary element in the equation that resulted in first the Business Partnership and then the governor becoming proponents of restructuring Minnesota schools. With these heavyweights—the Partnership represented the CEOs of the state's largest private corporations, and the governor had unrivaled political resources—taking a stand on the issue, the entrepreneurs had softened up and energized enough powerholders to give educational choice a real chance of passage in the legislative arena.

Get Ready for a Tough Fight

In Minnesota, political initiation of choice legislation was bitterly contested. The process began in January of 1985 when Governor Perpich announced his Access to Excellence plan for educational reform. Its cornerstone was a proposal that Minnesota parents and students—regardless of residence—be allowed to choose their public school district, with state funding to follow the student. Besides open enrollment (as the press termed it), Perpich also urged the expansion of existing postsecondary option programs. The governor's initiatives did receive glowing praise from the restructuring advocates. But vociferous reactions from other quarters made it clear that Perpich and his supporters were in for a bruising battle.

The two most influential Minnesota legislators, the House speaker and the Senate majority leader, early indicated their distaste for open enrollment. The key education chairs were publicly wary, voicing concerns and reservations. Other lawmakers expressed doubts about the policy and political fallout of the Perpich initiatives. But the most critical and concentrated flak came from the school board, superintendent, and teacher organizations. They blasted the choice plan as a "voucher" plan (a label that Perpich had avoided) and dismissed it as unsound in concept and unworkable in operation, and said that if implemented it would produce chaos in the state's schools.

Along with a host of concerns about implementation—most notably, about athletic transfers, desegregation regulations, and district planning—there were angry charges directed against the Perpich plan: It was not carefully thought out. It was "drastic" and "elitist." It was the first step toward voucher funding for private schools. It would lead to a mass migration of students. It would create winners and losers among public schools. Its hidden agenda was to force low-enrollment districts to reorganize. "The outcry against open enrollment," summed up one legislator, "was just incredible."

Nor could Perpich claim solid public backing for his proposals. State citizens seemed to be quite pleased with their schools. Although a few K–12 reform prescriptions—standardized tests and higher standards—were enormously popular, such was not the case with open enrollment. Indeed, public opinion polls indicated that a clear majority of Minnesotans disagreed with the Perpich initiative, hostility being most evident in rural, small-town areas (Craig, 1987). Here open enrollment was condemned as the forerunner of district consolidation, school closings, and community demise.

The big K–12 groups were hardly weak foes. They collectively had the access, resources, and networks to contest any educational issue; on some they held what amounted to a de facto veto over legislative decisions. The teacher unions had clout matched by few other advocacy groups, especially when it came to blocking a bill. Large memberships (spread statewide), campaign contributions, and grassroots organization buttressed an experienced, skillful cadre of lobbyists to make the political influence of organized teachers an electoral reality for Minnesota lawmakers. "The teacher unions," several said, "are the single most powerful interest group in the state" (Mazzoni, 1985).

Some establishment resistance was provoked by the way the choice plan had been formulated. Perpich had not consulted the educational organizations at all until the day before he made his announcement. Nor would he accept at any point their conditions for compromise. But had Perpich acceded to the conditions sought by the school board, superintendent, and teacher groups (the principal associations endorsed the choice idea), there would have been little policy innovation. Opponents wanted, at a minimum, that the postsecondary option be eliminated, that district officials retain authority to approve or reject student transfers, and that open enrollment—if it were to exist at all—be limited in scope and voluntary in nature.

Probably the chief reason that the Perpich initiatives triggered such a tough political fight was that they constituted a sharp departure from existing policy, a departure having major redistributive implications. They introduced a new first principle—choice as opposed to assignment—the full adoption of which would have entailed a fundamental shift in power from producers (school officials and educators) to consumers (parents and students). Such redistributive shifts are always likely to be resisted when they are viewed by established groups as involving revenues, jobs, status, and other valued stakes. Moreover, choice initiatives, even when confined as was Perpich's to the public schools, challenge fundamental ideals as well as fundamental interests. They spark heated debates about whether market competition expands or contracts excellence, equity, and efficiency in schools. They encourage a political process marked by ideological confrontation, not by pragmatic bargaining.

Combine Insider Power with Outside Pressure

Concerns and charges aimed at the Perpich plan—primarily at open enrollment—convinced the governor that politics as usual would not produce legislation. The educational establishment was largely opposed, many key lawmakers were resistant, and the citizenry was divided and skeptical. To overcome these obstacles, Perpich turned to the "outside game," taking his case to the grassroots and seeking to build public pressure. Specifically, he decided to visit high schools—mostly in rural Minnesota—visits that created ample opportunity to tout proposals, answer questions, and counter accusations.

The governor's high profile on the issue (some twenty schools were visited over two-and-one-half months) signaled to legislators and lobbyists his commitment to the reform cause. Perpich would fight for his educational program; it was a top priority in deed as well as declaration. The high school tours also attracted the media, both from the local area of the school being visited and from the Twin Cities metropolitan area. And, as the conflict between Perpich and his adversaries escalated, this media coverage became extensive, the open-enrollment issue often receiving headline treatment.

Perpich's "sell the public" approach certainly expanded the visibility of the choice initiatives and probably enhanced their appeal as well. Even opponents acknowledged that he could "make his ideas sound wonderful" and that the governor, assisted by Commissioner Ruth Randall (a Perpich appointee) and the Education Department, "really did a PR job on the tour." "He was successful," one conceded, "in framing that discussion so that opponents were made to look like foot dragging defenders of the status quo."

Besides his all-out campaign to arouse a grassroots constituency, the governor gave personal direction to a diverse coalition of organized supporters—including civic, business, parent, and educator groups—and he (and his staff) lobbied hard for the program. But outside pressure, in itself, was not enough to enact legislation; in fact, the choice initiative that was the focal point for this pressure—open enrollment—was defeated. The crucial element in the legislative success of the postsecondary option was a bipartisan alliance between Governor Perpich and House Majority Leader Connie Levi. It was Levi, more than any other actor, who was responsible for the options statute, first by nurturing it through the House and then, in the role of mediator, by assuring its bargaining success in conference committee (Mazzoni, 1988).

The significance of insider power was dramatically revealed by the fate of the choice proposals in the Senate, a body that had a sizable majority from the governor's own party. The principal author of Perpich's education bill was Senator Tom Nelson, chair of the Subcommittee on Education Aids. An expert in school finance, adept in committee bargaining, and respected by colleagues, Nelson became a persuasive champion for the choice initiatives. Yet neither his conviction nor skill could take these initiatives over all legislative hurdles. Senator Nelson did succeed with his subcommittee and with the full Education Committee. But the Finance Committee buried both open enrollment and the postsecondary option. There was no supportive senator of Connie Levi's stature to bolster Nelson's efforts; instead, he had to contend with varying degrees of opposition from Senate leadership.

Although outside pressure could not generate sufficient influence to overcome legislative opposition, this pressure was not without impact. It kept attention away from the postsecondary option and concentrated the controversy on open enrollment. Diversion was not an intentional strategy on the governor's part. His top priority was open enrollment; it was not just a stalking horse for postsecondary choice. The effect, however, was much the same.

Yet even if passage of the college option represented the politics of inadvertence for Governor Rudy Perpich, it represented the politics of opportunity for Majority Leader Connie Levi. The majority leader was ready (Levi had been crafting a postsecondary choice program since 1982, when her first bill in this area was passed); she was able (political savvy allowed Levi to exploit her many positional and personal resources); and she had influential backers (notably the Business Partnership). True, there were powerful adversaries. The K–12 groups denounced any proposal that siphoned state funds away from local school districts, and a few of these groups did seek to arouse their memberships on the issue. But they did not mount more than token resistance. Their lobbying resources were invested in fending off open enrollment and pushing for their own priorities. And they did not want to alienate the majority leader—a long-time ally on funding questions—over what was projected to be a minor program.

An analogy put forward by Kingdon casts a useful—if unusual—perspective on Representative Levi's opportunity, impact, and tactics; and by so doing it helps sum up another political lesson from Minnesota's experience in legislating choice. According to a source quoted by Kingdon (1984, p. 173),

> People who are trying to advocate change are like surfers waiting for the big wave. You get out there, you have to be ready to go, you have to be ready to paddle. If you are not ready to paddle when the big wave comes along, you are not going to ride it in.

From the perspective of this analogy, the choice impulse in Perpich's Access to Excellence speech swelled into a big wave. Voucher surfers, after testing the water, judged conditions to be improving but not likely to carry a big board. They decided, except for a minor launch, to wait for a more favorable tide. Open-enrollment surfers, though not quite prepared, sought to get out in front on the big breakers. Their daring carried them a surprising distance. But embroiled in crosscurrents, slowed by a resistant undertow, and unable to catch a broad-based surge, the board came up short. While this spectacular ride captivated onlookers, a postsecondary surfer, her board ready though largely unnoticed in the froth, maneuvered through the shoals into a protected cove. Here, safe from the storm, the board was quietly guided to shore. The moral: Innovation is not the art of surfing boldly at the crest but of paddling skillfully in the backwash.

Protect the Policy Breakthrough from Counterattack

Two basic strategies, according to Polsby (1984), for the political initiation of policy innovation are "meeting opposition head on and overcoming it" and "slipping an initiation by as a side issue or a nonissue." Governor Perpich tried the first in seeking open-enrollment legislation. It failed to achieve that end but it afforded necessary leverage for the second strategy, one that resulted in the enactment of the postsecondary option. But the "slipping by" strategy, whatever its effectiveness in finessing obstacles to innovation, sometimes produces a fragile product. The laws so enacted may have received meager discussion. Their decision processes may violate expectations of involvement. Their base of ownership may be narrow. Such policies invite and are vulnerable to counterattack. And, in Minnesota, choice proponents quickly found themselves on the defensive as education groups—with the school board, superintendent, and teacher organizations leading the charge—and local district officials launched a campaign against the options statute.

The counterattack began when school districts were faced with implementing the postsecondary enrollment statute by the fall of 1985. Whatever was lacking in the policy debate before the passage of this act—and it had received some discussion and media visibility (it was not, as widely rumored, sprung on the public at the last moment)—was made up for after its enactment. The law was engulfed in a firestorm of complaints. Educator and school district detractors protested that it took funding away from the K–12 system, made it difficult for local districts to plan, drained off the best students, eroded resources for high school programs, and encouraged unwise choices and other "abuses." Supporters responded that the law expanded options for a broad range of eleventh and twelfth graders, made efficient use of existing state facilities, helped parents and students pay for a college education, and fostered through intersystem competition the improvement of high school courses.

During the 1986 session, the K–12 groups sought to restrict and roll back the new initiative through legislative amendments. Seen as most crippling by option supporters was a proposal that would have enabled districts to bar students from participating if "comparable" courses were offered by their high school. (The Minnesota Federation of Teachers filed a lawsuit against the participation of religiously affiliated colleges.) Although political champions Majority Leader Levi and Senator Nelson were receptive to procedural adjustments and to some limitations, they strongly resisted amendments they thought would dismantle the fledgling program. Governor Perpich continued to express his enthusiasm for the college option, though distancing himself from the legislative controversy. And Education Commissioner Randall committed time, energy, and staff resources to facilitate implementing the act through its start-up problems.

For much of 1986, the postsecondary choice issue was embroiled in confrontation politics. Grassroots constituencies were activated, and intense pressure was brought to bear in the legislature. In the House, where Connie Levi held firm, the amendments were relatively minor. A floor amendment did have a provision to allow the participation of private school students inserted in the omnibus bill. Opponents had much more success in the Senate, where a comparability amendment was pushed through on a floor vote. Again, as is typical in Minnesota, the matter was resolved as part of conference committee tradeoffs, with Levi and Nelson having decisive influence. Private student participation was deleted, as was the comparability requirement. Some "fix-up" amendments were adopted. More importantly, the dual credit provision was modified. No longer were participating students at state expense to be able simultaneously to earn college as well as high school credit for their postsecondary courses. They could, however, receive college credit for these courses after enrolling in the postsecondary institution.

The postsecondary option had been protected. Its vital principles and provisions had been preserved. Majority Leader Levi and Senator Nelson had blunted the assault. They were aided by organized supporters (particularly the entrepreneurs, the League, and the Partnership), by hearing testimony and legislative contacts from an emergent client constituency (students offered compelling personal illustrations of educational benefits), by the determination of Commissioner Randall and her staff to get implementation off to a smooth start, and by a positive preliminary evaluation (a final evaluation was required by law to be ready for the 1987 session). Other factors also contributed to the continuation of the options program. It was popular (a November 1985 poll showed 48 percent of Minnesota adults approved, 29 percent disapproved, with 20 percent neutral). It was small (a reported 1,733 students—1.5 percent of public school eleventh and twelfth graders—exercised this choice in the fall of 1985). And, by state standards, it did not cost very much (funding transfers to postsecondary institutions—$2.1 million—were less than 1 percent in aggregate of aid payments being received by local districts).

Press for Incremental Extensions of Legislation

Politics as usual—that is to say, incrementalism—did not produce the postsecondary option. But once pressure, power, and finesse had combined to achieve that legislation, an incremental strategy could be used by restructuring advocates to expand the breakthrough. Perpich's creation of the Governor's Discussion Group in the summer of 1985 provided an arena for advocates to pursue that strategy.

After the 1985 session, Governor Perpich rethought his political approach to initiating educational reform. He did not want a repeat of the divisiveness caused by his Access to Excellence plan and hard-sell tactics, and he promised education groups that they would be consulted on all subsequent K–12 reform proposals. These proposals, however, were not to come directly from educators and school officials—or, as in 1984, from reformers. Rather, the governor demanded that initiatives reflect a consensus from his Discussion Group, a forum that regularly brought together all the major actors. Restructuring advocates and their establishment opponents were expected by Perpich to engage in face-to-face discussions, negotiate their differences, and hammer out a "visionary" plan they all could support.

Formulating by consensus an innovative plan for the governor was no easy matter. Discussion Group participants had engaged in an angry and polarizing conflict in the 1985 session over open enrollment, a conflict that intensified in the 1986 session over amendments to the postsecondary option. Fundamental disagreements continued to split the Discussion Group during its one-and-a-half years of meetings. These cleavages of philosophy and interest were sharpest whenever the restructuring advocates put new choice proposals on the table.

At times the likelihood of any choice plan coming from the Discussion Group looked slim. Even Governor Perpich appeared to have backed away from open enrollment. This occurred in the spring of 1986 at a meeting with officials from the state's school board, administrator, and teacher organizations who were screening gubernatorial candidates for the upcoming election. Perpich declared that, though he still personally believed in interdistrict choice, its advocacy had people "steamed up" and caused so much opposition that he would no longer push for it (Pinney, 1986, p. 1B). "No policy is worth pursuing," a staffer explained to the Discussion Groups, "that will divide the educational community." Whether or not this was just an election-year bid to win teacher union endorsement, which Perpich had renounced a year earlier during his policy conflicts with the unions, the governor's pledge added to the political problems faced by restructuring advocates. It became imperative for them to get a consensus-based plan from the Discussion Group that would release the governor from his pledge and enable him to press for open enrollment and other potentially controversial innovations.

Not until the fall of 1986 did the Discussion Group get down to give-and-take bargaining. The twenty-six participants, prodded by Commissioner Randall (she chaired the meetings), attempted to negotiate a document that Perpich could use as the basis for his proposals to the 1987 legislature. The advocates of choice did have some distinct bargaining advantages. Not only were they more determined to get an agreement, but they also were more unified, energetic, and assertive than their opponents. Seizing the agenda-setting initiative, advocates were able to secure Discussion Group agreement on a foundational statement that urged changing the K–12 system. "We had come to agree," said one, "[that] the system has to improve, and can improve. The central question became how that would happen . . . and what the state, specifically, should do to ensure that it happens." But while compromises were struck on other contested school reforms (such as testing procedures), educational choice remained a sticking point. Advocates insisted that expanded choice be part of any agreement. They were prepared, if necessary, to submit their own report to the governor. But several education representatives—notably those from the school boards association and the teacher unions—appeared to be equally determined that agreements not embrace new choice initiatives.

Three actions broke the deadlock (Mazzoni, 1986). The first was the strategic decision by advocates not to press for an "in-principle" endorsement of choice. "The decision was," in the words of one, "to focus on a few specific actions that might be taken in 1987, including some limited 'test' of open enrollment." The second action was the advocates' putting forward a bargainable proposal: retain the post-secondary option, test a controlled "second-chance" option for at-risk students, and make voluntary open enrollment available for all public school districts. The third action was the increased willingness of educator opponents to consider compromise. In the end, they were prepared to negotiate if choice programs were to be "voluntary," "limited," and "controlled."

By late December of 1986, matters seemed largely settled. The big trade had involved the most resistant of the teacher unions: the Minnesota Education Association (MEA). Its incoming president was willing to deal, after finding out that Governor Perpich would endorse only change initiatives coming from the Discussion Group. The MEA head demanded—and apparently received—backing from the reformers for union priorities on school district reorganization in exchange for accepting a program "piloting limited choice in public schools" (Kostouros, 1986; Astrup, 1986).

Yet when the Discussion Group met to decide on the final version of its report, understandings that advocates thought they had achieved came into question. Some opponents sought to reopen once-settled issues and to challenge other agreements. Back-and-forth exchanges became confrontational. The meeting, according to a reporter, "careened back and forth between collapse and compromise" (Kostouros, 1986). Discussion became most heated over the "second-chance" choice proposal, the proposal aimed at expanding education options for at-risk students. The MEA would not support it; other education representatives proposed restrictions. Under the pressure of a time deadline and anxious to bring a plan to the governor, Commissioner Randall resorted to her power as chair to push through compromises omitting the controversial provision.

The Visionary Plan signed by all Discussion Group members

contained a variety of general policy recommendations, including a proposal that "the Legislature . . . (1) continue testing the existing controlled choice program for eleventh- and twelfth-grade students, and (2) test a voluntary K–12 pilot choice program with appropriate assessment and evaluation . . . [and] financial assistance" (Governor's Discussion Group, 1986). Advocates had been successful in gaining protection for the postsecondary option, seen as being vulnerable because its two most powerful proponents (Connie Levi and Tom Nelson) were retiring from the legislature. Advocates had gained endorsement for K–12 open enrollment, albeit as a voluntary pilot program for school districts. But they had lost the "second-chance" option, and several were infuriated both by this deletion and by the process through which it had occurred. They sought, with much behind-the-scenes urging, to persuade the governor's office to promote this option. In Rudy Perpich, who was chairing the National Governor's Association task force on dropouts, they found a receptive audience.

Governor Perpich met with the Discussion Group in early February 1987. Although he had no specific proposal, the governor asked that more choice be recommended for dropouts and at-risk students. As a result of Perpich's request, the Discussion Group reconvened and decided on an addendum. It called on the legislature to require that school districts provide alternative programs for dropouts or at-risk students (to age 21), with these students being able to choose "any school district or other public alternative programs regardless of the school district of residence" (Governor's Discussion Group, 1987).

Several factors besides Perpich's personal intervention contributed to this outcome (Mazzoni, 1986). One was a laudatory evaluation of the first year of the Postsecondary Enrollment Options Act, an evaluation that came out just as the Discussion Group was to decide on the governor's request (Minnesota Department of Education, 1987). Another factor was a dramatic change in sponsorship of the second-chance provision. It was a top official from the superintendents' association, not the restructuring advocates, who offered the language that produced an accord. His sponsorship clearly made the proposal much more palatable to the educational group representatives.

The new choice initiatives recommended by the Discussion Group were incorporated in the governor's budget and legislative program. They then were passed as part of an omnibus bill in the House

(Senate committees were preoccupied with reforming the state's school funding formula), included in the conference committee report, and enacted by the legislature. All this activity took place with little disagreement. Incremental politics had replaced ideological confrontation on public school choice issues in Minnesota.

Restructuring advocates had used a new arena—the Governor's Discussion Group—to attain significant extensions of educational choice. They had given content and momentum to the group's deliberations; they had combined toughness in pressing for positions with reasonableness in advancing bargaining compromises. But the success of their actions also depended on people and conditions beyond their own energy, persistence, and skill. One was the willingness of educational representatives to moderate conflict and to seek consensus. It was such a leader who offered the specific basis for the at-risk initiative. Another was Commissioner Randall, who despite many difficulties and some criticism, managed to hold the group together and bring it to agreement. (Her top staff person functioned as honest broker between groups and a facilitator of their bargaining.) Most importantly, there was Governor Rudy Perpich. Although he occasionally waffled in his public pronouncements, the impulsive Perpich never lost his enthusiasm for open enrollment. He gave the Discussion Group its underlying agenda, appointed Commissioner Randall to chair its meetings, spurned participant attempts to deal directly with him on reform proposals, and interceded to obtain a vital addition to the group's plan.

A representative commission is rarely a promising way to initiate structural change (Plank, 1988). "Broadly representative commissions in education," Peterson (1983, p. 10) observes, " . . . [are] unlikely to agree on organizational reforms expressed in the most general terms . . . reorganization proposals have too discernable a set of political consequences." Given the tortuous negotiations in which the Discussion Group engaged to extend choice, it is hard to see how this forum could ever have initiated breakthrough legislation. That policy—the postsecondary option—did not come from pluralist bargaining; it was enacted in an atmosphere of confrontational pressure and through a process of legislative maneuver. Still, once an innovative policy is in law, it can—if protected—be used as the basis for substantial expansions. Such expansions of a structural reform, as is illustrated in the Minnesota case, are achievable outcomes for a representative commission. Yet even these incremental advances, as the Minnesota experience also shows, are quite problematic. They can require much staying power to attain.

Encourage Political Champions to Work Their System

This maxim was vividly demonstrated by Representative Connie Levi's pivotal role in the passage of postsecondary choice. Based on her personal experiences, Levi was determined to make a college option broadly available to high school students. For three years, she had been instrumental in the statutory evolution of this idea. She was both an influential political champion, becoming majority leader in 1985, and a deeply committed advocate. Once Levi had decided, with encouragement from the Business Partnership and other proponents, to assume the risks of being the chief House author of the governor's bill, she was able to work the legislative system effectively. Taking shrewd advantage of its side issue status, the majority leader shielded the postsecondary option through House committees and secured that option in conference committee negotiations (Mazzoni, 1988).

In 1988, Governor Perpich provided another example of a committed political champion working the system. To consolidate the 1987 gains on open enrollment, Perpich resorted to the insider finesse strategy. He rejected the high-profile approach of 1985 as both unnecessary and unwise—opponents could hold hostage proposals about which he appeared to care too deeply. Nor could he expect the Governor's Discussion Group, which had become more polarized, to bring him what he wanted. (After seven meetings, the group could agree on no more than a "reaffirmation" of the earlier plan and its addendum.) So Perpich decided to shift strategy gears. He had staffers privately contact key lawmakers, particularly Senate education committee leaders, to gauge support for bringing open-enrollment legislation to its logical conclusion. The governor's lobbyist admitted "If there was anything that got no [public] attention deliberately, it was this" (Orwall, 1988, p. 4C).

The choice amendment was not announced in a subcommittee meeting until the last stages of voting on the omnibus education finance bill. Until that occurred, there seemed to be little interest-group awareness, much less public awareness, of this amendment. Recalled a senator, "In part, opposition did not emerge to our amendment because the press did not realize it had passed. We did not try to hide anything, since we voted on it in open committee. But for whatever reason—maybe there was other news that day—it did not get coverage for at least a few days after it passed in open committee session; by that time, other news forced it out of the media."

The open-enrollment amendment moved quickly and with little protest through the Senate. Neither the governor and his aides, nor the restructuring advocates, some of whom expressed amazement at legislative developments, visibly engaged in lobbying. The education groups were taken aback; only the School Boards Association voiced much concern. "I couldn't convince people [legislators] the sky was falling," remarked a teacher union lobbyist in explaining why his organization did no more than raise "gentle" questions about the amendment. A governor's staffer explained, "When the opposition realized that few students would actually choose to leave their home districts . . . they became concerned with other priorities." But a lawmaker attributed different motives: "The [teacher] unions be-lieved they had sounded shrill in 1985, and [now] it was somewhat unseemly to oppose choice. . . . Besides, the public school groups all had other, more important items on their [legislative] agenda, items they might not get if they continued to oppose major political actors such as the Governor." As for lawmakers, their soundings indicated educational choice had become popular. Said one, "I know many [Senate] members from both parties who checked with their con-stituents before committing themselves. In most cases, they found grassroots support. . . . And where there was opposition, it was not vocal nor strongly held."

Like the other choice measures before it, open enrollment was the subject of negotiations and tradeoffs in conference committees. Resis-tance was greatest among House members from rural areas where interdistrict choice had long been condemned as the forerunner of "consolidation." But House leaders, with that body up for re-election in 1988, also wanted more money in the school aid formula than was contained in the Senate bill. The basic compromise was increased school funding for the House and the open-enrollment provision for the Senate. To mollify critics from small school districts, the program was to be phased in over several years. The conference report was enacted by the legislature without controversy. "To pass it without a whimper last night," said the amendment's chief author, "was just absolutely awesome. And it happened. . . . Not one word on the Senate floor . . . about the fact that we had mandatory open enrollment in our bill" (Reichgott, 1988, p. 2). What provoked in 1985 a political uproar was accepted in 1988 "without a whimper."

With open enrollment showing solid approval in public opinion polls (Craig, 1987), with many school districts becoming participants in the voluntary program (enacted in 1987), with only a relatively few students actually transferring to nonresident districts, and with legislators perceiving a growing client constituency for choice alternatives, it was not surprising that Minnesota lawmakers embraced another extension of the choice idea. Many legislative steps, beginning with postsecondary options, had already been taken toward that end. What data there were about the various choice programs suggested that, by and large, they were working—at least as far as participating students and their parents were concerned.

Many local school board members, administrators, and teachers continue to voice reservations, objections, and complaints about open enrollment (Orwall, 1989). And there are powerful legislative critics as well (for example, see McEachern, 1989, and Nobles, 1989), the most outspoken being the House education committee chair. Program flaws, they argue, include the transfer for athletic, social, and other nonacademic reasons of students into the selected schools; disrupted district planning due to the ease of student choice; and the undermining of the "left behind" schools and districts—especially small, poor ones—that lack resources to compete. These concerns do have political relevance, making procedural adjustments—and, perhaps, some restrictions—likely in the 1989 session. Still, the general policy direction appears to be set; public school choice has become an integral part of Minnesota's program for K–12 reform.

FINAL OBSERVATIONS ABOUT CHOICE POLITICS

Looking across the political history of educational choice legislation in Minnesota reveals other lessons for would-be reformers. One that is most obvious has to do with the tenacity of advocates. The key actors in Minnesota—the entrepreneurs, League, Partnership, Levi, and Perpich—stayed involved with the issue over time. "The major lesson from this," concluded a Senate education leader, "is that ideas are hard to kill in the political arena. Failure at one point can be turned into success later if you persist. The longer an idea is around, the more familiar it becomes and the less radical it appears." Minnesota's experience in legislating choice demonstrates once again that the politics of educational reform is not for dilettantes. Those who persist in policymaking are generally those who prevail.

A second obvious lesson has to do with political power. For all the softening up done by the policy entrepreneurs, Citizens League and Business Partnership, the clout of top state lawmakers—notably Governor Perpich and Majority Leader Levi—was required to enact, protect, and expand choice legislation. A governor, in particular, has enormous capacity to shape the agenda, captivate the media, deploy diverse strategies (Perpich used three fundamentally different ones), and press hard for innovation. As choice opponents in Minnesota found out, a powerful and determined governor, whether acting front or back stage, is a formidable protagonist.

Another lesson, or at least an observation, has to do with the importance for policymaking of institutional arrangements. In Minnesota, the conference committee—and choice bills always received final formulation by this body—has become the "Third House" of the state legislature. In this setting, a handful of legislative leaders and committee chairs—along with the governor—exert decisive influence over bargaining. Their compromises become the basis for a non-amendable report that the full legislature has little alternative but to accept. Although Minnesota's educational choice statutes did not originate in conference committee, committee procedures and practices did effectively insulate the reform against its lobbying foes and afforded a "policy window" (Kingdon, 1984) for strategically placed insiders to secure the innovation.

The fourth lesson, partly suggested by the third, has to do with basic political strategy. As long as K–12 policymaking is primarily confined to—and controlled by—the participants and processes of specialized education committees (and subcommittees), there is not much likelihood of significant restructuring legislation. These committees, as they typically function, predominantly reflect established interests, ideals, and conventions. Bargaining and logrolling on school funding and other policy questions take place within narrow limits, with the organization of public education being assumed as a given. Outcomes tend to be incremental adjustments of prevailing arrangements. For major structural innovations to occur, reform proponents must move their issue away from legislative "subgovernments" to other decision-making arenas. This arena shift may be to ones where a broader constituency can be mobilized (an aroused public becomes the power base to press for new departures) or to ones (the conference committee, for example) where supportive and influential lawmakers can exert critical leverage. In Minnesota, as has been said, the two strategies came together to produce a policy breakthrough. Other arenas, such as the Governor's Discussion Group, then could be employed to broaden the breakthrough legislation.

STATUS OF CHOICE IMPLEMENTATION

Beginning with the Postsecondary Enrollment Options Act in 1985, educational choice in Minnesota has been gradually extended to different groups of public school students. Options were first given to eleventh and twelfth graders to attend, if they chose (and were admitted to) a postsecondary institution. Then, in 1987, the High School Graduation Incentive and Area Learning Center laws offered "second chances" to those students experiencing problems in their resident school districts. Also, in that legislative session, a voluntary plan passed, expanding choice for K–12 students living in districts that agreed to open their doors. Finally, in 1988, a K–12 Enrollment Options Program was mandated for all public school districts in Minnesota.

Table 7-1 reports descriptive information and enrollment estimates for the five major choice programs. It shows that these programs have relatively small student enrollments; fewer than 2 percent of Minnesota's some 723,000 K–12 students elected these options in the 1988–89 school year. Participation has been greatest in the most mature program—implemented in the fall of 1985—in which some 6,000 eleventh and twelfth graders now enroll part or full time in a postsecondary institution (nearly half of the students enroll in the state's extensive community college system).

Present enrollments in choice programs, however, may not predict their future enrollments very well. Implementation of these programs is just beginning, and the most far-reaching reform (that is, mandated K–12 open enrollment) will not involve all Minnesota school districts until 1990–91. Nor can definitive statements be made, at the moment, about how well the new choice programs are working, because no comprehensive and in-depth investigation has been undertaken.

Table 7-1

Educational Choice in Minnesota: Five Major State K–12 Programs

Program	Year Enacted	School Year Implemented	Students Participating (Est. by School Year(s))	Institutions Participating	Direct State Appropriation
Postsecondary Enrollment Options—11th & 12th grades (M.S. 123.3514)	1985	1985–86	5,400 (1987–88) 6,000 (1988–89)	285 public school districts 80 postsecondary schools (1987–88) 285 public school districts 80 postsecondary schools (est. for 1988–89)	$ 75,000[e]
Area Learning Centers (M.S. 129B.52–129B.55)	1987	1988–89	4,045 (1988–89)[a]	18 centers (est. for 1988–89)	$150,000[f]
High School Graduation Incentives (M.S. 126.22)	1987	1987–88	1,400 (1987–88)[a] 1,800 (1988–89)	[c]	00

K–12 Open Enrollment— voluntary (M.S. 123.3515)	1987	1987–88	140	(1987–88)	95 (1987–88)	$ 50,000[e]
			435	(1988–89)	153 (1988–89)	00
K–12 Open Enrollment (M.S. 120.062)	1988	1989–90 (larger districts) 1990–91 (all districts)	2,500	(1989–90)[b]	162 (est. for 1989–90)[d]	00

[a] Since one of the options that can be chosen by students eligible for High School Graduation Incentives is an Area Learning Center, the latter program includes students also counted in the former. At this time, state program staff are unable to specify an unduplicated figure for Area Learning Centers. A 1988 amendment to the incentives law expands eligibility to certain low-income or jobless adults (21 or over) who have never graduated from high school. These adult students are not included in estimated participants for 1988–89.

[b] An estimate based on applications forwarded to the state early in 1989 indicating intent to enroll in September 1989.

[c] All school districts may accept eligible students unless enrollment would upset racial balance restrictions (established in state rules), or space is unavailable. At this time, the state cannot determine the number of districts accepting students under this program.

[d] In the first year of implementation (1989–90), only 162 of Minnesota's 435 school districts will have enrollments large enough (more than 1,000 pupil units) to be under the mandated program. These 162 districts, however, enroll about 84 percent of the state's K–12 students. In addition, 127 smaller districts will be voluntary K–12 open-enrollment sites during the 1989–90 term.

[e] Transportation aid for needy students.

[f] Grants for four exemplary centers.

Evaluations of the postsecondary option, and informal surveys of students in the other choice programs, suggest, however, a satisfied—indeed, enthusiastic—group of participants.

A 1986 evaluation of the postsecondary option—by far the most thorough survey that has been done (Minnesota Department of Education, 1987)—found that 95 percent of the participating students indicated satisfaction, with over 60 percent saying they were very satisfied. The survey also revealed that the majority of student participants found postsecondary courses more challenging than those in their high schools, received a grade of B or higher, and—contrary to predictions from opponents—most of these students enrolled in "academic" courses (for example, English, literature, algebra, and calculus).

Questionnaire surveys and anecdotal evidence from participants in voluntary K–12 open enrollment also suggest highly satisfied students (Minnesota Department of Education, 1988b). In addition, a survey of parents provides evidence as to why they chose to enroll their children in another district. Most respondents (44 percent) said they chose a new school for curricular and academic reasons; 26 percent to be closer to home, work, or day care; 23 percent because of more options and better facilities; and 21 percent for social or psychological benefits (Minnesota Department of Education, 1988b). Descriptive information collected about the K–12 program disclosed that 90 percent of the students choosing to leave their resident districts were white (only about 8 percent of the state's students are minority), an almost equal number of males and females participated, and—perhaps surprisingly—slightly more than half transferred to small districts (Minnesota Department of Education, 1988b).

Informal interviews of students in the recently implemented "second-chance" options—area learning centers and high school graduation incentives—reveal mainly success stories. These students, by law, are eligible to transfer out of their resident districts only if they are having specified problems (for example, drug use, low grades, and absenteeism) or have dropped out of school. Dropouts, it should be noted, made up more than half of the estimated 1,400 students who enrolled under the incentives program in the first semester of 1987–88 (Minnesota Department of Education, 1988a).

Broad-based and longitudinal evaluations will be needed before one can say that the individual success stories associated with choice programs are widespread, let alone are typical. Certainly, this sort of evaluation is required before arriving at valid assessments about the institutional impact of injecting market dynamics into Minnesota's K–12 system. And this impact is central, for as an advocate has observed (Kolderie, 1988), "Choice is seen in Minnesota not as an end in itself but as a means to a better education. . . . It has been developed by the state as the mechanism by which it can cause its schools to improve." Whether education choice will have a substantial improvement effect, particularly in upgrading schools for the vast majority of students who do *not* move, remains to be seen. Again, however, some early indicators are promising: new cooperative courses involving schools and postsecondary institutions, markedly increased advanced placement offerings, and the rapid spread of "education districts" (regional cooperatives among local school districts) in rural Minnesota.

THE NEXT STEP—NONPUBLIC SCHOOLS?

Since 1985, the policy focus in Minnesota has been on creating options for parents and students within public education. The voucher issue (involving private school funding) has been largely eclipsed by the public school choice debate. And the statutes that have been enacted provide for only marginal private school participation. Under the Postsecondary Enrollment Options Act, eleventh and twelfth graders can take nonsectarian courses at private colleges; and any student eligible for the High School Graduation Incentives Program can elect to attend a nonpublic, nonsectarian alternative (for example, a street academy) that has a contractual relationship with a local school district. (The nonpublic alternative is guaranteed just 50 percent of public school funding.)

Expanding educational choice to include a larger role for private schools could become an important issue for the Minnesota legislature. The chief agenda setter on choice policy—Governor Perpich— has urged "blurring the lines" between public and private systems in responding to the needs of students who are not learning in their current public school programs. Drawing on a recommendation from his Discussion Group, the governor has proposed in his 1989 budget that private nonsectarian alternatives offering education for dropouts and at-risk students receive 90 percent state funding. He also has proposed that these students be able to attend any nonpublic nonsectarian program, even if not under school district auspices, that can gain approval of the State Board of Education (Perpich, 1989).

Perpich's proposal for expanded private school involvement is targeted at a specific student population. It does not call for education vouchers that could be used generally in nonpublic schools (nor do vouchers appear to be getting much political momentum from any other quarter). Still, the governor's initiative may be seen as a step toward the kind of choice system envisioned by Minnesota's non-public school advocates. As one supporter commented,

> It is important that this state has established the principle of choice, even if we have so far been excluded. But it must be recognized that parents and students have very restricted choice—that is, they can go to this public school or that one. That's like choosing between this brand of grape jelly and another one. Grape jelly is grape jelly!

It is hard to say if private schools will ever become major providers in Minnesota's marketplace of educational choice. But the choice system has been steadily growing, the academic problems of troubled youth are serious, nonpublic alternatives are available in many—notably urban—settings, and organized advocates (such as the Citizens for Educational Freedom) persist in their legislative efforts to increase the varieties of state-supported "jelly" available in the educational marketplace.

Governor Perpich is not the only influential agenda setter on K–12 policy issues. The organization with the most impressive long-term track record in this regard—the Citizens League—has recently issued a new report (Citizens League, 1988). It urges the establishment of "chartered schools" as the next major step in the evolution of educational reform. These public schools, chartered either by a school district or by the state, would be "different" from conventional ones in the way they delivered education and, within broad guidelines, they would be "autonomous" (pp. ii–iii). Along with the league, several of the prominent policy entrepreneurs are vigorously promoting the chartered school as a vehicle to inject significant structural differentiation into the emergent choice system. The softening-up process has already begun on this policy innovation. Its outcome, of course, is problematic. But past political performance—and current issue networks—argue that this latest entrepreneurial thrust be taken seriously, outside as well as inside Minnesota.

REFERENCES

Astrup, Robert. Unpublished memorandum to Minnesota Education Association local association presidents and MEA Board of Directors, 23 December 1986.

Berman, Paul. "The Next Step: The Minnesota Plan," *Phi Delta Kappan* 67 (1985): 188–193.

Brandl, John. "Three Strategies for K–12 Education," *Minnesota Journal* 1 (1983): 1, 4.

Citizens League. *Rebuilding Education to Make It Work*. Minneapolis, MN: Citizens League, 1982.

Citizens League. *Chartered Schools = Choices for Educators + Quality for All Students*. Minneapolis, MN: Citizens League, 1988.

Craig, William J. "Open Enrollment in Public Schools," *CURA Reporter* (University of Minnesota) 17 (1987): 7.

Governor's Discussion Group. *Visionary Plan for Governor Rudy Perpich*. St. Paul, MN: Minnesota Department of Education, 1986.

Governor's Discussion Group. *Addendum to Visionary Statement*. St. Paul, MN: Minnesota Department of Education, 1987.

"Half of States Show Interest in Giving Students and Parents More Choice," *State Education Leader* 7, No. 4 (1989): 7.

Kingdon, John W. *Agendas, Alternatives, and Public Policies*. Boston: Little, Brown, 1984.

Kolderie, Ted. *Competition as a Strategy for Public School Improvement*. Minneapolis: Public Services Redesign Project, University of Minnesota, 1985.

Kolderie, Ted. "The Essential Principles of Minnesota's School Improvement Strategy," *Equity and Choice* 4 (1988): 47–50.

Kostouros, John. "Whose Vision Is It, Anyway?" *City Business* (December 31, 1986): 5, 9.

Mazzoni, Tim L. "The Policymaking Influence of the State School Lobby: A Minnesota Study." Paper presented at the Annual Meeting of the American Educational Research Association, Chicago, 1985.

Mazzoni, Tim L. "State Policymaking and Public School Choice in Minnesota: From Confrontation to Compromise," *Peabody Journal of Education* 63 (1986): 45–69.

Mazzoni, Tim L. "The Politics of Educational Choice in Minnesota." In *The Politics of Excellence and Choice in Education*, ed. William L. Boyd and Charles T. Kerchner. London: Taylor and Francis, 1988.

Mazzoni, Tim L., and Sullivan, Barry. "State Government and Educational Reform in Minnesota." In *The Fiscal, Legal, and Political Aspects of State Reform of Elementary and Secondary Education*, ed. Van D. Mueller and Mary P. McKeown. Cambridge, MA: Ballinger, 1986.

McEachern, Bob. Testimony to the U.S. House Subcommittee on Elementary, Secondary, and Vocational Education. Presentation to Oversight Hearings on Parental Choice, St. Paul, Minnesota, 16 February 1989.

Minnesota Department of Education. *Postsecondary Enrollment Options Program Final Report*. St. Paul: Minnesota Department of Education, 1987.

Minnesota Department of Education. *Initial Impacts of High School Graduation Incentives.* St. Paul: Minnesota Department of Education, 1988a.

Minnesota Department of Education. *School District Enrollment Options Program.* St. Paul: Minnesota Department of Education, 1988b.

Nathan, Joe. *Free to Teach.* New York: Pilgrim, 1983.

Nobles, James. "Choice Doesn't Complete the Education Task," *Minnesota Journal* 6 (1989): 3.

Orwall, Bruce. "Open Enrollment Gets Perpich Kudos," *St. Paul Pioneer Press and Dispatch*, 27 April 1988, p. 4C.

Orwall, Bruce. "Critics Contend Evidence of Its Success Still Lacking," *St. Paul Pioneer Press and Dispatch*, 19 February 1989, pp. 1A, 12A.

Perpich, Rudy. *1990–91 Proposed Biennial Budget: Education Aids and the Department of Education.* St. Paul: State of Minnesota, 1989.

Peterson, Paul. "Did the Education Commissions Say Anything?" *Brookings Review* 2, No. 2 (1983): 3–11.

Pinney, Gregor. "Perpich Abandons Open Enrollment Plan," *Minneapolis Star and Tribune*, 21 May 1986, p. 1B.

Pipho, Chris. "Switching Labels: From Vouchers to Choice," *Education Week* 8, No. 19, 1 February 1989, p. 27.

Plank, David N. "Why School Reform Doesn't Change Schools: Political and Organizational Perspectives." In *The Politics of Excellence and Choice in Education*, ed. William L. Boyd and Charles T. Kerchner. London: Taylor and Francis, 1988.

Polsby, Nelson. *Political Innovation in America.* New Haven, Conn.: Yale University Press, 1984.

Reichgott, Ember. "How Legislature Dealt with Open Enrollment," *Minnesota Journal* 5 (1988): 2.

Roberts, Nancy, and King, Paula. "The Process of Public Policy Innovation." In *Research on the Management of Innovation*, ed. Andrew Van de Ven, H. Angle, Cambridge, MA: Ballinger, in press.

Snider, William. "Parley on 'Choice,' Final Budget Mark Transition," *Education Week* 8, No. 17, 18 January 1989, p. 74.

CHAPTER 8

School Choice: Unwrapping the Package

Ann Bastian

The debate around school "choice" has become both encouraging and troubling in the past year. Those of us with strong commitments to public education have reason to celebrate the retreat from choice concepts that allow public funding for private schooling, such as vouchers and tuition tax credits. We have won an important battle in centering the choice debate within the public school arena.

But there is reason to pause, as well. Increasingly, school choice has become the principal focus of efforts to restructure schools. The mass media have been quick to extol its virtues, usually with the suggestion that choice won't cost any money. Business leaders like the marketplace aspects of choice, politicians like its populist resonance. School choice has become more than this year's buzzword—it has become the top item on the education agenda in over twenty states. For useful surveys of school choice, see Education Commission of the States (1988), Zerchykov (1987), and National Parent Teacher Association (1988).

Given the potency of the prescription, we need to be much clearer and more specific about the pros and cons of choice—its purposes, scope, conditions, and record of performance—before we swallow any magic pills. We cannot afford to be simplistic. School choice actually means different things in different places, and different things for different people. In fact, choice is the rationale behind a myriad of labels: magnet schools, charter schools, alternative concept schools, unzoned schools, open-enrollment plans, controlled choice plans. Whenever choice is invoked, we need to know exactly what we're getting in its name.

THE CHOICE MODELS

Public school choice concepts raise many good questions: How do we create programs suited to students' diverse interests and talents, getting past the factory mode in education? How do we help parents feel more invested in their child's school, more supportive at home and in the classroom? How do we motivate teachers and administrators to assess squarely the strengths and weaknesses of their schools and make real changes? How do we reduce the role of bureaucracy, which has been inexorably standardizing and monotonizing the teaching and learning process? How do we rescue the children—approximately *one-third* of our student population—who are now being underserved and utterly demoralized in failing schools?

These are the right questions, but how well do choice plans answer them? In theory, choice means that schools will earn their enrollments, thereby encouraging a wider range of educational options and spurring deficient institutions to self-improvement. Schools that do not meet parent or student preferences, or do not live up to their program goals, will be faced with declining enrollments. Presumably, the result would be a mix of decent schools, and poorly functioning schools would simply go out of business.

Yet theory is not always the same as practice—there are often intervening realities. Take, for example, New York City, which offers striking examples of how promising and how damaging (and how different) choice plans can be.

New York City's East Harlem school district, Community District 4, has become famous throughout the country, and paramount in the literature, as the place where choice works for poor and minority youngsters. All of its middle schools (seventh to eighth grades) are schools of choice, along with three path-breaking unzoned elementary schools and a new alternative high school (Price and Stern, 1987; Meier, 1987).

It must be stressed that choice works well here because it is part of an overall school improvement process that has been underway in District 4 for fifteen years. Choice was an important ingredient, not the motive force, of change. Choice was not introduced overnight, but expanded school by school, as teachers themselves developed new programs and approaches. Each school of choice has been constructed as a small and relatively personalized unit. Alongside choice, District 4 has developed an exemplary parent information program and strengthened the guidance capacity of teachers and counselors in the feeder elementary schools. Moreover, District 4 is a densely populated area where all schools are reasonably accessible.

Perhaps most important, choice in District 4 developed out of collaboration among school people in the district, not competition between them. The district itself plays an important role in coordinating the program, to ensure that choice offerings are complementary and coherent among the schools. Enrollment is neither selective nor random; school directors collectively decide on student assignments to the middle schools after applications are submitted.

Despite all the plusses, District 4 is not a perfect model. It should be noted that the district's bilingual schools are segregated from its schools of choice, as are special education programs. The only performance data available for New York City schools are standardized test scores, which show District 4 rising from the bottom rank among districts (thirty-second) to the middle range (sixteenth) but within the district there remain very wide fluctuations of test performance.

We hear a lot about East Harlem's positive experience with choice, and not much about the New York high school magnet plan, which is the more common variety of choice and the other side of the coin. Here is a citywide choice plan based on magnet schools competing with comprehensive neighborhood high schools. Over time, the system has evolved four tiers: elite academic high schools, specialized theme schools, vocational schools, and neighborhood high schools.

These tiers represent a strict hierarchy of resources, opportunity, and results. The best schools are selective, through both formal admissions procedures and informal barriers to entry. The worst schools are dumping grounds for children who don't apply to magnet schools, don't get into magnet schools, or don't succeed in schools of choice. Although magnet schools are more or less racially integrated, the neighborhood high schools are entirely segregated; their students are members of minorities and are poor.

These schools on the bottom could break any teacher's heart and regularly do. They are falling apart, physically and socially, and producing dropout rates of 50 to 80 percent for black and Latino students. The choice hierarchy is reinforced by middle school programs that do not prepare low-income students to compete or that do not inform parents about their children's options (or prerequisites); counseling ratios are commonly 600 to 1. This is an example of false choices, because not all options are open and not all options are equal.

If the New York City examples are suggestive of the promise and the pitfalls of choice, the much-heralded Minnesota model prompts unanswered questions. The Minnesota Enrollment Options Plan allows students to enroll in any (participating) public school in the state. The plan takes into account some of the objections to choice: low-income students have transportation subsidies; schools can't selectively accept or reject transfers, although they can set space limits.

But it's hard to match the acclaim accorded the Minnesota model with actual results; the program barely exists. By next school year, it is expected that 2,500 students will participate, out of a total enrollment of 700,000. That is simply too small a sample to say the program is working, that it is stimulating widespread school improvement and coping with the stress of major student shifts.

Two more states, Iowa and Arkansas, have recently adopted statewide choice and twenty more are considering variations of the model. As statewide programs are weighed, the paucity of the record should be kept in mind. So should some of Minnesota's distinct advantages: the state provides 60 percent of school funding, funding disparities between districts are not great, the population is relatively homogeneous, and the quality of schools is generally good and not highly uneven.

CONCERNS AND CONDITIONS

The record shows only one thing thus far: choice is a complex, double-edged issue, not a quick fix for school improvement. Nothing inherent in the choice concept makes it automatically achieve such goals as quality, diversity, and democracy in education. To figure out if a choice plan is going to benefit, damage, or simply distract a school program, educators and parents and citizens should be looking very closely at how the plan is constructed and how well it suits the specific circumstances of the local school community. *What we do know is that if choice is genuinely pursued as a way to serve quality, equality, and diversity in schooling, then it cannot be separated from a comprehensive agenda for school improvement and it cannot be divorced from the resource question.*

Optimally, choice will follow from a restructuring program where all students have quality alternatives from which to choose, all families will be fully informed of their options, all staffs will be engaged by and trained for their school mission, and every participant will have equal access, both physical and cultural access, to the school of choice.

In the absence of ideal conditions, a number of potential problems must be assessed in establishing any choice plan. First and foremost, we should be concerned about the potential for the further segregation of students along the well-entrenched lines of class, race, gender, and handicapping condition. This is not only an issue of whether choice plans are nonselective, or randomly accept nonresident applicants.

What if there are not enough "good schools" to go around, as in New York City and the majority of other urban systems? How far will students have to go to find a good school, and how many spaces will be open? What kinds of kids will have the stamina to strike out on their own—and who will be left behind? How will kids feel about leaving their neighborhood, and how will they be accepted by those already "at home" in the good school?

How will parents understand what options are available and what schools are really right for their child? How will parents get to this school or influence its policies, beyond signing the enrollment form? Why will the schools such students leave behind be any better off or more compelled to change, when they are already dumping grounds for the educationally dispossessed—and know it?

To put these concerns more formally, we need to consider the potentially negative impacts choice can have on equal opportunity, accountability, and the democratic governance of schools. Each of these concerns is important in its own right, and is seriously compounded when choice goes beyond district boundaries.

EQUITY IMPACTS

The probable negative impacts of choice with respect to equity may be summarized as follows:

• Students and teachers may be "creamed," so that chosen schools garner high achievers, while poorer schools are drained of resources and left to languish.
• Schools competing for enrollment may increase informal screening and sorting mechanisms—through preferential recruitment, complex application procedures, or "pushing-out" processes—to bolster the school's achievement profile.
• Choice may unduly place the onus of achievement on the individual student who has opted out of the local school. Choice may be particularly stressful or prohibitive for poor and minority students, if they are required to depart from cultures of peer and family solidarity and adopt the individualistic modes of achievement that mark white, middle-class ("mainstream") performance values.
• Parent involvement may decrease, rather than improve, if the school of choice is outside the residential community, which is a known universe of other parents and children. Practical barriers to parent access, such as time and distance, may also increase disproportionately for poor families.
• Civil rights mandates and desegregation plans may be eroded if choice allows specific waivers to apply or if changing enrollment patterns make integration efforts wholly artificial. Although choice plans often include stipulations to observe integration orders, it is also true that such court orders have been legally undermined and diminished in recent years. In New York City, the decaying neighborhood high schools are left with the main responsibility for providing mandated services to LEP (limited English proficiency) and special education students.

ACCOUNTABILITY IMPACTS

Possible negative impacts of choice with regard to accountability include the following:

- Schools may stress public relations and packaging over program innovation and substance in promoting enrollments for their schools. Joe Clark is not the only PR principal in the nation.
- Reliance on standardized testing as a measure of student and school performance may significantly increase as schools compete. This worry cuts very deep, because we are already in danger of sacrificing comprehension and critical thinking to test-driven systems of teaching and learning. Moreover, we are not close to eliminating cultural bias from standardized testing. It is not reassuring to find Minnesota's governor, Rudy Perpich (1989), touting his choice plan by saying, "Choice, *supported by testing*, will create a marketplace for education that is accountable and responsive to the individual needs of our students."

GOVERNANCE IMPACTS

Possible negative impacts of choice with regard to school governance include these:

- Where choice is geographically extensive, as in statewide plans, parents may no longer be taxpayers and voters in the districts their children attend and may be disenfranchised from the political governance process.
- Where choice requires any significant shifting or instability of teaching staff, it may undermine reforms to increase teachers' authority over the school program; school-based management may become a strictly administrative prerogative. Teacher choice may be negated by parental choice.
- Schools that are not residentially based may be less influenced by and integrated with community life, in ways that potentially make them less responsive to or less supported by education constituents. This isolation from community life is particularly damaging to minority students and families.
- Extensive choice may actually place more control in the hands of state administrators and less in local schools and districts, if there are significant and unstable enrollment shifts, expenditures, staffing, and transportation logistics to manage.
- Funding disparities between schools and districts may also

widen with enrollment disparities, if states do not substantially increase their portion of funding, decrease reliance on local tax bases, and equalize aid to schools. In funding and performance, poor districts could simply get poorer, not necessarily better.

I believe there are reasonable remedies to some of these problems with choice, although the correctives require much greater caution and commitment than most choice plans demonstrate thus far. The fundamental issue is whether or not choice is developed in the spirit of improving all schools for all children. But here we cannot rely on rhetoric alone. We have to look at the contexts for choice, both the educational and political contexts.

Our assessment must include a recognition of what choice cannot accomplish. Rehabilitating inner-city schools, revitalizing rural schools, recruiting a talented and representative teaching corps, lowering class size, rebuilding decaying school plants, modernizing curricula and pedagogy, extending youth support systems—to do all this for every community and every school in need is going to require intervention on many fronts and a much greater investment of tax dollars. Choice in itself doesn't solve any of these problems. Choice is not a substitute for adequate funding or qualified teaching. You can only be sure that anyone who says choice works without costing anything doesn't mean fair choice.

If we assess choice as one factor in a total reform agenda, we must also assess if it is part of a hidden agenda. Is choice being pushed by legislators to circumvent battles over rural school consolidation? Is choice being offered to justify disinvestment in failing urban systems? Is choice a "new, improved sorting machine" to replace the increasingly discredited mechanisms of standardized testing and tracking? (Moore and Davenport, 1988)

Is choice among public schools intended as the opening wedge for funding private and parochial school options? Or is choice simply today's vehicle of convenience for political careerists and educational entrepreneurs? Again, the answers are not embedded in choice itself, but in the very specific circumstances under which it is put forward.

Finally, there is a philosophical wrinkle in assessing the merits of choice that strikes a personal chord. Some of the strongest proponents of choice like to talk about creating a school marketplace. They envision an educational system akin to a private enterprise system, where competition spurs schools on to excellence and consumers call the shots.

I'm not sure which marketplace they have in mind, but the one I'm familiar with, here in the real world, works a bit differently. It is a marketplace where competition not only produces winners, but losers as well. It is a marketplace where consumers do not have equal buying power, reliable product information, or very much control over what gets produced. In recent years, with massive deregulation, it is a marketplace that has created immense polarizations of wealth and well-being.

Frankly, I am offended by the proposition of David Kearns, CEO at Xerox, that "an economic model of education is both more democratic and more responsive than a political model" (Kearns and Doyle, 1988). I happen to think it is a particular strength of the U.S. educational system that it is governed by constitutional and electoral processes, and not by the "invisible hand" of the marketplace.

I happen to believe that education is an entitlement of free citizens, not a commodity for consumers. I don't applaud an educational system that structures achievement in terms of winners and losers, whether it be a school or the students in it. I don't look forward to schools as service centers or employment agencies; I envision them as community institutions, serving the goal of democratic empowerment.

So it doesn't help me analyze the real impacts of school choice, as a system of enrollment, by extolling the virtues of the marketplace. Let's keep public education as a public enterprise, a common good creating common ground, and see how we can increase the options and diversity within it. Let's have choices that represent all we know about good schooling available in every school and district. Let's *not* fulfill Ronald Reagan's departing prophecy: "Choice works, and it works with a vengeance" (Snider, 1989).

REFERENCES

Education Commission of the States. "Overview of State Public School Choice Activity." Denver: Education Commission of the States, 1988.

Kearns, David, and Doyle, Denis. "Winning the Brain Race: A Bold Plan to Make Our Schools Competitive." San Francisco: Institute for Contemporary Studies, 1988.

Meier, Deborah. "Success in East Harlem," *American Educator* 5 (Fall 1987): 299–300.

Moore, Donald, and Davenport, Suzanne. *The New Improved Sorting Machine*. Chicago: Designs for Change, 1988.

National Parent Teacher Association. "Guidelines on Parental Choice—An Educational Issue." Chicago: National Parent Teacher Association, 1988.

Perpich, Rudy. "Policy Issues on Lawmaking Agenda," *Education Week* 8 (11 January 1989): 20.

Price, Janet R., and Stern, Jane R. "Magnet Schools as a Strategy for Integration and Reform," *Yale Law and Policy Review* 5 (Spring–Summer 1987): 299–300.

Snider, William. "Parley on 'Choice' . . . Final Budget Mark Transition," *Education Week* 8 (18 January 1989): 24.

Zerchykov, Ross. *Parent Choice: A Digest of the Research*. Boston: Institute for Responsive Education, 1987.

CHAPTER 9

School Choice: The New Improved Sorting Machine

*Donald R. Moore and
Suzanne Davenport*

SCHOOL CHOICE AND STUDENTS AT RISK

A lead story in *Education Week*, 21 September 1988, observed that "many consider the most pressing concern facing American education" to be "the growing number of students 'at risk' of leaving school prior to graduation or without the skills needed to get a job."

Research on which this chapter is based was carried out under contract with the National Center on Effective Secondary Schools, School of Education, University of Wisconsin-Madison, which is supported in part by a grant from the Office of Educational Research and Improvement (Grant Number G008690007). Any opinions, findings, and conclusions or recommendations expressed in this publication are those of the authors and do not necessarily reflect the views of this agency or the U.S. Department of Education.

Copies of the full study report, *The New Improved Sorting Machine*, and related publications are available from Designs for Change, 220 South State Street, Suite 1900, Chicago, Illinois 60604, 312-922-0317.

187

In the nation's large cities, rapid economic change has eliminated many stable manufacturing jobs previously available to young people lacking basic skills, so that most new jobs with any future require at least ninth-grade levels of reading, writing, and math. Yet a large percentage of urban students are not reaching even these minimum skill levels and are thus unemployable, even though labor shortages for literate workers are developing in many major metropolitan areas (U.S. Department of Labor and U.S. Department of Education, 1988). If the nation is going to address this escalating human and economic crisis, urban school systems must radically improve their capacity to produce competent graduates.

At the same time, increased student choice about which public school to attend is being advocated as a potent strategy for improving the quality of education, and has become an extremely popular reform in those big cities with large concentrations of students at risk. The competition engendered by public school choice, we are told, is the engine that will power major improvements in school quality (Nathan, 1989b; Kearns and Doyle, 1988). But will school choice perform as advertised, especially in the big cities where the failure of our schools is most acute?

In a two-year research study, Designs for Change analyzed the implementation of school choice at the high school level in four large cities: New York, Chicago, Philadelphia, and Boston. As we summarize here, the results are disturbing. In these school systems, school choice has, by and large, become a new improved method of student sorting, in which schools pick and choose among students. In this sorting process, black and Hispanic students, low-income students, students with low achievement, students with absence and behavior problems, handicapped students, and limited-English-proficient students have very limited opportunities to participate in popular-options high schools and programs. Rather, students at risk are disproportionately concentrated in schools where their fellow students are minority, low-income, and have a variety of learning problems. And these low-income neighborhood schools—serving the very students these urban school systems must begin to educate adequately—characteristically exhibit low levels of expectation for their students, deplorable levels of course failure and retention in grade, and extremely low levels of graduation and basic skills achievement.

In the school systems that we studied, school choice schemes have become a new form of segregation, in which students are segregated based on a combination of race, income level, and previous school performance. Yet while meaningful school choice is beyond the reach of the majority of students, the supposed existence of choices creates an illusion of fairness.

Nor are the defects we found in the school choice schemes in these cities the result of easily remedied flaws in design. Rather, the inequities that we documented flowed from powerful political and organizational dynamics that often created gross inequities even in programs that appeared open and fair on paper.

At the very least, study results underscore the need for rigorous analysis and regulation of choice systems and for involvement of parents of students at risk and their advocates in designing and monitoring them. At most, subsequent research and experience may show that school choice presents so many dangers that it should not be pursued as a significant strategy for urban school improvement.

FOCUS OF THE STUDY

Our analysis of school choice was part of a larger research study focused on understanding student placement and labeling at the high school level in four large school systems: New York City, Chicago, Philadelphia, and Boston (Moore and Davenport, forthcoming). With respect to school choice, we were especially interested in analyzing (1) the overall configuration of high schools and high school programs available for students entering high school, (2) the admissions processes by which students ended up in various types of schools and programs, (3) the characteristics of the students in various schools and programs, and (4) the subsequent rates of success for students who attended various schools and programs.

In this chapter, we review study results about these issues that are most pertinent to assessing the realities of school choice in big city school systems, and we then discuss related implications for evaluating public school choice as a strategy for improving the quality of urban schools.

The study included more than three hundred local interviews, collection and review of a variety of pertinent research reports from the four cities, and the research team's own analysis of data concerning the characteristics of students in various types of high schools. The study was advised and assisted by a panel of educators, researchers, and child advocates drawn from the four cities.

HIGH SCHOOL ADMISSIONS: RECENT HISTORY

During their eighth-grade year, most students in the four cities had the opportunity to apply to any one of a large number of high schools and high school programs. Students ended up in a neighborhood or district high school that served their place of residence unless they pursued and secured admission elsewhere. Historically, most big-city students have not faced the extensive menu of options for high school that they do today; before 1970, except for students attending selective exam schools and vocational schools, most students simply moved from their neighborhood junior high to their neighborhood high school.

Beginning in about 1970 and continuing into the 1980s, all four school systems steadily established more options high schools and programs (or "options" or "magnet schools" or "schools of choice") as alternatives to the neighborhood high school. Such options, for example, focused on higher achievers (as did the long-existing exam schools), embodied a particular educational philosophy, addressed an area of student interest (such as the arts), or emphasized preparation for a particular occupation. They were either entirely separate schools or separate programs *within* existing neighborhood high schools. Among options programs within schools, some were operated as entirely separate schools that were simply housed at the neighborhood school and some were course sequences within the existing neighborhood high school program.

Although these high school options sprang from multiple sources, a major impetus for establishing them on a substantial scale was the effort of urban school systems to develop a less controversial alternative to mandatory student busing to remedy racial segregation. The proponents of options (or magnet schools, as they have been most frequently called in connection with school desegregation) argued that students could be enticed to attend desegregated schools if they voluntarily chose to attend because the desegregated school offered an attractive educational program (Bennett, 1989).

The net result of the movement for options has been a dramatically increased array of such options at the high school level in each of the four cities:

- *Example*: In New York, eighth-grade students in 1984–85 were given a catalog over 300 pages long describing options schools and programs. They chose from 261 different schools and programs that were listed on their high school application. Their choices included, for example, Edward R. Murrow High School for Communications, Manhattan Center for Science and Mathematics, Aviation High School, and Academy of Finance (New York City Board of Education, 1986).

- *Example*: In Chicago, eighth-grade students could apply to seventy-six high school Options for Knowledge programs for fall 1986, including Lindblom Technical High School, the International Baccalaureate Program at Kenwood Academy, Word Processing and Typesetting at Amundsen High School, and Allied Health Preparatory at DuSable High School (Chicago Public Schools, 1986).

- *Example*: In Philadelphia, the school district's *Options* booklet for 1987–88 listed forty-four high school choices, including the Parkway Program, Bodine High School for International Affairs, Motivation Program at Edison High School, Bartram Business Magnet Program, the Roxborough/Randolph Skills Hi-Tech Magnet Program, and the Saul High School of Agricultural Sciences (School District of Philadelphia, 1986).

- *Example*: In Boston, eighth-grade students could apply to twenty-five magnet high school programs for 1984–85, including Boston Technical High School, Music Magnet Program at Madison Park High School, Umana School of Science and Technology, and Urban Retrofit at Dorchester High School (School Committee of the City of Boston, 1984).

At first glance, catalogs of available options might suggest that the typical entering high school student in these school systems had a substantial opportunity to attend a school tailored to his or her interests and needs. In reality, however, these options schools and programs have created and legitimated a highly stratified and inequitable system of education.

CHARACTERISTICS OF STUDENTS IN VARIOUS TYPES OF HIGH SCHOOLS

Through the high school choice systems that operated in these four school systems, most students ended up attending six types of schools: nonselective, low-income schools; nonselective low- to moderate-income schools; nonselective moderate income schools; selective vocational schools; selective magnet schools; and selective exam schools. Table 9-1 indicates the distribution of students among these six types of high schools in the four cities.

Although theorists about public school choice envision choice systems in which students with diverse characteristics have equal access to schools of choice (Nathan, 1989a), this ideal was very seldom in evidence in these four cities. For example, Table 9-2 presents data concerning the percentages of students with various characteristics attending the six different types of high schools in Philadelphia. As Table 9-2 indicates, low-income students, black students, Hispanic students, special education students, bilingual students, and students with attendance problems were systematically underrepresented in academically selective schools, but heavily concentrated in low-income and low- to moderate-income nonselective schools.

Weighing all the evidence about the composition of these six types of high schools in the four cities, the research team found the consistent underrepresentation of students at risk that is summarized in Table 9-3. Exceptions to these patterns occurred almost exclusively when parents of students at risk or their advocates conducted sustained vigorous campaigns for reforms in high school admissions.

Table 9-1
Six Types of High Schools

Types of High Schools	New York	Chicago	Philadelphia	Boston
Nonselective low-income				
Number of schools	25 schools	18 schools	7 schools	5 schools
Student enrollment	62,391 students	28,614 students	11,718 students	4,356 students
% total system enrollment	24.4 %	25.8 %	20.4 %	26.4 %
Example	Theodore Roosevelt High School	DuSable High School	Franklin High School	Charlestown High School
Nonselective low- to moderate-income				
Number of schools	25 schools	18 schools	7 schools	4 schools
Student enrollment	73,069 students	27,109 students	18,294 students	4,576 students
% total system enrollment	28.5 %	24.5 %	31.9 %	27.7 %
Example	Louis D. Brandeis High School	Lakeview High School	Overbrook High School	South Boston High School
Nonselective moderate-income				
Number of schools	26 schools	18 schools	7 schools	4 schools
Student enrollment	71,988 students	33,910 students	15,955 students	3,014 students
% total system enrollment	28.1 %	30.6 %	27.8 %	18.3 %
Example	Benjamin Cardozo High School	Kenwood Academy	Northeast High School	West Roxbury High School
Nonselective school totals				
Number of schools	76 schools	54 schools	21 schools	13 schools
Student enrollment	207,448 students	89,633 students	45,967 students	11,946 students
% total system enrollment	81.0 %	80.9 %	80.1 %	72.4 %
Selective vocational				
Number of schools	9 schools	6 schools	4 schools	Not applicable
Student enrollment	16,555 students	11,870 students	6,072 students	
% total system enrollment	6.5 %	10.7 %	10.6 %	
Example	Aviation High School	Chicago Vocational High School	Dobbins Voc- Tech High School	

continued on page 194

Table 9-1 *continued*
Six Types of High Schools

Types of High Schools	New York	Chicago	Philadelphia	Boston
Selective magnet Number of schools Student enrollment % total system enrollment Example	9 schools 19,295 students 7.5 % Edward R. Murrow High School	1 school 2,497 students 2.3 % Whitney Young High School	3 schools 1,977 students 3.4 % Carver High School for Engineering & Science	Not applicable
Selective exam Number of schools Student enrollment % total system enrollment Example	4 schools 12,689 students 5.0 % Bronx High School of Science	2 schools 6,775 students 6.1 % Lane Technical High School	3 schools 3,363 students 5.9 % Central High School	3 schools 4,545 students 27.6 % Boston Latin School
Selective school totals Number of schools Student enrollment % total system enrollment	22 schools 48,539 students 19.0 %	9 schools 21,142 students 19.1 %	10 schools 11,412 students 19.9 %	3 schools 4,545 students 27.6 %
Total citywide Number of high schools Student enrollment	98 schools 255,987 students	63 schools 110,775 students	31 schools 57,379 students	16 schools 16,491 students

THE HIGH SCHOOL ADMISSION PROCESS

Students ended up in the various types of high schools and programs indicated earlier as the result of a complex admission process that included the following (sometimes overlapping) steps: (1) recruitment and information-gathering, (2) application, (3) screening, (4) selection of students offered places, and (5) final student acceptance. Investigating each step in this process highlights the many points at which formal requirements, informal requirements, staff discretion, and parent or student initiative affected the final result, typically to the detriment of equitable admissions.

Table 9-2
Characteristics of Students in Six Types of Philadelphia High Schools

Types of High Schools	Percent Low-Income	Percent White	Percent Black	Percent Hispanic	Percent Special Education	Percent Bilingual	Percent Student Absence
Nonselective low-income	58.0	3.0	79.0	15.0	14.5	2.8	28.0
Nonselective low- to moderate income	36.0	12.0	78.0	7.0	12.4	1.8	25.0
Nonselective moderate-income	20.0	54.0	42.0	2.0	11.9	0.5	17.0
Selective vocational	34.0	25.0	67.0	7.0	2.9	0.2	14.0
Selective magnet	19.0	37.0	54.0	4.0	2.0	0.7	11.0
Selective exam	11.0	39.0	45.0	3.0	0.4	1.4	7.0
All high schools	34.0	26.0	64.0	7.0	10.6	1.4	21.0

Note: The percentage in each cell is the percentage of that type of student in that type of school in Philadelphia. Thus, the upper-left cell can be read as follows: "In Philadelphia, 58.0% of the students in nonselective low-income schools are low-income students." The last row on the table presents system-wide averages. Thus, the lower-left cell can be read as follows: "In Philadelphia, 34.0% of all high school students are low-income students."

Table 9-3
Differences Between Students Admitted to Nonselective Versus Selective High Schools

Nonselective Low-Income and Low- to Moderate-Income High Schools Typically Admit—	Selective Vocational, Magnet, and Exam High Schools and Programs Typically Admit—
High percentages of low-income students	Moderate percentages of low-income students[a]
High percentages of black and Hispanic students	Moderate percentages of black and Hispanic students[a]
Low percentages of white students	High percentages of white students compared with their overall enrollment in the school district[a]
High percentages of students who read two or more years below grade level	Very low percentages of students who read two or more years below grade level
High percentages of students who have been held back for poor performance and thus enter high school overage	Low percentages of students who have been held back for poor performance and thus enter high school overage
High percentages of students classified as handicapped	Very low percentages of students classified as handicapped
High percentages of students with limited English proficiency (LEP)	Very low percentages of students with limited English proficiency (LEP)
High percentages of students with a history of poor attendance	Very low percentages of students with a history of poor attendance
High percentages of students with previous behavior problems	Very low percentages of students with previous behavior problems

[a] Not true for selective vocational schools.

Identifying critical dynamics of this process that shaped the composition of various high schools was a central focus of the study, in which we relied on school system procedure manuals, interviews with school principals, counselors, and student advocates familiar with the admissions process, and existing studies of admissions in the four cities (for example, Smith et al., 1986; Allen, 1986; Advocates for Children, 1985). Here are a few key conclusions.

Most Families Did Not Understand the Process

An interview study conducted in New York (Smith et al., 1986) confirmed an observation that we heard consistently: most students and parents did not understand the high school admissions process. The majority of students either did not apply or filled out an admissions form with little understanding of the complexities that would determine their chances of success. Those who did not apply were often unaware of the brief periods during which applications were accepted, which in some instances amounted to a single week or day. Many who did apply did not know much about the nature and quality of the specific options available, about the previous coursework they should have taken to qualify themselves for a particular option, about the odds of admission to particular programs, or about the strategies that brought success in the admissions process.

Given this lack of understanding of the process on the part of most families, those families who took the time and had the connections to master its intricacies were at a major advantage. They could help students prepare for admission to a desired high school beginning in elementary school by ensuring that the student took the proper courses. They could master the written and unwritten rules of the application process, and exert influence to secure their child's admission to a desired school. Study consultants characterized the admissions process as one in which the successful parent often had to serve as "advocate and negotiator." An article by a magnet school parent knowledgeable about Chicago's admissions process described how parents succeeded in securing magnet school admissions for their children:

Magnet hunting has turned into the great middle-class trauma, and this time of year, as applications fall due, parents around the city gather to swap theories, network, bewail their fate, and to listen once again to the tales of parents who beat the system. . . . Some go through the official lottery system, but others improve their odds by applying personal clout, by inventing nonexistent siblings and minority ancestors for their kids, or by mortgaging their souls to the PTA (Halperin, 1988).

Those families who were poor, had themselves failed in school, moved frequently, or didn't speak English were unlikely to be among those who could help their children complete this intricate admissions process successfully (Price and Stern, 1987; Advocates for Children, 1985).

Junior High Counselors Played a Crucial Role

Given the complexity of the admissions process, junior high counselors and other junior high educators who took a special interest in a student played a crucial role in determining who was admitted to high school options. Urban student-counselor ratios are often as high as 500 to 1, giving counselors little time to spend with individual students (College Entrance Examination Board, 1986; Lee and Ekstrom, 1987; Steinberg, 1988). Further, counselors spend time disproportionately on higher-income and higher-achieving students (College Entrance Examination Board, 1986). In New York, for instance, junior high school students were estimated to receive an average of twenty minutes of guidance counseling about their application to high school (Educational Priorities Panel, 1985). Since junior high counselors were among the few people who fully understood the admissions process, their decision to help a student whom they viewed as promising gave that student a major advantage. Such counselors could encourage a student to apply to particular options, set up interviews with representatives from the options high school when they visited the junior high, aid the student in completing the application, and use their personal influence with the options high school to help secure admission.

Frequently, junior high counselors developed working ties with particular receiving high schools, and junior highs attempted to build their reputation through their success in placing students in high-status options schools and programs (Advocates for Children, 1985). Thus, it was in the interest of junior high staff to recommend and encourage students to apply to high school options who had a good chance to succeed and to discourage "risky" students from applying.

Selective Recruitment

Options high schools and programs often engaged in selective recruiting at moderate-income neighborhood junior high schools, at selective junior high options schools and programs, and at parochial and other private schools, whether or not the recruiting schools had selective admissions criteria. These practices, often based on a network of established relationships between junior high counselors and high school recruiters, worked to the disadvantage of schools serving many students at risk.

- *Example.* The selective magnet schools and programs in Chicago (such as the International Baccalaureate high school programs) recruited heavily from selective elementary school programs, favoring students who had completed previous coursework that was available only in these selective schools. Thus, students who failed to secure places in selective magnets in kindergarten had greatly decreased opportunities for admission to magnet high schools later on.

Unclear and Questionable Admissions Standards

Typically, the admissions processes for most high school options were not subject to strong management and policy setting from top school system administrators and from school boards during the period we studied. Rather, as noted earlier, individual schools were able to exercise a great deal of discretion in deciding whom to admit. The lack of a coherent set of system-wide policies and active efforts to enforce them led to significant inequities.

First, admissions standards formally advertised by options schools and programs were often different from those actually employed in the student selection process:

- *Example*: In 1986, all but six of Chicago's forty-four separate magnet schools were supposed to have nonselective admissions criteria. However, inquiries at many supposedly nonselective schools indicated that they had instituted additional unstated admissions standards, such as grade-level reading achievement (Allen, 1986).

Second, operating without central guidance about their admissions criteria, options schools and programs made subjective judgments about what admissions criteria were appropriate. A basic principle of equity in a number of areas of the law (one that is well established, for example, in the employment field) is that entry-level test procedures must be shown to be related to subsequent success. Further, even when some selectivity is justified, selection methods and criteria employed in identifying qualified applicants must be no higher than the minimum needed for adequate performance (Advocates for Children, 1985). However, widely used selection methods for options schools and programs, such as reviews of past work, student and parent interviews, locally devised tests, and reviews of behavior records and attendance records have almost never been empirically justified by options schools and programs as necessary for adequate student performance, but have nevertheless been adopted based on the subjective judgment of the school's staff.

- *Example*: Admissions criteria for similar programs within a school system often varied widely (for example, among programs that taught computer skills), seemingly based primarily on the numbers of students who applied versus space available and not on the skills needed for adequate performance in the program (Advocates for Children, 1985).

Third, as part of the admissions process, great weight was attached to achievement scores on standardized tests of achievement, with a student's high school admission often hinging on small differences in tested achievement. Yet in many instances, the achievement tests employed to make these individual placement decisions were not initially developed by the test makers with this intention, and they did not have reliability and validity appropriate for this task (Radwin et al., 1981).

Fourth, we consistently found that whether or not an option had significant *academic* admissions standards, much importance was placed on screening out students with previous attendance and behavior problems:

- *Example*: In a New York study of admissions, the researchers reported that "Good attendance is unquestionably the single most common admissions criterion. Of the fifty schools interviewed, forty-three said that they considered absences or lateness in evaluating student applications" (Advocates for Children, 1985).

Fifth, academically selective schools typically did not admit handicapped or limited-English-proficiency (LEP) students during the years studied. Only in New York, where child advocacy groups had pressed for more admission of handicapped students to selective vocational and selective magnet schools, did the percentages of handicapped students in these schools approach system-wide averages (Advocates for Children, 1985).

A Consistent Bias Toward Choosing the "Best" Students

Given the discretion exercised in recruitment, screening, and selection, there was an overwhelming bias toward establishing procedures and standards at each step in the admissions process that screened out "problem" students and admitted the "best" students, with "best" being defined as students with good academic records, good attendance, good behavior, a mastery of English, and no special learning problems.

- *Example*: In 1984–85, New York's "educational options" programs were required to admit 25 percent of their students from among applicants testing more than six months below grade level in reading, 25 percent from students testing more than six months above grade level, and 50 percent from those testing in between. However, these schools consistently ended up with student bodies ranking well above the city-wide and national reading averages, since they consistently chose the students scoring the highest in each of the three required achievement ranges (Advocates for Children, 1985).

The student stratification resulting from the bias toward selecting "the best" is apparent in the study data summarized earlier in Table 9-3.

Three main explanations for this selection bias were indicated by our interviews and by relevant research. First, research about teacher preferences indicates that, given a choice, most teachers prefer to work with high-achieving students and to avoid "problem" students (Gamoran and Berends, 1987). The rapid uncoordinated development of options programs has given educators a chance to exercise this preference.

Second, schools in all four cities were publicly recognized as "good schools" if their achievement scores were high compared with other schools; they are not judged in light of the progress that they made with their students (High Schools Principals Association, 1986). Thus, the easiest way to build a reputation as a good school and avoid a reputation as being a bad one was to recruit high-achieving students and avoid admitting low-achieving students. As the president of the New York City Principals' Association put it, the present system encourages schools "to seek excellence through a selection process rather than through the effectiveness of an educational program" (Kriftcher, 1986).

Third, white and middle-class families, who were best positioned to exert political influence in these cities and who grew to see options high schools and programs as an avenue for providing a good education for their children, worked diligently to structure the options system in a manner that gave their children a competitive advantage in securing options admissions and to resist or to blunt changes in the admissions system that would open them up to a broader range of students. For example, proposals for modest changes in the admissions requirements for New York's popular education option schools led to a well-organized, vocal campaign in opposition (Price and Stern, 1987).

Most Students Were Turned Down

As the selection process unfolded, with the number of parents and students expressing a strong desire to attend options schools and programs greatly exceeding available places, the end result was that most applicants were not admitted to any options high school or program.

• *Example*: In 1984–85, 90,000 students entered New York high schools. They made a total of 380,000 choices of schools that they would like to attend. Yet only 32,000 applicants received and accepted a choice. A school system committee established to investigate the high school admissions process concluded, based on student interviews, that typically, "after submitting an application, the next thing applicants heard was a letter of rejection" (Smith et al., 1986).

• *Example*: In 1983–84, the following percentages of applicants were accepted at some of Chicago's selective high schools: Lane Tech (55 percent), Young Magnet (9 percent), Prosser Vocational (21 percent), Dunbar Vocational (48 percent) (Chicago Board of Education, 1984). At selective elementary school magnets, acceptance percentages of 3 percent to 5 percent have been typical (Halperin, 1986).

The small percentage of students accepted and the fact that few or no students were accepted from many low-income neighborhood junior high schools meant that many students entered high school with a feeling that they were, as one teacher put it, "second-hand goods." Further, as students from low-income junior highs became aware that their older siblings and friends had not been able to win seats in high school options, teachers reported that the possibility of gaining admissions to these options was viewed with increasing cynicism from year to year.

IMPACT ON OTHER SCHOOLS

Beyond the impact of options high schools and programs on the students who attended them, the development of options had important impacts (1) on the rest of the high schools in these systems (high schools that were required to accept all students who resided within their attendance area) and (2) on the junior high schools whose programs and allocation of limited resources were shaped by the junior high's need to prepare students for the high school admissions process. Several conclusions about these impacts are discussed as follows.

Siphoning Off the "Best" Students, Parents, Teachers

To the extent that the most capable students who lived in the attendance area of a nonselective high school gained admission to options high schools and programs, these options drained the neighborhood school of their highest-achieving and best-behaved students, leaving the nonselective schools to deal with even higher concentrations of the students with the most serious learning problems, as reflected in Table 9-3.

Further, selective schools often were granted special prerogatives in selecting staff, which worked to the disadvantage of neighborhood schools.

- *Example*: Heads of options schools and programs established in Chicago were initially given the right to select their teachers, drawing off the best staff from other schools in the system and transferring out those teachers currently teaching at the school whom they didn't want. These unwanted teachers were then able to exercise their seniority rights to take positions in nonselective high schools, sometimes "bumping" popular teachers in these neighborhood schools who had less seniority.
- *Example*: A number of failing neighborhood high schools in New York have been closed and reopened as selective options schools under the leadership of new principals who had substantial discretion in choosing staff. As in Chicago, the teachers who had previously worked at the school were dispersed to other neighborhood high schools.

Finally, neighborhood high schools often lost those active and well-connected parents who could have worked to improve and aid their children's neighborhood high school. The parent advocacy skills, negotiation skills, political connections, and willingness to work for the school that were often so helpful in securing admission to options were lost to the neighborhood high school. And the principals of options schools and programs fully recognized the benefits of having aggressive and well-connected parents in their school and frequently admitted students based on their parents' qualities.

Sending Back Students Who "Don't Work Out"

Frequently, high school options formally or informally sent students who didn't meet their expectations back to their neighborhood schools.

- *Example*: The official policy of such option schools in Philadelphia as Bok Area Vocational-Technical High School, Carver High School of Engineering and Science, and Central High School was that students who seriously violated the discipline code or failed two or more major subjects for a second year were transferred back to their neighborhood high school (School District of Philadelphia, Desegregation Office, 1987).

Similar policies have previously been in force in Chicago and New York. Although these policies have been revoked, people interviewed reported that informal practice has continued to send students who "don't work out" back to their neighborhood school.

Resource Allocation

In dealing with the most difficult students, neighborhood schools faced a host of obvious and not-so-obvious problems that ideally required additional resources to be properly addressed. As the president of the New York City Principals' Association stated about the neighborhood high school that he headed,

> Money is always in short supply, but particularly in those schools which service needs unfamiliar to educational option programs. For example, during the 1981–82 school year we had 2,700 un- or under-immunized youngsters. . . . Additional guidance and health services are required to overcome the potential and actual problems found in young people whose families are struggling not for prosperity, but for survival. (Kriftcher, 1986)

Yet neighborhood schools frequently came off second best in the allocation of school system resources, as compared with options schools and programs. Sometimes, sizable differences in per pupil expenditure favored the selective school.

- *Example*: In 1988–89, the Chicago Public Schools spent an average of $2,304 per pupil on those schools with less than 30 percent low-income students (the schools where most of the options programs to promote integration were housed), but only $1,995 on schools with between 90 percent and 99 percent low-income students, even though schools were supposed to receive supplementary state funds for each low-income student, over and above their basic per pupil allocation (Chicago Panel on Public School Policy and Finance, November 1988).

At other times, the differences were much smaller and subtler, but the cumulative effect was great. The selective school might, for example, receive small amounts of discretionary funding not available to the neighborhood school, first priority in getting its boiler repaired, first priority in receiving its allotment of supplies and in putting in its orders for new books.

Over-the-Counter Admissions

Options schools and programs typically had definite enrollment limits, and they could make clear plans for the coming year because their teaching staff and student body were essentially set by early summer. In contrast, neighborhood schools dealt with a constant process of student enrollment and withdrawal (called "over-the-counter admissions" in New York). As the schools of last resort, they were required to admit whomever came in the door in September or any subsequent month. Thus, the neighborhood school acted as a buffer to the selective school, allowing it to escape any obligation for dealing with fluctuations in enrollment.

- *Example*: As a result of integration requirements in New York, some options schools could not, in 1984–85, admit more than 50 percent minority students. Because they were able to attract fewer white students than would allow them to use their building to capacity, these options schools had empty classrooms. Meanwhile, nearby neighborhood schools were operating at well over 100 percent capacity because they had to enroll minority students who could have been served in the option school's empty classrooms (Rabb et al., 1987).

Pressure in Neighborhood Schools to Focus on Serving High-Achieving Students

Because selective high schools and programs created a major system-wide focus on high-achieving students, both neighborhood high schools and junior highs that wished to build a good reputation were frequently forced to do so by competing for and catering to high-achieving students, rather than by upgrading the quality of education for the majority of their students. Principals of neighborhood high schools who wished to build a good reputation often concentrated on creating selective magnet programs or advanced tracks and courses appealing to the high-achieving students. And school principals and guidance counselors then spent a large proportion of their limited time in a recruitment battle with selective schools.

Further, junior highs sought to build their reputations by preparing students to attend selective high schools, and then they allocated scarce counseling resources in seeking to place their top students in selective schools.

- *Example*: A leaflet for King Magnet Middle School in Boston advertised: "Join a Winning Team—The King! High % of Students Admitted to: Boston Latin School, Boston Technical School, Boston Latin Academy."

Thus, the development of options indeed introduced competition into these urban school systems, but the incentives that the options schools and programs created have typically not been to pursue overall school improvement, but rather to focus more attention on top achievers.

Impact on Student and Staff Morale

Most abstract but extremely important, the growth of high school options created a prevalent feeling among educators and students across these urban school systems that students who didn't make it into a selective high school program (unless they attended an exceptional neighborhood high school) were second rate and that the notion that the bulk of these students could master high school work was "unrealistic," even though students attending neighborhood high schools constituted the clear majority of students attending these big city school systems. These sentiments are reflected in a letter written by a New York parent to a local student advocacy organization, which said, in part:

> I have two children. One (my son) attends an elite (public) school. . . . My daughter, on the other hand, must spend her days at a (public) school for throw-aways. An emotional crisis caused her to have poor attendance in the ninth grade. She did not make an elite school. She didn't even make an "op ed" school. . . . So now, she is in a school where all the kids have serious attendance and academic problems. While the kids are "enrolled," they have really dropped out. Everyone in the place has problems—and I think the worst problem is that these kids are totally isolated from kids who will stay in school and achieve. My son says that when kids misbehave in his school, the threat is that they have to go to my daughter's school. . . . Maybe someone might care about "holding pens or rejects!" Maybe kids who need help should be in a viable institution and occasionally see an achieving kid. I wish I lived in the suburbs where both my kids could go to the same school. My daughter's shame about herself, her classmates and her school are a problem that no better teachers, better curriculum, and more accountability can overcome (Price and Stern, 1987).

QUALITY OF SELECTIVE SCHOOLS

Without question, there are dozens of high school options of outstanding quality in these four school systems, options that are providing students with an excellent educational experience:

- *Example*: Da Vinci Science-Math Research Institute at Benjamin Cardozo High School in New York in 1987–88 won more Westinghouse Science Awards than any other public high school in the country. This magnet program not only admitted outstanding science students but also a like number of students who were below-average in past achievement, but who benefited from the inquiry-oriented science program at the school.
- *Example*: Whitney Young High School in Chicago is an academically selective magnet school whose racial composition mirrored the school system. It has consistently competed on an equal footing in academic contests with suburban Chicago high schools that are, by reputation, among the best in the nation.

Limited Evidence of Program Effectiveness

Despite such clear-cut examples of effectiveness, however, few studies have been done in any of the four cities (or nationally) to assess the quality of the educational options that have been established, to determine whether the options have brought their students to higher levels of achievement than they possessed when they entered these schools, and to determine whether these schools have differential impacts on different subgroups of students. As noted earlier, schools gained reputations in these systems primarily by exhibiting above-average achievement results as compared with other schools, even if these results were an artifact of the school's selectivity. (Even nationally, limited data are available about the impact of options schools. In his "Survey of Magnet Schools," Blank (1983) concludes that magnet schools that implemented high-quality programs were not necessarily selective and that magnet schools in general had higher levels of achievement than did nonmagnets. However, in making the latter observation, the researchers were not able to separate out the impacts of the magnet school programs from the impacts of initial student selection.)

Evaluation of program effectiveness is especially pertinent given the selective admissions practices of these schools and the allocation of good teachers and extra resources to them, which run counter to well-established principles of educational equity. If any case can be made for giving options schools and programs higher-achieving students and extra resources, it should be based on clear evidence that these schools and programs are achieving significant results. But these issues have not been systematically investigated as the basis for continuing and expanding options.

Opportunistic Implementation

In the four cities, we found major variations in program quality among options schools. Similarly, in his national study of magnet schools, Blank (1983) documented great variation in their educational quality. In a widely cited study of the implementation of reforms, Berman and McLaughlin (1978) distinguished between a "problem-solving" approach to implementing an innovation (in which the focus is on improving educational quality for students) and an "opportunistic" approach to implementation, in which the innovation is adopted primarily to receive added funding or to gain some other prerogative. As has been the case with other types of innovations, options schools and programs have been established with both orientations. Further, study consultants observed that, as the number of options has grown, an increasing percentage have been of doubtful educational quality and appear to have been established primarily for opportunistic reasons.

In the four school systems studied, establishing an option school or program may offer the following kinds of advantages: additional funding, opportunity to appoint a program coordinator, opportunity to hire additional staff, opportunity to transfer existing school staff judged unacceptable, opportunity to screen out difficult students, opportunity to screen students applying to the school who come from outside the school's neighborhood attendance area, extra funds for staff development and planning, improved physical facilities and equipment, and priority in obtaining books, supplies, and repairs.

Study consultants and child advocates whom we interviewed described a number of specific schools in which the establishment of an educational option consisted of renaming an existing school program or department, with no significant change in its methods of operation. Further, such instances of opportunistic implementation with few or no increased benefits to students were proportionally more frequent in those programs housed in nonselective low-income and low- to moderate-income schools, as compared with options programs housed in nonselective moderate-income schools and as compared with selective vocational, magnet, and exam schools. Thus, having a program called a Science-Math Institute in both a low-income and a moderate-income high school can provide the appearance of equal opportunity—but not its reality.

OUTCOMES FOR STUDENTS AT RISK

The current study was not designed to assess causal relationships between placement in a particular type of school and student outcomes. Nevertheless, the study highlights radically unequal outcomes among the various types of high schools that have been created by school choice, and extremely deficient outcomes for students at risk. The nature of current outcomes is illustrated by Table 9-4, which

Table 9-4
Student Outcomes in Six Types of Chicago High Schools

Types of High Schools	Percent of Freshmen Failing English	Percent of Freshmen Failing Math	Percent of Dropouts in Class of 1984	Percent of Seniors Reading at or Above National Average	Percent of Seniors Reading Below Minimum Competency	Percent of 1984 Graduates Reading Above National Average
Nonselective low-income	39	47	49	11	53	4
Nonselective low- to moderate-income	33	38	39	27	32	14
Nonselective moderate-income	23	32	29	39	22	24
Selective vocational	24	30	25	30	19	20
Selective magnet	12	15	13	73	3	57
Selective exam	15	20	13	85	2	66
All high schools	29	36	35	35	28	19

presents data about course failure, dropout, and reading achievement in Chicago in the six different types of high schools analyzed in the study. As Table 9-4 indicates, 39 percent of ninth graders in nonselective low-income high schools failed English and 47 percent failed math, a pattern that has persisted over a period of years. Further, 49 percent of students dropped out of these nonselective schools, but even so, only 11 percent of the seniors who remained read at or above the national average for high school seniors, while 53 percent of these seniors read below minimum competency; that is, at the junior high level.

Combining dropout and reading achievement data for Chicago's Class of 1984 that are presented in Table 9-4, 6,700 students comprised the original entering class in Chicago's eighteen nonselective low-income high schools, but only 300 of them (4 percent of the original class) both graduated and could read at or above the national average. Among the rest, 3,300 dropped out and 1,500 who graduated were reading below the ninth-grade level, even though they were high school seniors. Thus, 72 percent of the original class either dropped out or graduated reading so poorly that they were unlikely to find an entry-level job with any future. Available data for low-income high schools in the other three cities indicate similar results. Clearly, more than a decade of school choice in these four cities has not engendered the kind of overall school improvement envisioned by school choice advocates.

THINKING ABOUT THE POTENTIAL OF SCHOOL CHOICE

When key results from the present study have been presented to advocates of public school choice, they have characteristically responded with two related arguments. First, they argue that the four cities studied "designed" their choice programs improperly and that these defects could be overcome if "every school became a magnet school" and other design changes were made. Second, they point to examples of public school choice programs that are allegedly more equitable and thus allegedly prove that choice can simultaneously bring about high educational quality and equity. The preceding discussion of our research results suggests several ways in which these counterarguments fall short.

The research literature of the past two decades on the implementation of reforms consistently indicates that creating educational programs that help children learn better is far more than a design problem. Powerful beliefs and preferences of those charged with implementing a reform, established organizational routines, and existing political arrangements work to pervert the aims of program designers (Sabatier and Mazmanian, 1979; Elmore, 1978). In our research, we repeatedly saw how many such dynamics undermined the equity of school choice programs. For example, the following forces systematically undermined equity:

- The preferences of most teachers for working with high-achieving and well-behaved students and avoiding students at risk.
- The widespread belief among educators that many students in low-income neighborhood schools are uneducable and that the best that can be done is to "save a few."
- The myriad subtle ways in which the admissions processes for options schools can screen out students at risk, even when the process appears fair on paper.
- The rewards systems operating within school districts, which recognize schools that recruit and focus disproportionate resources on high-achieving students, rather than schools that bring their entire student bodies, including low-achieving students, to higher achievement levels.
- The persistent political pressure that middle-income parents of all races exert to shape the policies, practices, and individual admissions decisions of options schools to benefit their children.

One of the most frequently offered remedies for the kind of multi-tiered educational systems that we documented is "to make every school a magnet school." But again, it takes more than a formal policy decree to turn this concept into a set of schools that are, in fact, equitable and effective in their day-to-day practices. Indeed, each of the cities studied has been rapidly expanding the number of options schools and programs, so that they already claim that they are seeking to make every school a magnet school. Unfortunately, as noted earlier, many of the options available to students at risk that have resulted from this rapid expansion merely entail the renaming of existing programs or course sequences, without any corresponding improvement in their quality, and reflect the establishment of the options program for opportunistic reasons unrelated to the effort to provide better learning programs for students.

The second and related response to our findings from the advocates of public school choice is to cite repeatedly one of a small number of public school choice programs that have allegedly avoided the problems that we documented. By far, the most frequently cited example is the system of junior high school choice that has been established in District 4 in East Harlem (Fliegel, 1989). Clearly, the East Harlem program represents a sincere long-term effort to improve education in an inner city neighborhood, and it has resulted in a number of excellent schools. Yet despite all the attention it has attracted, the program has yet to be subjected to rigorous research analysis that would justify citing it as a national model, and data already available about the program raise significant questions about the extent of its effectiveness and equity. Here are some important questions about the East Harlem program that require further investigation:

- The East Harlem choice program consists of twenty-four options, several of which are repeatedly cited for their excellence and achievement. But the admissions process for these programs depends on individual admissions decisions by program staff, and several of the programs are highly selective. This is the very system of selection that we have seen repeatedly abused at the high school level in the four cities we studied. Is this discretionary selection system really more equitable in East Harlem, and if so, do the reasons for its greater equity have any general application?

- The percentage of students in District 4 reading at grade level has increased from 15.9 percent in 1973 to 62.6 percent in 1987, and the relative standing of the district's achievement scores compared with other districts has improved (Fliegel, 1989). Yet, city-wide, the official achievement scores in grades 2 through 9 have risen from 33.9 percent in 1971 to 62.7 percent in 1987, and furthermore widespread skepticism has been expressed about the validity of these test results (Radwin et al., 1981). Do the District 4 results reflect what its students would achieve in an independent assessment using a test with which the district was unfamiliar?

- There are extreme variations in the reading and math scores among the various options in District 4. For instance, in 1986, the percentages of seventh-grade students reading at or above grade level in alternative concept schools ranged from highs of 97.7, 97.3, and 90.0 percent to lows of 30.0, 36.8, and 42.1 percent (Price and Stern, 1987). These results suggest a high degree of initial selectivity, and a failure to educate students in some nonselective options schools. Are the students who are most at risk really benefiting from the choice program, or are benefits accruing disproportionally to students who are already better off?

- Both students who require special education and students who require bilingual education are excluded from the District 4 choice programs; they attend separate schools (Price and Stern, 1987). The exclusion of handicapped and limited-English-proficient (LEP) students was one of the major inequities observed in the other choice programs that we studied. Why are these at-risk students excluded, and what is the impact on their performance?

- District 4 simultaneously claims that more of its graduates are admitted to selective exam high schools and that their choice program attracts many students from more affluent neighborhoods outside their district (Fliegel, 1989). To what extent are improved achievement results and high school admissions results an artifact of the migration into the district of these more affluent students?

- The architects of the District 4 program stress that it began with a long-term commitment to improve the schools in the district, and that school choice was only one element in the strategy (Fliegel, 1989). As with the reform of the Cambridge Public Schools (Peterkin and Jones, 1989), another example frequently cited as evidence of the success of choice, it is not clear what elements of the overall reform strategy have been most important in bringing about the improvement that has occurred. How important is the school choice component of the District 4 strategy, and what is the relevance of District 4's multifaceted strategy for other school districts that view choice, in and of itself, as the primary catalyst for change?

Clearly, the East Harlem program has significant virtues and merits further study. But neither East Harlem, nor the handful of other examples repeatedly cited by public school choice advocates, provides solid evidence that public school choice represents an effective strategy for improving big-city education on a wide scale.

RECOMMENDATIONS

The present study makes it clear that high school options have great potential for increasing educational inequality, creating a new form of segregation based on a combination of race, income level, and previous success in school. In the four school districts studied, school choice has become a new improved sorting machine. At the least, study results call into fundamental question the naive view that loosely structured choice systems will yield improved schools for all students through "competition." The competition that frequently occurs in such circumstances is primarily among students, not schools, with admission to a selective school out of reach for the average urban student.

As they are currently being implemented in the four cities studied, options schools and programs represent a major assault on the opportunities of the nation's most vulnerable children. Further, despite the current enthusiasm for public school choice among educators and policymakers, there is little evidence that choice brings higher levels of achievement for students (especially students at risk), once students' initial levels of achievement are taken into account. This combination of well-documented risks and unproven benefits suggests that, at the minimum, public school choice must be stringently regulated and that it should be viewed as only one subsidiary part of an effective and equitable effort to improve public schools.

Thus, study recommendations spell out a series of changes in the governance and oversight of options schools and programs that are essential if school choice programs are to operate within minimum standards of fairness and if their strengths and weaknesses are going to be systematically assessed. However, correcting the inequities and dangers of choice may not be feasible, and this possibility should be carefully weighed through additional analysis of the implementation and impact of public school choice programs.

Recommendations: Strengthening Interest Groups Who Support Equity

The most important change that will improve the fairness of the school choice process in school systems like those studied is also perhaps the most difficult to make. Unless the interests of students at risk are represented in the policymaking and in the monitoring and implementation of policy that shape the admissions and program development processes, many of the other changes recommended here are not likely to affect the day-to-day experiences of students. Active parents of students at risk and advocates for these students must reach some parity of involvement and influence with the well-organized middle-class parents who are already active in shaping the admissions process to benefit their children; otherwise, more stringent formal procedures will be of little use because they will be circumvented.

Inequities in school choice are particularly likely to develop when a choice program is established *in isolation*, with a general faith that competition will improve school quality. From the standpoint of equity for students at risk, it is essential that carefully controlled choice be pursued as *one facet* of a serious overall effort to improve educational quality for all children.

Recommendation 1. Procedures should be established through which active parents of students at risk and advocates for these children can participate in decision making about the quality of these children's educational experiences, including the design and implementation of school admissions.

Recommendation 2. School choice should be employed as a subsidiary component of an overall effort to improve the quality of all schools, with a particular focus on improving the education of those students most at risk of school failure.

Recommendation 3. Independent parent and citizen advocacy organizations should make the admissions process for options schools and programs a major focus for investigation and advocacy, and foundations and other independent funders should support such activities.

Recommendations: Assessing the Equity and Effectiveness of Options

Our analysis indicates that options have typically grown up under loose mandates that give wide discretion for the school-level design of their admissions procedures. With few exceptions, such discretion has consistently been used to the detriment of the students with the greatest learning needs. More systematic and equitable alternatives to the development of public school choice can be derived from an analysis of the shortcomings of the programs that we studied, as well as from the experience of those who have established more equitable options programs in smaller cities, such as Cambridge, Massachusetts (Peterkin and Jones, 1989).

Recommendation 4. School districts should institute moratoriums on the development of additional options schools and programs, pending (1) a review of systematic data about their characteristics and their impact and (2) the development of comprehensive procedures for monitoring their operation and expansion that include strong safeguards to promote equity. Parents of students at risk and advocates for these students should have a decision-making role in this reappraisal.

In general, the school systems studied have significant research and evaluation capabilities and regularly collect data about many key issues pertinent to assessing the impact of public school choice, such as the characteristics of students attending various types of schools and programs, the staff and financial resources allocated to these schools and programs, and the performance gains of students attending them. Yet none of the four school systems studied has regularly analyzed such data to clarify key issues concerning their options schools, used the results for planning and policymaking, and made such results public. Most of the data presented in this chapter have been pieced together from a variety of school system reports whose purpose was not to illuminate the operation and effectiveness of options. In many instances, the failure of school systems to analyze such data themselves and make it public constitutes a conscious effort to avoid examining difficult questions of equity concerning programs that are popular with influential constituencies.

Recommendation 5. Through analyzing data already available and through inexpensive sampling studies, school systems should provide themselves and the public with information useful in further illuminating such key issues as the characteristics of students attending various types of options high schools and programs, the resources allocated to such schools and programs, and their impact in boosting student achievement, including the achievement of specific student subgroups. Such data should be collected and analyzed both in the moratorium period recommended earlier and on an ongoing basis.

A systematic analysis of existing options should form the basis for making decisions about the future of individual options schools and programs. The following recommendations are aimed at building on any strengths of specific options that can be systematically documented, while eliminating or minimizing inequities.

Recommendation 6. Options that are effective, but have selective admissions requirements, should be moved toward increased diversity of admissions, making changes in admissions procedures as spelled out below. Options that, based on evaluation, are ineffective should be placed on probation and closed if they do not improve.

Recommendation 7. School systems should give top priority to developing new options schools and programs that meet the needs of a representative cross section of a school system's students, including an equitable percentage of students with handicaps, limited English proficiency, past academic failure, and attendance and behavior problems.

Recommendations: The Admissions Process

School-level discretion in the admissions process has consistently been used to introduce inequities for students at risk. As documented earlier, these inequities are not oversights, and solutions to these problems must take powerful organizational and political dynamics into account.

Recommendation 8. All aspects of the admissions process should be subject to strong system-wide rules and aggressive enforcement, with parents of students at risk and their advocates having decision-making roles in the design and oversight of these systems. Key steps in the admissions process should be administered centrally, rather than left to school-level discretion.

Recommendation 9. The basic assumption of the admissions process for options schools and programs should be that students have a right to apply based on interest and that the school or program has a positive responsibility to ensure a student body representative of the school system as a whole (for example, through a stratified random selection process).

Recommendation 10. Options schools and programs should be required to justify any restrictive admissions requirements as essential for performance in their program and should keep these requirements to a minimum, choosing students randomly from among minimally qualified applicants. Admissions procedures and requirements that are inherently unreliable as predictors of program success and/or inequitable, such as student and parent interviews, behavior records, school-developed tests, and requirements for previous coursework, should be prohibited system-wide.

Impact on Other Schools

Our analysis indicated a number of detrimental impacts of options schools and programs on nonselective schools, as well as some strategies for school improvement tested in options programs that could be productively employed in strengthening nonselective schools.

Recommendation 11. As part of a comprehensive review of the role of options in a particular school district, the school district should identify and eliminate or minimize detrimental impacts of high school options on nonselective schools in such areas as loss of capable students, loss of capable staff, resource inequities, formal or informal procedures for sending students back to their neighborhood school, and creation of incentives for neighborhood schools to place undue emphasis on recruiting and educating high-achieving students.

Recommendation 12. Prerogatives historically granted to options schools and programs that have proven useful in their efforts to build an effective school program (such as flexibility in staff selection, staff training, upgrading of facilities, and discretionary funding) should be identified and applied to the improvement of neighborhood schools.

IN SUMMARY

Public school choice is a reform strategy whose advocates have thus far failed to prove that it can bring about the widespread school improvement that is essential in the nation's big cities. School choice has proven risks and unproven benefits for students at risk, and has typically represented a new and more subtle form of discriminatory sorting at a time when the economic survival of our cities depends on across-the-board improvements in educational results. The burden of proof now clearly rests on the advocates of public school choice to show that it can lead to significant equitable school improvement in more than a few isolated situations, and that its risks can be eliminated on a widespread basis as a matter of actual practice and not merely on paper.

REFERENCES

Advocates for Children. *Public High Schools, Private Admissions: A Report on New York Practices.* New York: Advocates for Children, 1985.

Allen, Martha. "Nonselective Magnet Schools Use Selective Criteria." *Chicago Reporter,* 15 (1986): 6–8.

Bennett, David A. "Choice and Desegregation." Paper prepared for the Conference on Choice and Control in American Education, University of Wisconsin-Madison, 1989.

Berman, Paul, and McLaughlin, Milbrey Wallin. *Federal Programs Supporting Educational Change,* Vol. 8: *Implementing and Sustaining Innovations.* Santa Monica, CA: Rand Corporation, 1978.

Blank, Rolf K. "Survey of Magnet Schools: Analyzing a Model for Quality Integrated Education." Final report of a national study for the U.S. Department of Education. Washington, DC: U.S. Department of Education, 1983.

Chicago Board of Education. *Annual Desegregation Review 1983–84, Part II: Recommendations on Educational Components.* Chicago: Chicago Board of Education, September 1984.

Chicago Panel on Public School Policy and Finance. *Illegal Use of Chapter 1 Funds by the Chicago Public Schools.* Chicago: Chicago Panel on Public School Policy and Finance, November 8, 1988.

Chicago Public Schools, Department of Equal Educational Opportunity Programs. *Options for Knowledge Programs.* Chicago: Chicago Public Schools, Department of Equal Educational Opportunity Programs, 1986.

College Entrance Examination Board. *Keeping the Options Open: An Overview, Interim Report of the Commission on Precollege Guidance and Counseling.* New York: College Entrance Examination Board, 1986.

Educational Priorities Panel. *Lost in the Labyrinth: New York City High School Admissions.* New York: Educational Priorities Panel, 1985.

Elmore, Richard F. "Organizational Models of Social Program Implementation." *Public Policy* 26 (Spring 1978): 185–227.

Fliegel, Sy. "Parental Choice in East Harlem Schools." In *Public Schools by Choice: Expanding Opportunities for Parents, Students, and Teachers,* ed. Joe Nathan. St. Paul, MN: Institute for Learning and Teaching, 1989.

Gamoran, Adam, and Berends, Mark. *The Effects of Stratification in Secondary Schools: Synthesis of Survey and Ethnographic Research.* Madison: National Center on Effective Secondary Schools, University of Wisconsin, 1987.

Halperin, Marj. "The Lottery." *Chicago* 37 (December 1986): 159–161ff.

High School Principals Association. *High School Principals Association Issues Paper: High School Admissions.* New York: High School Principals Association, 1986.

Kearns, David T., and Doyle, Denis P. *Winning the Brain Race: A Bold Plan to Make Our Schools Competitive.* San Francisco: Institute for Contemporary Studies Press, 1988.

Kriftcher, Noel N., to Arthur Auerbach. New York Board of Education, March 5, 1986.

Lee, Valerie E., and Ekstrom, Ruth B. "Student Access to Guidance Counseling in High School." *American Educational Research Journal* 24 (1987): 287–310.

Moore, Donald R., and Davenport, Suzanne. *The New Improved Sorting Machine.* Designs for Change, 220 S. State St., Suite 1900, Chicago, IL 60604. Forthcoming.

Nathan, Joe. "Choosing Our Future." In *Public Schools by Choice: Expanding Opportunities for Parents, Students, and Teachers,* ed. Joe Nathan. St. Paul, MN: Institute for Learning and Teaching, 1989a.

Nathan, Joe, ed. *Public Schools by Choice: Expanding Opportunities for Parents, Students, and Teachers.* Minnesota: Institute for Learning and Teaching, 1989b.

New York City Board of Education. *1986–87 Directory of the Public High Schools.* New York: New York City Board of Education, 1986.

Peterkin, Robert, and Jones, Dorothy. "Schools of Choice in Cambridge, Massachusetts." In *Public Schools by Choice: Expanding Opportunities for Parents, Students, and Teachers,* ed. Joe Nathan. St. Paul, MN: Institute for Learning and Teaching, 1989.

Price, Janet R., and Stern, Jane R. "Magnet Schools as a Strategy for Integration and School Reform." *Yale Law and Policy Review* 5 (1987): 299–300.

Rabb, Harriet, et al. *Promoting Integration in the New York City High Schools.* New York: Education Law Project, Columbia Law School, July 1987.

Radwin, Eugene, et al. *A Case Study of New York City's Citywide Reading Testing Program.* Cambridge, MA: The Huron Institute, 1981.

Sabatier, Paul, and Mazmanian, Daniel. *The Implementation of Regulatory Policy: A Framework for Analysis.* Davis, CA.: Institute for Governmental Affairs, 1979.

School Committee of the City of Boston, Department of Implementation. *Student Assignment Information, Boston Public Schools 84–85.* Boston: School Committee of the City of Boston, Department of Implementation, 1984.

School District of Philadelphia. *Options for Learning.* Philadelphia: School District of Philadelphia, 1986.

School District of Philadelphia, Desegregation Office. "Special Admissions Schools for September 1988, Use of Form EH 38. (File N. 400)." Philadelphia: School District of Philadelphia, October 13, 1987.

Smith, Frank, et al. *High School Admissions and the Improvement of Schooling: A Report of the University Consultants.* New York: Smith, Frank, et al., 1986.

Steinberg, Adria. "Guidance and Counseling: Too Little, Too Late?" *Harvard Education Letter* 4 (1988): 1–5.

U.S. Department of Labor and U.S. Department of Education. *The Bottom Line: Basic Skills in the Workplace.* Washington, DC: U.S. Department of Labor and U.S. Department of Education, 1988.

CHAPTER 10

Is More or Less Choice Needed?

Joseph G. Weeres

The concept of choice currently embraces sets of policy options ranging from school-based management to tuition vouchers. In response to the question raised by the title of this chapter, I argue that more choice is needed within many school districts in the form of site-based management, but that interdistrict transfers and tuition vouchers are neither politically necessary nor socially desirable. My analysis is divided into two sections. First, I argue that schools already function as markets, and, contrary to much of the literature in support of choice, the difficulties confronting education today largely represent *consequences* of these market arrangements. Second, I propose ways of offsetting some of the negative political externalities produced by these market arrangements.

SCHOOLS AS MARKETS[1]

Advocates of choice frequently pit their proposals against "the one best system," the description of school governance coined by Tyack (1974). Chubb and Moe (1988), for example, juxtapose much of their argument for a voucher system against this metaphor. Although the phrase aptly described school administration at the turn of the century and perhaps does so today in a diminishing number of big-city school districts, it fails to capture the larger pattern of school governance that evolved after World War II. Reformers, concerned with reducing the spheres of influence of big-city political machines, and being responsive to the political demands of a growing middle class, sponsored the proliferation of suburban governments around the big cities. The effect has been to create a market in which individual choice about where to live and do business shapes the politics of education in most school districts. The chaotic consequences of this arrangement were masked for decades by the expansion of the marketplace, which allowed individual self-interests to converge around the gains to be accrued from growth. Individual choice pushed out collective political decision making. But when growth inevitably ended, as it has for an increasing number of communities, the logic of individual choice threatens to overwhelm the capacity of school districts to provide coherent educational services. To see why this occurs, let's begin with the hypothesis that has been a cornerstone of urban economics for over a quarter-century.

The Tiebout Hypothesis

In 1956, the noted economist Charles Tiebout hypothesized that the distribution of suburban governments would conform to the economic principles of large-scale markets. In large competitive markets, the convergence of individual choices by both consumers and suppliers tends to transform the market into isomorphic groups. Tiebout reasoned that, in a market of rapidly proliferating local governments, individual citizens would choose to reside and do business in communities that offered the highest level of governmental services for the lowest tax rate, and governments correspondingly would seek to attract the most financially capable taxpayers by offering baskets of governmental services (police protection, roads, schools, parks, and so on) tailored to these potential residents. The intersecting of the supply and demand curves would result, he argued, in a distribution of relatively small, internally homogeneous communities, stratified from one another by the median income of residents and the quality and level of governmental services.

Generally speaking, empirical data about the subsequent growth of metropolitan areas support Tiebout's model (Zudrow, 1983), but there are, as I discuss later, important qualifiers. In theory, stratification based on income and taste ought to produce relatively stable politics, because residents already have expressed a set of preferences about the kind of governmental services they want and are willing to pay for through their residential decisions. This stability is most secure at the top part of the wealth scale, where the market is not price sensitive. These communities have sufficient slack taxpaying capacity to be able consistently to exclude (through zoning and other devices) the kinds of less affluent residents who might not as easily be able to pay for a high level of governmental service or whose social status might discourage other potential buyers. The economic status of these communities tends to be stable, and that makes it easier for the schools to match educational services with citizen demands.[2] These are not the citizens who are demanding more choice. They already have quasi-private school districts.

But as one moves down the income ladder, the market becomes more price competitive, and chaotic, resulting in greater internal heterogeneity within local communities and more unstable politics. School politics in these communities tends to parallel a pattern of economic growth and decline. It is from these communities that the voices for choice have grown the loudest.

The Politics of Economic Growth

Historically, most communities have followed an economic growth pattern associated with the law of diminishing returns. Initially, communities grow by building houses and businesses on what was once farmland. This process of growth promotes consensus, and stability, in politics because it helps order individual preferences about the economic gains to be accrued through participation in this economic growth.

Businesspeople, for example, stand to gain through increases in the value of their landholding and the large number of customers who will live in proximity to their businesses. In order to secure these benefits, however, they need to influence the governmental agencies that will regulate the growth. City councils and planning commissions develop master growth plans, enact zoning restrictions, offer zoning variances, establish tax rates, and make a host of other decisions that businesspeople need to know about, and, if possible, influence in order to maximize their own individual economic returns on community growth. School boards also participate in shaping growth through the location of school sites. Land adjacent to these sites typically rises in value relative to other locations, and the quality of the schools constructed influences the value of surrounding property. It is during this growth stage that business participation in both city and school politics is most pronounced.

Homeowners also benefit by economic growth. As the community becomes more attractive to prospective homebuyers through the provision of better governmental services (such as roads, parks, sewers, and schools), existing homes increase in value. The costs of many of these governmental improvements, however, typically are deferred by issuing long-term bonds. Individuals who reside in the community during the early phase of growth can earn an economic rent off these deferred debts, because their homes typically increase in value immediately, and the governmental debt is paid off over a much longer period of time. This condition affords existing homeowners an opportunity to accrue an economic rent by selling their houses and moving out of the community, and letting subsequent homeowners pay off the long-term governmental bonds.

Under these circumstances, most residents, both businesspeople and homeowners, have a vested interest in economic growth and the governments that regulate it. They are more willing to pay taxes because it will bring them personal economic benefits through increases in property values and business sales. They will contribute their time and energy to government, by volunteering for governmental service and participating in community-building endeavors, because it is in their individual economic self-interests to do so.

These conditions make it relatively easy for political leaders to pull together stable political coalitions around the notion of community growth. By enacting governmental policies that promote growth, and thereby enhance individual economic interests, politicians and school boards usually can earn the right to rule, and secure a significant measure of political legitimacy. Policies can be assessed in terms of their effects on growth, and those that are perceived to be economically dysfunctional can be rejected with the certainty that most residents will support developmental policies (Peterson, 1981).

From the period following World War II through the mid-1970s, most communities grew incrementally, developing parcels of land serially until all the land in the community held housing or business properties. This process of incremental growth nurtured the politics of community building, giving communities time to form norms necessary for political consensus. It also was an era in which the overall metropolitan market was expanding. Federal subsidies for roads and freeways made large areas accessible for the construction of new cities and communities. Families of the baby boomers were presented with a diverse menu of governments from which to choose.

Beginning in the early 1970s, however, economic forces began to work against these processes. The construction industry had become sufficiently capitalized so that it had the financial resources necessary to take a community through a full growth cycle in a matter of a few years. Under these conditions, virtually all the economic rents associated with growth go to the builder, not to individual homeowners and local businesses. Also, a crowding-out effect began to emerge where existing communities already had consumed most of the accessible and desirable land within the metropolitan area. This condition reduced the number of emerging growth communities, and made it difficult for citizens to hop from one community to another to catch the next growth wave. A major side effect was the emergence of no-growth coalitions. Existing residents saw that their opportunities to relocate in another growth community were curtailed, and that they would have to pay for, rather than pass on to incoming community members, the long-term governmental debt associated with building the city's infrastructure. As a consequence, politics in an increasing number of communities has taken on characteristics associated with that of economic decline, where the absence of strong political structures for aggregating preferences into collective decisions results in unstable governance.

The Politics of Economic Decline

After growth ends, the composition of most communities becomes increasingly heterogeneous. In Tiebout's pure theory, the market should clear and residents should reshuffle, and governments should redesign their service packages, to re-establish internal homogeneity within each community. But this doesn't happen, because most individuals and businesses cannot move from one location to the next that easily. The costs are too high, and a crowding-out effect that precludes such moves already has taken hold in many metropolitan areas. Local communities also typically hedge their bets on growth by developing more diversified economies and housing stocks than Tiebout's model predicts. It frequently is in the individual economic interest of elites, though not necessarily that of the city as a whole, to extend growth by creating density via the construction of apartments and condominiums, all of which tend to attract a more heterogeneous population. Also, as the housing stock and economic infrastructure age, communities find it increasingly difficult to recruit replacements of equivalent taxpaying capacity for people who leave.

The municipal reform movement left local governments ill equipped to manage these social and political cleavages. By encouraging the development of a suburban marketplace, reformers created circumstances whereby people assessed their relationship to local government in terms of their individual self-interest. These market conditions work against the ability of citizens to express civic interests, by making manifestations of public-regarding action irrational in a world of exit and choice (Olson, 1965). At the same time, reformers weakened the capacity of local governments to order preferences other than by means of growth coalitions. They pushed out the political parties ("let's keep politics out of education"), and eroded a sense of community political consciousness by separating school and city governmental structures. They permitted the establishment of a host of metropolitan agencies such as water districts that cut across existing local government jurisdictions. The proliferation of these local governments makes the lives of individuals so functionally divided—they may reside in one city, work in another, and spend their leisure time in several others—that it precludes the sense of community identity so necessary for the mobilization of public-regarding interests. School politics under these conditions, and in the absence of growth, produces unstable majorities on school boards, and circular social choices.

After growth ceases, many of the individuals who previously contributed to the maintenance of the local government don't have much economic incentive to do so. Business leaders, who often formed the core of growth coalitions, typically withdraw from school board politics, and focus their involvement in specially created urban redevelopment agencies and enterprise zones, separate local governmental entities outside the purview of electoral politics. Ordinary citizens, too, begin to vote their self-interest by turning down bond and tax referenda, because the provision of more governmental services will not enhance their property values.

The failure of school bond and tax initiatives often signals a diminution of trusteeship behavior among school board members. Whereas under conditions of growth, admission to the board often was controlled by local elites, and represented the honor of being annointed, it now increasingly becomes subject to direct electoral politics. Previously sponsored board members find themselves effectively challenged by candidates representing special interests. The cleavages engendered by economic growth and decline pit homeowners against businesspeople, long-time residents against newcomers, and social class against social class. Trustee boards dissolve into individuals who represent narrow constituencies associated with intensely held single issues. The expression of a broader public civic interest is rendered mute by the logic of markets and the weakness of reform government.

School board elections, as a consequence, yield victories to candidates who cannot retain office. Special-issue constituency candidates attempt to impose their preferences on the school system, which, in turn, sets off a cycle of circular social choices, as one majority on the board is replaced by another. The capacity of districts to formulate and maintain a coherent educational program is undercut by these electoral circularities. Parents and teachers circumvent the hierarchy of authority within the administrative structure and take their cases directly to members of the board. Principals and other administrators forge political relationships with special interests, and attempt to influence district policy outside the normal chain of command. As a consequence of these destabilizing forces, superintendents get caught up in the cross fire, and a procession of executives moves in and out of the district.

In these unstable political circumstances, school superintendents frequently attempt to protect themselves by centralizing authority and emphasizing the formal elements of bureaucratic structure. They also seek to secure a measure of authority by bringing in county counsels to participate in board deliberations, and attempt to justify school policies by coupling them to expressed professional norms, state and federal regulations, and court decisions (Meyer and Scott, 1983).

Much of this centralization stems from the inability of unstable majorities on school boards to legitimate discretionary behavior on the part of school personnel. The vulnerability of the boards to community voice manifests itself as the closing up of supervision and bureaucratic control through the elaboration of rules and regulations. Conformity is imposed, not because of some agreement about higher-order values as advocates for choice sometimes argue, but because the community is unable to make collective political decisions.

Federal and state agencies periodically have intervened in this process to try to bring some coherence to the educational programs offered by local districts, and to redress some of the inequalities produced by the coincidence of school district boundaries with the taxpaying capacity of citizens. These efforts usually have been confounded by local control, and the logic that drives decisions in that market context (Peterson, 1981). The result has been a confusing array of functional responsibilities that have made it increasingly difficult for local citizens to feel in control of the kinds of services provided by their local schools. It is within this context that demands for more choice have arisen. The market arrangement of public education already has conferred on them many choices, but, at the same time, has resulted in such a diffusion of political power that the choices often have become so particularistic and bereft of coherence as to call into question the viability of the common school.

In the early 1960s, this syndrome of political instability and circular social choice was confined mainly to the big cities. In the early 1970s, it engulfed the inner ring of suburbs. Today, a significant portion of residential communities displays this pattern of politics, and only the most wealthy (who can exclude themselves from market price competition) and those with strong bonds of internal social interaction are likely to avoid the political externalities that result from the arrangement of public schooling as markets with weak governance systems. It is not surprising, then, that debate has arisen about how schooling might best be arranged, and whether more or less choice is needed.

CHOICE OPTIONS

A significant by-product of the current political arrangement of public schooling is that while it has created a market that offers choice as to residential location among diverse school districts, it correspondingly has generated a broad base of political support for public education. Citizens in the more affluent school districts feel that they gain sufficiently from their tax dollars to support the extension of public education to those who are fiscally less well off. Moreover, the "lumpy" character of the choice mechanism, and the dynamics of urban development, also have had redistributive effects within school districts as their populations have become more heterogeneous, both economically and ethnically.

But, as we have seen, this heterogeneity now threatens to overwhelm the governance system. Unstable majorities on school boards, and circular social choices by these boards, have weakened the capacity of many districts to formulate and maintain coherent educational services. Some critics are now advocating that the response to this condition should be a further decomposition of the market, either in the form of privatization and the creation of a voucher system, or the establishment of an interdistrict transfer plan whereby parents could choose to send their children to a district other than the one in which they reside. I argue, however, that neither of these alternatives is desirable, and that by simultaneously initiating a program of school site-based management and strengthening the capacity of the governance system to make collective political decisions—ironically by constitutionally *limiting* the scope of school board prerogatives—the current arrangement of public schooling can be adjusted to better serve the educational needs of our society.

Weaknesses of Voucher and Interdistrict Proposals

Albert Hirschman (1986) has argued that the appropriateness of market solutions as alternatives for governmentally administered programs depends on the nature of the good or service to be provided. Market solutions, he points out (p. 88), work best under the following conditions: (1) there are differences in preference that are widely recognized as equally legitimate; (2) citizens generally are knowledgeable about the quality of services and can evaluate and compare them; (3) purchasers can move freely from one supplier to the next, and can learn from experience; and (4) there are many competing providers. In the case of education, these conditions seldom are simultaneously present, and both vouchers and interdistrict transfer proposals are likely to run into difficulties. As Hirschman notes, parents are often ill informed about quality, comparison shopping is difficult, the transaction costs of shifting from one supplier to the next are high, and basic education serves public, as well as private, interests (see also Boyd and Kerchner, 1988; Krashinsky, 1986).

The apparently unavoidable rock that scuttles voucher proposals is equity. Under the voucher scheme, it becomes individually economically rational for taxpayers to bid down the value of the public financed voucher, and transform public education into a welfare system. Under the current arrangement, public and private goods are jointly supplied. The suburban marketplace allows citizens to purchase a level of service they want, but at the same time secures a measure of political support for public education generally, and for fiscal redistribution, either through state equalization or intradistrict transfers. In this respect, the provision of public education is akin to Social Security. There is strong general support because almost everyone benefits.

Privatization, however, would decouple these choices by making the benefits less lumpy. Even though the value of the voucher might be set at a relatively high level initially, the provision of services privately would lead to the realization among the more affluent that they could secure these same services without providing subsidies in the form of vouchers (or tax credits) to the poor. They could substitute their own dollars for the voucher coupon and obtain the same level of service. There would be no direct individual incentive to subsidize the education of the poor. Inevitably, the value of the voucher would be eroded through inflation, because political support for its enhancement would diminish. In these circumstances, public schools would necessarily become, and be perceived as, the provider of last resort (Boyd, 1987).

Privatization, in other words, would operate too efficiently. Once set in motion, it would begin a public decision-making process that would make educational opportunity virtually coterminus with social class. The inequality would be greater than under the current arrangement because more variability in social class exists among individuals than among school districts. In such a system, the option of choice for the less affluent would be severely limited.

Interdistrict transfer plans are likely to fail for a quite different reason: they won't work. Theoretically, they are designed to make the current arrangement more (market) efficient by allowing schools and citizens to cross school district boundaries to find each other. This possibility has intellectual, and possibly great political, appeal. But in practice few parents are likely to take advantage of these opportunities: the costs of transporting their children are too high. Few parents will have the time to drive their children to distant schools, and even fewer, now that almost all spouses of childbearing age work, will be able to pick them up after school. High school students might be able to take advantage of the option, but even this group is likely to be constrained by desires to attend schools with their friends. The system would require massive school busing, and those costs are likely to outweigh any gains in productivity that would accrue through a better match of consumer preferences and school programs.

School Site-Based Management

School reform frequently takes on the attributes of a social fad. One important reason relates to the weak instruments for collective political decision making that exist within the current arrangement of public schooling. School administrators and community activists seize on reforms as opportunities to build political coalitions for change around a set of policies other than those associated with community growth. The movement toward excellence and choice in education offers another such opportunity, and one that may acquire sufficient political support to permit a restructuring of school governance around management based on school site.

This alternative to vouchers and interdistrict transfer plans, I believe, is not only more politically feasible, but also potentially can redress the central weakness in the current system of school district governance—namely, a tendency toward circular social choices. Analytically, circularity manifests itself as a lack of ultimate responsibility. Its origins lie both in the administrative structures most school districts have adopted, and in the authority relationships that have evolved between school boards and school superintendents.

The administrative structure of most school districts resembles what Williamson (1970) terms a "unitary organizational form." School district organizations typically have evolved through a process of functionally divided labor. The superintendent delegates much of his or her administrative responsibility to three assistant or associate superintendents (business, personnel, and instruction) and their staffs who, in turn, supervise and coordinate activities within the school sites. As federal and state governments have intervened to subsidize various school reform efforts, administrative appendages have been grafted on to this basic structure (such as Chapter 1, special education, and driver's training). The divisibility of function has made such organizations remarkably adaptable to accommodating these interventions without fundamentally altering the basic structure, yet the structure necessarily has become quite complex.

It is well known that this type of organizational structure is susceptible to loss of control, particularly as the size and complexity of the organization increase. Control loss manifests itself as problems of coordination. Because the organization has a functional division of labor, all the elements that comprise the organization must work in unison for the organization to realize its common purposes. The introduction of a new reading program, for example, requires that all three divisions—personnel, business, and instruction—cooperate to implement the program smoothly and effectively. New textbooks must be ordered, in-service programs organized, substitute teachers arranged so regular teachers can attend workshops, new teachers screened for the appropriate pedagogical approach, testing procedures revised to take into account the instructional emphasis of the new program, and so forth.

To assure cooperation, superintendents build a management team: a relatively small group of managers whose primary responsibility is to share information in implementing the centrally defined policies of the organization. The trust, loyalty, and shared purpose of the team facilitate coordination. The superintendent's cabinet typically meets regularly, often weekly, and most organizational initiatives and problems are filtered through this group. The hand-picked team helps the superintendent bridge the structural elements that divide the organization.[3]

At the same time, however, the team approach can magnify a major structural weakness of the unitary structure: the identification of cause-effect relationships when all the parts of the structure are functionally interrelated. The norms, which evolve as members of the team interact over time, can lead to the the denial or minimalization of unfavorable information about organizational performance ("Achievement scores are down because parents are too permissive at home"), and impose sanctions on members who attempt to identify cause-effect relationships that are under the jurisdiction of a member of the team ("I think they're down because we're hiring too many unqualified teachers").

In a stable political environment, superintendents usually can mitigate the adverse effects of these norms by personally initiating new ideas, legitimating internal criticism, or simply restructuring the group. But as districts become more heterogeneous, and board politics more unstable, the disparate demands impinging on the management team can imperil its capacity to functionally integrate the divided labor into a coherent structure. Unlike the special programs financed by state and federal governments, which often can be deflected into tangential divisions, board demands frequently impact the main structure directly. Because of the functional interdependency of its parts, accommodating these demands often requires wrenching change to the entire unitary structure. After a few cycles of these changes, contradictions emerge within the structure as the organization is unable to adapt fully, and personal loyalty to the group ("being a team player") becomes the primary rationale for action by central office administrators. Centralized control devolves into governance by committee.

Superintendents in these communities often do not have sufficient authority to fully sort out these contradictions. Nor can the board, because its members also are vulnerable to shifting political currents within the community. Furthermore, because board members individually represent narrow constituencies with intense preferences, they feel impelled to cross the boundary between policy and administration that municipal reformers had drawn. Individual members bypass the superintendent and begin going directly to site and central office administrators for information or to give advice or to inspect school programs. Administrators also sometimes establish particularistic relationships with individual board member and community constituencies, further complicating the integrity of the administrative structure.

This governance system lacks ultimate responsibility. No one really is in charge. The muddled educational programs that result offer school clients few (socially) desirable choices.

Management based on school site offers the possibility of simultaneously re-establishing client choice and curricular integrity. It would
afford school districts greater flexibility in accommodating the increasingly heterogeneous populations that comprise communities.
Many of the features of such a system are familiar: A multidivision
administrative structure is substituted for a unitary one. School sites
within the district differentiate themselves according to the modality
or content of service (educational philosophy, pedagogical method,
approach to student learning style, and so on). Sites are allocated the
bulk of discretionary district resources, and make decisions regarding
their use. Parents can cross existing attendance boundaries to send
their children to the school of choice. Individual schools gain a
measure of self-determination in shaping their unique culture and
service product, but must attract a clientele or suffer foreclosure.
Parents have more choice among schools, but less voice once inside.
Site-based management would give the individual schools the autonomy that Chubb and Moe contend is so necessary for school effectiveness.

The major tradeoff for citizens, however, would be at the board
level. By itself, site-based management won't work in districts en-
snared in social choice circularities. A concomitant change is needed
in the governance system of school districts to stabilize the political
environment. Chubb and Moe (1988) are correct in asserting that if
the schools are failing, the most probable culprit is the environment,
not the schools. The answer, however, is not privatization, as they
advocate, but strengthening the governance system.

To accomplish this, the boundary between policy and administration that was initially set by municipal reformers at the turn of the
century, and that was enforced by social norms that hold under
conditions of community growth but collapse under decline, needs to
be established constitutionally. State legislatures must intervene to
formally prescribe a policy role for the school board and an administrative one for the superintendent. Boards currently make too many
decisions, hold too many meetings, and, in many districts, consume
virtually all the time of the superintendent. Their powers need to be
limited to approval of a general budget, selection of the superintendent, negotiation of labor contracts, authorization of site-based curricular options, expulsion of students, and perhaps a few other matters
of broad policy. The board probably should not meet more than eight
to ten times a year. Such a policymaking role might induce more

community leaders once again to serve on boards, which would further reinforce a broader community perspective.

The authority of the superintendent, likewise, needs to be strengthened to assure a point of ultimate responsibility within an administrative structure that now is frequently so permeable that accommodation to every political interest has become acceptable professional practice. To curtail circumvention by clients and school employees, superintendents need more formal control over operations of the district, including personnel decisions. To exercise this authority, and to make public intervention more lumpy, superintendents require term contracts of at least three years in length. Without an increase in the superintendent's authority, it will be impossible to retain the curricular integrity of the choices offered by the school sites, or to empower the teachers and principals who must create more effective learning environments.

State education agencies can foster site management by offering fiscal and status rewards for schools that exhibit superior performance. In California, the cash awards the state confers on schools that score above their social class expectancy bands appear to have mobilized many school sites to improve the quality of instruction. Public schools spend a miniscule amount of their revenues on research. The state education agencies can facilitate more reflective practice by making research funds available to districts and schools. It is abundantly clear that there is no single, identifiable educational production function. People learn in different ways, and schools need to find out what works with the specific clientele they serve.

These changes in the governance structure will not solve all the problems associated with the arrangement of public schools as markets. A more profound transformation of the social and economic environments surrounding schools in our most economically depressed communities, for example, surely will be needed. But all of us will benefit by the extension of more choice for parents, if the options available are public schools with strong internal identity. Creating stability in the governance system is a first necessary step.

NOTES

1. Elsewhere (1988), I present a more formal theoretical analysis of, and offer some supporting empirical data for, the argument contained in this section.

2. Politics in these communities is not always without conflict, because well-educated residents can disagree about the kinds of services they want their districts to provide. In general, though, the discord rarely threatens the districts' capacity to provide a coherent educational program, mainly because they have sufficient slack financial resources to circumvent zero-sum political decisions.

3. Sponsorship in the administrative promotion process usually accompanies an organizational structure built around a functional division of labor. Sponsorship helps solve potential coordination problems by getting people into administration who share common perceptions about organizational purpose and the means for its realization.

REFERENCES

Boyd, William L. "Balancing Public and Private Schools: The Australian Approach and American Implications," *Educational Evaluation and Policy Analysis* 9 (1987): 183–189.

Boyd, William L., and Kerchner, Charles T., eds. *The Politics of Excellence and Choice in Education*. New York: Falmer Press, 1988.

Chubb, John E., and Moe, Terry M. "Politics, Markets, and the Organization of Schools," *American Political Science Review* 82 (1988): 1065–1088.

Hirschman, Albert O. *Rival Views of Market Society*. New York: Viking, 1986.

Krashinsky, Michael. "Why Educational Vouchers May Be Bad Economics," *Teachers College Record* 88, No. 2 (1986): 139–151.

Meyer, John, and Scott, W. Richard. *Organizations and Environments*. Beverly Hills, CA: Sage, 1983.

Olson, Mancur, Jr. *The Logic of Collective Action*. Cambridge, MA: Harvard University Press, 1965.

Peterson, Paul. *City Limits*. Chicago: University of Chicago Press, 1981.

Tiebout, Charles M. "A Pure Theory of Local Expenditures," *Journal of Political Economy* 64 (1956): 418–424.

Tyack, David. *The One Best System*. Cambridge, MA: Harvard University Press, 1974.

Weeres, Joseph G. "Economic Choice and the Dissolution of Community." In *The Politics of Excellence and Choice in Education*, ed. William L. Boyd and Charles T. Kerchner. New York: Falmer Press, 1988.

Williamson, Oliver. *Corporate Control and Business Behavior*. Englewood Cliffs, NJ: Prentice-Hall, 1970.

Zudrow, George R., ed. *Local Provision of Public Services: The Tiebout Model After Twenty-five Years*. New York: Academic Press, 1983.

CHAPTER 11

The Politics of Educational Choice

Thomas Jones

In 1980, "school choice" was only a minor player on the stage of education politics. By the end of the decade, however, choice had a starring role, though it was not yet widespread in state legislation and local practice. This chapter offers an analysis of the ideas shaping school choice as a political movement. It proposes that much of the movement's political strength derives from declining faith in the traditional, neighborhood-based, comprehensive school ideal. That ideal is being challenged by growing allegiance to the model of the private school.

Underlying this shift in school models is a declining faith in the powers of government to improve schools through regulation or resources. There is a growing faith in the salutary effects of market competition among schools. Differing conceptions of "school improvement" have colored the movement's personality and will shape its prospects. These conceptions are likely to be magnified as the choice movement grows.

THE COMPREHENSIVE SCHOOL IDEAL

Although the situation may be changing in the present decade, U.S. educational history has been a tale of triumph for a single model of government-controlled schooling, the comprehensive school. Until recently all the basic questions seemed settled; school organization was a given to work within, not a matter for examination and analysis. Government would both administer and finance education from kindergarten through (at least) the twelfth grade. Schools would be organized into small geographic areas, or school districts, that provide for the education of children at each grade level. Local policies, and usually a local tax levy as well, would be set by elected board members resident in the district. Schooling would be available to all children without charge and without regard to a child's economic, social, intellectual, emotional, or physical condition. Districts would assign children to the closest neighborhood school appropriate for their age.

Curriculum at each school would be as broad as possible within budget constraints, designed to serve the diverse wants and needs of all families in the neighborhood. An elementary school might have a special program for junior scientists, if many of the parents were engineers. Or it might offer special tutorials in reading or math, or a breakfast program, if many of the parents were poor and unemployed. But basically there should not be much difference among schools. And if major differences were found, schools were, by definition, inequitable. Such inequities were a cause for political concern and the subject of subsequent "needed reform."

The comprehensive character of schooling was even more vital at the high school level. High schools would offer a variety of academic, business, and technical tracks under one roof, plus a "general" education program for those who weren't sure. Often these four would break down into still more specific tracks for purposes of instructing children according to their effort and ability. But in every case the neighborhood school would be the appropriate school for each child.

The comprehensive school ideal related not just to curriculum but to sociology as well. Every school would serve all conceivable "types" of children: rich and poor, bright and slow, black and white, handicapped, non-English-speaking, and so on in the same elementary or high school. Accommodation for different talents and interests of children would be made through the widest possible diversity in curriculum offerings so that whatever the child's future ambition, the neighborhood school would offer the appropriate preparation.

That the system of academic tracking just described would undermine the sociological side of the U.S. public school ideal was a fact obvious to all. Occasionally an ambitious school principal would seek to abolish tracks. But since families have different objectives for schooling, tracking in some form usually would return, or more likely never disappear at all.

Life requires developing one's talents to the full, but life also requires getting along with all different types of people. Schooling, in sum, must be a balance between a social and an academic preparation for life. Pupil differentiation through tracking within schools, combined with an identical social mix among schools, was the right balance, according to the public school ideal.

Still, there was the difficult matter of those who did not share this public school consensus: those people who had wanted religiously based schools, socially exclusive schools, or educationally distinctive schools geared to a focused curriculum or a unique pedagogy. Crucial to the comprehensive school ideal was the concomitant right of people with these exotic preferences to choose other forms of schooling if they wished. This right was sacred and guaranteed. But private tastes must be distinguished from the public interest. The separation between tastes and interests was a very clear and distinct one, and could be discerned readily on the basis of school type. The public interest was served only by public schools (that is, comprehensives). Since private schools were not part of the public interest, logically it followed that they should not be financed by public monies.

Problems with This "Settled View" and the Solutions

None of this is to say that there weren't problems with this settled view. There were problems galore! But the problems were considered to be the result of how the system was implemented and managed, not of its fundamental assumptions. For example, complaints about the inadequacy of the curriculum and instruction at any particular school could be viewed as evidence that more instructors and more course offerings were needed at that neighborhood school site. Across different schools, there was the problem that some children—particularly poor children—weren't learning very much. This problem showed the need for more research about the teaching-learning process. In addition, a longer period of teacher training was needed, and better systems of evaluation and accountability should be implemented. These required more teacher trainers, more educational evaluators, and more school accountants.

Still, large numbers of parents were disaffected by the moral tone of public schools. Drugs, sex, and permissiveness were frequently discussed. But these problems only showed that schools needed an even broader curriculum to deal with these matters and more government regulation to enforce this curriculum. Then, too, there was the problem of which levels of government should finance education and how to share the burdens among them. The need for more administrators and planners to coordinate the whole process was clear and evident to all.

These problems come down to the same thing really: more people and more money. And so, of course, schools needed people who study ways of getting more people and more money, too. As long as this view of school problems predominated, the comprehensive school ideal was still in place.

Segregation of Classes and Races

Perhaps the most intractable problem for U.S. public education has proven to be school segregation by race and class. In recent decades, schools have been segregated not so much by direct educational policies—these had been changed by legislative and court orders in the 1950s and 1960s—as by U.S. patterns of housing.

Over many decades, the education system had engaged in a sort of tacit war with housing patterns. Families able to do so had moved away from city centers in an effort to find "good" public schools—ones without difficult children and without social problems. School quality was directly related to local housing values. Over time these patterns of housing segregation, both economic and racial, had proven to be controlling.

In recent decades, three diverse social interventions have been designed to solve the segregation phenomenon within the framework of the U.S. comprehensive school tradition. The first and oldest of these was the integration of political communities: the combination of many smaller political jurisdictions into a single larger one. This solution applied not only to school districts, but to other units of local government as well. Its motivation was based partly on segregation considerations and partly on considerations of rationalization and efficiency in government.

This solution produced metropolitan governments in a few large cities such as Jacksonville, Florida, and Indianapolis, Indiana (although schools were not included in the latter case). In education, these movements were most successful in smaller places, producing "central" schools, "jointures," or "union" school districts in many parts of the country, and creating some integration as a by-product. The movement also spawned the growth of larger suburban high schools, able to deliver a larger array of specialized courses.

The centralization movement fitted within the framework of the comprehensive school ideal because it enabled high schools, especially, to draw from larger, more heterogeneous catchment areas. In the process, however, "neighborhood" was redefined, becoming something less personal and more remote. The regional school movement was successful at a price. The price was expansion, expansion of "neighborhood" in many cases beyond any reasonable definition.

Probably the best testament of the limited success of the regionalization movement was the growth of the second movement: racially based school assignment. Although there is considerable disagreement as to the extent that forced busing caused "flight" to suburbs in the North and to private schools in the South, it is nonetheless very clear that government intervention did not reverse the prevailing housing trends. The policy produced the derogatory epithet, "forced busing," and again, private wants in the housing market proved more powerful than express government policies.

In 1954, the Warren Court said that segregation by race for educational purposes is "inherently unequal." This was first and foremost a constitutional finding. But insofar as its educational origins are concerned, the finding can be related to implementation of the sociological side of the comprehensive school ideal. Subsequent judicial decisions in the decade of the 1960s expanded the definition of illegal segregation to include school districts outside the South that had no history of legally enforced segregation. These decisions perhaps may be viewed by future educational historians as an attempt to enforce the socioeconomic population mix of the comprehensive school ideal despite prevailing patterns of housing. Forced busing was one manifestation of the problem in implementing the comprehensive school ideal. Because sociological balance had to be mandated by the courts, the implication was that it could not be achieved any other way.

The third attempt to deal with the problem of neighborhood segregation of racial and income groups has become the most direct predecessor of the public school choice movement: the magnet school. The magnet school idea was spawned in part through the failures of forced busing. In its original conception, the magnet was to be a "supergood" comprehensive school—a school so good that children from all social classes would want to attend. Because the number of applicants would by definition exceed the number of places, the school could select applicants from all races and classes. (More will be said later about the evolution of the magnet school idea to its present form—one based on curriculum specialization.)

The magnet school idea was really little more than the "more people/more money solution" to the education problem, mentioned in the preceding section, dressed up in new garb. But this plan too served in its way to undermine the comprehensive school ideal. According to its detractors, the magnet school achieved its desired mix not by shifts in the (all-important) neighborhood housing pattern, but by "creaming" the most industrious pupils from neighborhood schools. According to this line of thinking, the pupils who are willing to travel considerable distances out of their neighborhoods to attend the magnet are very often the smart and able ones, particularly if their local school is not so good.

Although each of these three major reform movements has aimed at implementing the comprehensive school in its ideal form, each has resulted in rendering the concept increasingly obsolescent. The first redefines "neighborhood" beyond any reasonable approximation. The second policy tries to overcome neighborhoods' sociological imbalance by selective exporting and importing of children. And the third policy may segregate some schools more in order to desegregate "showcase," magnet schools. All three, however, retained the essence of the comprehensive concept, envisioning a diverse social mix and a broad curriculum within each school.

Despite the best efforts, reforms of these three types have had little lasting success so far. The metropolitan government movement has not been much heard from in recent decades. School assignment on the basis of race is still tied up in the federal courts. Only the third option—the magnet school—still seems politically viable. But its political viability rests on two crucial points (1) the new language of "the market," and (2) a shift from a comprehensive curriculum to a specialized curriculum. But this is getting ahead of the story.

In sum, the U.S. school ideally would have neighborhoods sufficiently alike that significant differences occur within schools but not among them. Ideally, in every school the social composition would be diverse and the curriculum would be extremely varied. The intractability of the housing problem has thwarted this ideal. Social strategems to achieve it have tried to work around the housing obstacle to achieve the desired pupil mix.

School Improvement and the Science of Education

A second major type of solution offered for "the education problem" has been enriched resources and more research. Financial aid and generous staffing plans are devised in an attempt to ensure that schools in poverty areas would be as well resourced and, whenever possible, even better resourced than wealthy suburban schools. Under this strategy, deridingly called "ghetto enrichment," the hope was that comprehensive, neighborhood-based public schools could purchase higher-quality schooling for a price.

The resource enrichment strategy depended on the settled view that school improvement was a technical endeavor. Pupil achievement differences could be measured and then manipulated (in the best sense of the word, of course) through social and educational interventions to achieve the desired results. Improving U.S. schools, in this respect, was much like sending someone to the moon. And exactly that analogy was often drawn.

What was required was people and money, plus scientific research filling in the details of how to do it. The social and educational interventions sought by the school improvement researchers nearly always required additional resources. Thus, the administrator's and the practitioner's requirements fit together nicely. These requirements provided the theme for the play: more people-more money. Politicians might not always attend to each scene, but at least they knew the plot outline.

The villain of the piece was the Coleman Report (Coleman et al., 1966). After 1966, compelling scientific evidence documenting the substantial and general successes of various educational interventions became very hard to find, although specific exceptions can always be found. It took twenty years, but by the 1980s the "fact" that school financial resources, teacher characteristics, class size, and facilities don't much affect pupil achievement is now so widely "understood" that it has become almost a banality.

This chapter is no place to argue the question of whether or not there has been, now is, or ever can be, a scientific basis for educational improvement. It is high irony that the Coleman Report, which relied on technical and empirical procedures, resulted in discrediting the view that school improvement results from those same sorts of procedures. But that is exactly what happened. The Coleman Report's effects were very important politically. If school improvement is no longer simply a technical endeavor—if it no longer depends simply on more people, money, or scientism—then other premises for political and governmental activity must be found.

By the last third of the century, then, shifts in view could be discerned, as deficiencies in the technicist solution were becoming increasingly evident. There was growing consensus that school problems were increasingly invulnerable to remediation through people and money alone.

The Organizational Problem

Another conception of school problems related not merely to housing segregation, technicism, and the finance of the present system. Under this third conception, the problem was an organizational one.

The successful functioning of neighborhood-based, government-operated, comprehensive schooling had depended fundamentally on links to its constituent neighborhood. Diversity within the school had to be kept within the bounds of tolerance as defined locally. Putting the conundrum another way, comprehensive schools not only have to be diverse enough to represent the population as a whole, they have to be homogeneous enough to be governable.

Governing adults in the larger society is one thing. Governing children during their most impressionable years, and in intimate daily associations with one another, is quite another. The problem is particularly challenging when it is remembered that school administrators and teachers have three clients—the child, the parent, and the (nonparent) taxpaying public—each with very different wants and expectations.

Until mid-century, educators handled the problem of the client in three somewhat contradictory ways. First, they claimed the autonomy associated with professional expertise. Educators claimed to know what was best for the client (however defined). Second, they held to a view of institutional separateness—the school should be above politics and outside markets. And third, education dealt with the idiosyncratic wants of the particular local communities through compromise and accommodation, thereby, in effect, responding to the wants of its more powerful clients.

The quintessential figures in shaping the first of these responses were the progressive educators, especially John Dewey. Dewey wrote that the school should be what the "best and wisest parent" wants for his or her child. Dewey himself felt he was in a position to know what the best and wisest parent wanted. But by the 1980s a better-educated public had come to challenge the degree of professional autonomy represented in Dewey's attitude. The professional educator was no longer a "crusader," but a conciliator and implementer, someone with the ability to carry out whatever the public wants.

As long as the school was "above politics," it could claim to be an independent and detached force, serving society, to be sure, but doing so from the view of what it thought right. School was a place that offered opportunities; it did not necessarily promise results. Dewey's view had essentially been that education's role was to lead to sharper and more ethically informed individual judgments.

But by mid-century the view was changing that schools were a unique institution, separated in a sense from the rest of society. The ever-widening quest for more resources pushed schools further into the political arena. Every conceivable interest group laid claim to education's purse. School administrators were taught in their preparation programs about the "myth" of the apolitical school. And if there was any doubt left, the political protests of the nation's high school and university students in the late 1960s and early 1970s clarified very forcefully the point that schooling was a political enterprise.

The result was heightened expectations and contradictory political-educational agendas. Schools must always reflect the latest developments in the science of education. They must prepare children according to their parents' aspirations while simultaneously reforming the social structure. They must meet every conceivable special need of any politically definable set of pupils. Schools must assure good jobs, develop social sensitivities, provide opportunities for individual self-discovery, and be academically rigorous—all within the confines of one building. If the family wasn't satisfied with the child's progress on all these dimensions, it had to change houses to get a different school. And even if the family did change houses to get a different public school, it would be a school with exactly the same pressures as the old school.

School arrangements settled locally were, by the 1970s and 1980s, giving way to state or national considerations. In their daily operation of schools, administrators had to attend to a variety of unpopular concerns. Occassionally these were curricular, but most often they had to do with concerns reflecting pupil treatment and school values.

The clearest case is racial segregation practiced in the schools of the Old South until after mid-century. This was a racially based school assignment policy if there ever was one, based on the views of the prevailing local social order. In this case, the interests of a racial minority, abetted by nationally based politicians and the federal judiciary, prevailed in a legal sense (although often not, as we have seen, in a housing sense) over the wishes of local establishments. There are many other examples as well. People opposed to "nonsectarian" prayer in schools used nationally based legal counsel to prevail over those local school boards that wanted it. Selection of texts and library books frequently pitted localities against constitutional considerations articulated by the courts. Even such formerly routine administrative matters as haircuts, dress codes, spankings, and locker searches were no longer based on local considerations alone but on legislative and constitutional ones.

The point is not whether governments handled some or all of these controversies properly. The point simply is that schools increasingly had to follow national laws and court orders; yet they still had to depend on local communities for affection and support. And this aid some localities were increasingly reluctant to give. By the 1980s, the ties between school and community were becoming attenuated. Greater social diversity was the comprehensive school ideal, to be sure, but diversity also created unprecedented stresses and strains.

The comprehensive school was supposed to be a microcosm of the society in one house and under one roof. The underlying idea was to apply the principles of adult society to children and adolescents.

Many learned lectures and journal articles appeared dealing with the "infinitely complex" questions of governance and control. Should "reform" be "top down," from the federal and state levels? Or should it be "bottom up," emphasizing teacher autonomy and the "professional" nature of education? Emphasis always was placed on an administrative or a legislated solution within the confines of the government-operated public school.

In all this, it seemed to many teachers that U.S. public education had reached a state of hyperactivity. School improvement was so involved with reform of classrooms through organizational strategies that the teaching act and the content of education had been obscured. The pace of change itself had become an impediment to good learning.

In sum, the comprehensive school depended on certain assumptions and preconditions regarding the nature of education, social, and curricular diversity; a belief in improving education by applying scientific techniques; and a view of school governance that replicated the larger adult democracy. To the extent that these beliefs were becoming increasingly obsolete in the 1980s, political and educational leaders began to look for new models and metaphors.

THE MARKET AS "SOLUTION"

In the 1980s, the question of schools' academic standards was a national preoccupation. Large segments of the population felt that school was too easy, that children should be "stretched" in a way that local neighborhood schools were not doing. The problem in inner cities was particularly acute.

U.S. society was changing, creating new tensions for the schools. Arguably the most important of the social changes was the perception of national economic decline. For the thirty years or so following World War II, the United States had been by far the world's richest nation. By the mid-1970s, oil price shocks, inflation levels unprecedented in this century, and the economic recovery of Europe and Japan meant that the United States was not quite so well off in relative terms. Although standards of living were still rising, the rate of economic growth was lower than in many other industrialized nations. What was most worrying was not the present, but the future.

U.S. schools had been given much of the credit for past national successes. They must now take a share of the blame for national failings, too. Evidence of school failure was not lacking. International comparisons of school achievement across the world showed that U.S. schools were inferior.

There was a feeling that school standards had declined along with U.S. economic power. Virtually anyone was "given" degrees and diplomas, leading to an adult workforce that no longer took as much pride in its products or services. Surely the next generation would have to work harder, work longer, and work "smarter" than in the past. In its report, the National Commission on Excellence in Education (1983) stated that traditional schooling patterns and the attitudes of professional educators had put "a nation at risk":

> Our once unchallenged preeminence in commerce, industry, science, and technological innovation is being overtaken by competitors throughout the world. . . . The educational foundations of our society are presently being eroded by a rising tide of mediocrity that threatens our very future as a nation and a people. What was unimaginable a generation ago has begun to occur— others are matching and surpassing our national attainments (p. 5).

Schools, though, had been imbued with informal, child-centered, learning philosophies and self-paced instructional methods.

Although it was not necessarily the intention of the document's writers, *A Nation at Risk* ultimately produced greater public interest in and awareness of school choice. It is perhaps from the publication of that document that historians will date the movement of school choice into the thinking of the educational mainstream. *A Nation at Risk* called for more rigorous high school graduation and college admission requirements, more study of academic basics and less study of life skill subjects, a longer school day and school year, and rigorous standards for measuring educational results. In most important respects, the message was not new. Calls for rigor and the association of educational problems with social failings have been heard in every decade.

What was different about *A Nation at Risk* was the proposed remedy. No technicist solutions were offered; no new spending or research programs were suggested. Here, in an official government document of major import, the problem was not identified with "too few people, too little money, too little scientism." The problem was simply too little effort toward excellence. Education's problems were much like those in the business sector. The federal government wasn't bailing out business with money and jobs (in most cases), and it wouldn't follow this strategy for schooling, either. The education system was enjoined simply to "pull up its socks."

Structural reform proposals grew out of state-sponsored follow-up studies. The main ones had to do with teacher career ladders and merit pay for teachers. In these reforms, "good" teachers would be identified and rewarded with more pay and higher status. Education could not count on more money *in toto*, but the best people would be well rewarded. In these state-sponsored initiatives, particularly, market-oriented thinking replaced resource-based technicism.

Against this background, the attention of much of the mainstream U.S. public was drawn to school choice, although it was by no means a new idea. Academics of the left, such as Christopher Jencks, and of the right, such as Milton Friedman, had argued for many years for their very different versions of choice. The Reagan administration had always advocated the most radical form of school choice: tax credits for parents paying private school fees. Minnesota had adopted a tax deduction that applied to private schools, which was sustained by the U.S. Supreme Court in 1983. But "choice" was still a radical word around schools, considered by many people to be a thinly veiled attempt to secure government aid for private schools.

THE PRIVATE SCHOOL: A NEW MODEL FOR PUBLIC EDUCATION?

Under the school choice scenario, children would not be assigned to a particular school based on a neighborhood catchment area. They would be allowed to select their preferred school from among several. Schools would "offer" their services and parents would "choose" them. By implication, bad schooling would not be chosen by anyone and would not survive. The discipline of the market, it was assumed, would lead to educational improvement.

Choice would encourage schools to distinguish themselves from one another. Education would become more like professions such as medicine and law, where people have some range of options among providers of those services and providers have some choice of clients.

An interest in private schooling, then, and the emulation of at least some of its aspects, colors the politics of school choice and influences thinking. Private schools already are schools of choice in several senses of the term. Attendance is usually not based on a particular neighborhood catchment area. Private schools operate in a market environment, in the sense that they are always competing with "free" public schools. Parents select on the basis of whether or not the private school offers what they want for their child. And bad private schools do go out of business. The Coleman Report, among other studies, argues that some of these elements lead to higher levels of academic performance.

But private school use is limited according to parents' ability and willingness to pay. Private schools can and do practice a very direct form of pupil selection, which is very rare in public schools. As we have seen, pupil selection for public schools is done through the indirect means of the housing market.

Both for reasons of cost and selectivity, private schools are used by only about 11 percent of the nation's pupils. They tend to have a religious affiliation, a more focused curriculum, and serve a social niche rather than a broad cross section of the population. For many choice advocates, then, the question is how to appropriate and modify private school principles to improve mass education.

The overturning of one paradigm and its replacement with another is thought not to be a rational event, a revolution in a theory brought about by the conclusions of objective inquiry, but a change in the attitudes of the intellectual class. Although this change is generated by continuing dissatisfaction with the growing failures of the old paradigm and the belief that the new one is superior, the switch of the intelligentsia to a new way of thinking seems to be very subjective in nature. According to Barry (1987, p. 4) paradigms are always internally consistent. They are challenged only by interpretations of events that are external to prevailing ways of thinking.

In the present context, the belief that more governmental manipulation, more personnel and spending, or more empirical research will improve education has been the prevailing paradigm of this century. And it is certainly a consistent one, and fundamentally incapable of being disproved. In support of that paradigm, many—doubtless most—U.S. comprehensive schools work well, structured just as they are.

But comprehensive schools are in trouble insofar as they are no longer affectionately regarded by the communities they serve, insofar as they seem not to be responding to the demands for academic excellence, or are not developing new solutions to the segregation problem. Insofar as the language of the market has dramatic resonance, and the perceived failures of schools shadow their accomplishments, the comprehensive school model may safely be called the "old paradigm."

That said, the political future of the school choice movement is still much in doubt. The next few acts of the political drama have not been written. It is possible, however, to identify some common elements in the thinking of advocates of school choice and to see how variations with regard to those elements lead to different plans for implementing school choice.

Choice proponents agree in their opposition to the present government assignment to one particular neighborhood school. That concept would be modified or abandoned. Schools would draw children from different neighborhoods; children from any one neighborhood would have the right to attend any one of a number of different schools at government expense.

Agreement on this point, however, is only at the most general level, and various choice plans illustrate where disagreement arises. Some people want to provide choice within a larger comprehensive school. That is, "minischools" would be set up within a single building. The child would still be bused to school in the normal manner of a catchment area. Choice would extend only to which internal minischool the child wished to attend. Classes, schedules, and possibly even extracurricular activities would be based on the minischool. This approach is the only one feasible in a small school system implementing choice on its own. (Larger school systems and more densely populated areas offer greater potential.) Minischools may also appeal to those who want to make some concessions to the choice movement, but wish to retain existing organizational routines insofar as possible.

The minischool is the most limiting of all choice plans from a physical space standpoint, and indeed may not be much different from a tracked comprehensive school. Limitations are due to the fact that school administration and facilities may be shared (though not necessarily); a distinctive school ethos may or may not be harder to develop within school buildings than among them. Choice is so new that concerns associated with implementation have not yet gotten much attention.

A second type of plan implements choice among different school buildings within the same public school district. Here, possibly, the school would be able to create a more distinctive environment and differentiate itself from other public schools in a way that would be more difficult under the minischool concept. Intradistrict choice still implies quite substantial limitations on choice. In most experimental plans, teachers are still hired from the school district's central office. They can be transferred from one school to another, but presumably employment would be based on the total enrollment in the district, not the popularity of any one school.

A third type of plan involves the possibility of choice among public schools in different school districts. At this level, the administrative and personnel implications have more competitive possibilities. School districts are entirely different local organizations, more like competitive firms in the private market. Administrators and teaching staffs could (if they wanted to) compete with one another more fully than in the two other plans with schools operated by the same employer. Still, however, teachers under the third type of plan would all be in the same statewide unions and under the same state regulations.

Wishes of some parents could not be accommodated under a system of district competition; hence there is another alternative that seemingly requires minimal government regulation. Choice could be extended to any school, public or private, presumably including religious schools. It would break the "monopoly" that government-run schools now have. This approach is often identified with the school voucher concept and educational tax credits proposed by the Reagan administration.

Choice plans that include private schools have not only to cross political hurdles but constitutional ones as well. Direct government financial aid to private schools has been declared unconstitutional in most contexts. In this regard, the 1983 Mueller decision may be helpful. The U.S. Supreme Court ruled that a state income tax deduction for parents' school costs was legal, if the deduction applied to both public and private school parents. The decision has given some hope to proponents of full choice, although inclusion of private schools is still divisive politically. More will be said about this in the concluding section.

Here it should be noted that many private schools would rather not have government aid because they fear that strings would be attached. Government regulation would require private schools to be much more like public schools, a result most users see as unfortunate.

All choice plans would permit and encourage schools to develop some degree of high-profile specialization—in the sciences, community studies, or the performing arts, for example. Schools would no longer be compelled to offer a comprehensive curriculum approriate for all conceivable pupil wants. In this respect, the old comprehensive school curriculum is replaced by a new form of magnet school.

By implication, pupil academic specialization will prevail over generalism; early career direction will prevail over more exploratory types of "balanced diet" learning experiences. The importance of this change can hardly be overemphasized. I return to it immediately hereafter.

Not only is there an element of pupil option here; there is an element of school incentive as well. The presumption is that each school would have to differentiate itself from others in order to attract students.

Private education has always been associated with curriculum specialization, although curriculum focus is by no means the full *raison d'être* of private education. Therefore, public school choice advocates seem to have adopted the full private school position on this point. They are at sharp variance, however, with the basic view of the comprehensive school.

As we have seen, an important element of the comprehensive school—the point on which heretofore there was no compromise—is that the curriculum be comprehensive in the school as a whole. The comprehensive curriculum was desirable partly for its own sake. Children are not sure what they want to study, they need to try a large number of different things, and therefore early specialization would be bad. It was better to have uniformity among schools and specialization within them—or such, at any rate, was the established view.

But the second traditional assumption underlying a comprehensive curriculum was that specialized curricula would inevitably lead to social selection. Middle and upper classes would specialize in the academic subjects; poorer children would specialize in subjects such as vocational courses and sports, where the emphasis is in performance.

In light of these traditional positions, it is possible that some public school choice programs will not really offer that much new curricular choice. Children specializing in, say, fine arts may want (or be required to study) some science or language. Vocational schools will offer traditional English, social studies, and so on. Operationally,

choice may come down to offering one or two specialized courses that
would have been options in a comprehensive school anyway. Or
choice may be reflected in the content within the common
curriculum—including more stories about science in a technological
high school English class, for example.

A second speculative possibility is that the traditional position of
comprehensive school proponents has been wrong. Different social
classes do not have different curricular aspirations. If this is so, then
schools could be distinctive in their curricula but still comprehensive
in their social makeup. This is indeed the hope of most advocates of
school choice. But it is not the historic and reasonably well-
documented view.

The most likely possibility is that advocates of school choice have
not really thought this through. At any rate, it is quite surprising how
little attention had been devoted to the curricular implications of
public school choice, given its marked departure from the U.S. school
ideal.

*Choice implies a faith in market mechanisms. More people, money, and
scientific research will not, by themselves, lead to school improvement, choice
advocates believe.* This is not to say that the "solution of more" is always
to be rejected, but only that the traditional levers of government
intervention will not work by themselves.

Parents and children are ultimately the best judges of educational
quality. They want different and better schools, if only government
would allow the market to provide them. School excellence and better
pupil test scores will occur if families are permitted to choose the
education they think best. In this sense, the choice movement very
much reflects the social assumptions of Adam Smith's "invisible
hand" applied to schooling, and, again, mirrors very closely the
historic principles of private schooling.

Choice advocates disagree on the desirable extent of government
control over the market mechanism. Should the market be relatively
controlled or relatively free? Assuming some market mechanisms are
desirable, just how far do you go?

One crucial line of demarcation is the inclusion of the traditional,
not-for-profit private schools. If most religious schools should get
assistance, what about government aid for parents using exclusive
private boarding schools, or profit-seeking schools? Would or should
schooling become a business like a law office or a beauty shop? These
are dubious adventures even for some proponents of the free market.

Then there is the point that schooling still would not be financed by the private market, but by some level of government. If local governments finance schools, as they usually do now, would one locality have to collect taxes that would have to be used when children cross into other local school districts? Would schools be financed wholly by government or could they charge fees? These questions create a whole new range of variations.

School choice advocates are united in their belief that market mechanisms will close bad schools with low achievement results. But the opposite case is more controversial. What happens when any particular school is so good that market demand exceeds the number of places available? Should the school be able to select the children it wants? Selectivity is one of the main criticisms of some magnet schools and private schools. It raises anew the issue of stratification according to intellectual ability or social class. Several choice alternatives would theoretically prohibit schools from choosing pupils while allowing pupils to choose schools. The practicality of this limitation is doubted by some.

The point here is not to review all the alternative plans, but to suggest that the areas of agreement are only at the broadest and most abstract sort of levels. School choice is more a way of thinking about solutions to policy problems than a single plan or statutory enactment. And this is what makes choice so unsettling. It is not a reform that is likely to be implemented quickly or neatly. Choice challenges the settled questions regarding the role of government, the organization, and the mission of education.

The wide range of implementation possibilities also has the result of dividing the movement politically. Many who would endorse public school choice oppose the inclusion of private schools. Others feel that choice plans without inclusion of private schools are window dressing, or are counterproductive. Political support for choice in principle is always greater than for any specific proposal.

School Choice in Britain

Developments overseas, and particularly in the United Kingdom, provide examples and insights that may influence U.S. developments. The British government of Margaret Thatcher has overcome the political obstacles and enacted national school choice legislation going quite far toward the free market. British families have the right to choose among local schools and among local education authorities. Money follows the child; revenues go to another local education authority (LEA) if the family so chooses. Each school has its own governing board with substantial control over budgets and staffing; teachers work for the school and may be dismissed by individual schools. There are possibilities for teacher pay supplements above the national salary schedule, or for extra staffing for enterprising schools.

The British Parliament is also requiring a national curriculum to be taught in every primary and secondary school. Although this curriculum provides considerable latitude from school to school, it does tend toward government control, thereby limiting market forces to some extent. LEAs will continue to operate, for the time being at least, with greatly diminished powers. Individual schools may choose to become completely independent of their LEA and take supervision directly from the central government (Haviland, 1988).

As in the past, Britain continues to make substantial financial provision for children attending the schools operated by various private and religious bodies. There are essentially two types of private schools. "Voluntary" schools accept some level of government controls but have full government finance. Voluntary schools may not charge fees. "Independent" schools also usually have some history of religious affiliation, but they do charge fees and have fewer government controls. The British government "assisted-places scheme" pays fees for low-income students attending the independent schools.

School systems of New Zealand, parts of Canada, the Republic of Ireland, Holland, France, Japan, and Australia—among others— offer greater school choice than does the United States. These countries also have different systems of government and a different history from our own. In all these countries, school choice is a politically contentious issue, but so is the absence of choice in the United States. Although the experiences of other nations will continue to generate interest in the United States, it may be safely assumed that U.S. decisions will not be forced by events abroad.

DIFFICULT CHOICES: POLITICS OF EDUCATION IN THE 1990S

The school choice political drama is still very much in progress. The remaining acts have yet to be written, much less played out. But if the preceding analysis is correct, three main protagonists are emerging clearly. First, there are the guardians of the old order, the comprehensive school as it presently is. They will continue to view school improvement in terms of the technicist paradigm—as needing more people, more money, and more research.

Second, there will be the advocates of the private school model. Markets fit in with what they want, but markets are not the ultimate aim. In their view, school improvement derives from a matrix of forces: the home, the religious faith, and a school independent enough from government to operate in accordance with its own ideals.

Third, there are those protagonists who view school improvement in terms of pupil test scores and international competitiveness. Yet they also place a high value on school integration, technicism, and organizational reform. Their strategy is essentially curricular. They believe parents would choose wisely among competing public schools, if they had the opportunity to do so. Aside from the comprehensive curriculum, however, they would leave most other elements of the government school in place.

In the 1980s, these multiple views of school improvement were politically beneficial for the choice movement. The movement knew what it was against, but did not have to agree on what it was for. Different proponents were able to argue for a free market and a strong government in an uncertain mix. In the decade of 1990s, they will have to sort this out.

Only speculation can be offered about what decisions will be made in the future. The most compelling observation is that many interests support the present system. Local governments will not easily give up their monopoly powers over schools. Upper-income people paid for their houses in suburban school districts with the expectation that lower-income groups would be excluded; the last thing some of them want is for nonhomeowners to gain access to "their" schools. Teachers and school administrators have shown very little interest in competing with each other for students and funding. Private schools are politically weak and, as noted earlier, divided as to the efficacy of state aid. Most advocates for the poor are still ideologically wedded to the comprehensive school ideal.

Probably the federal government's stressed financial condition will limit action options at that level. Different states will proceed with school choice in their own fashion. Some will experiment with variations of the three plans mentioned earlier; others will retain their present systems indefinitely. Change will proceed slowly. Intraschool and intradistrict choice will be tried first. Interdistrict choice and private school inclusion will take somewhat longer. Catchment areas and comprehensive schools are likely to remain the norm for most U.S. children for many years to come.

REFERENCES

Barry, Norman P. *The New Right*. London: Croom, Helm, 1987.
Coleman, James S., et al. *Equality of Educational Opportunity*. Washington, DC: U.S. Department of Health, Education, and Welfare, 1966.
Haviland, Julian, ed. *Take Care Mr. Baker*. London: Fourth Estate Press, 1988.
National Commission on Excellence in Education. *A Nation at Risk*. Washinton, DC: U.S. Department of Education, 1983.

CHAPTER **12**

Progress, Problems, and Prospects of State Educational Choice Plans

Joe Nathan

This chapter describes the dramatic progress of an idea. It is a simple concept: families and educators should to allowed to choose among public schools. Over the last several years, this notion has been endorsed by the nation's governors, and by a clear majority of the general public. After briefly reviewing the rationale for expanded public school choice, I examine recent developments in four broad areas: (1) general public interest in public school choice, (2) state and the federal government response, (3) new research on existing choice

Some of the research cited in this chapter was carried out with assistance from a grant from the U.S. Department of Education, Office of Planning, Budget, and Evaluation. Opinions expressed are not necessarily those of the department or its staff.

programs, and (4) prospects for expansion of state efforts to promote choice among public schools.

RATIONALE FOR MORE PUBLIC SCHOOL CHOICE

There are three basic rationales for public school choice: (1) expansion of opportunity for parents, students, and educators; (2) recognition that there is no one best program for all students or educators; and (3) use of controlled competition to help stimulate improvement among schools. The debate is not about whether educational choice is a good idea. The real question is whether state and local policymakers will narrow affluent families' educational advantage. This society accepts educational choice for the rich. Affluent families can send their children to private schools or pay tuition to another public school district. They can move to an exclusive suburb and send their children to a "public" school where the price of admission is the ability to purchase a home for several hundred thousand dollars and pay real estate taxes.

These arguments are familiar to those who have followed debates about educational vouchers, in which tax funds would pay for students to attend public, private, and parochial schools. For many people, choice among *public* schools is an acceptable compromise. In Minnesota, for example, groups that oppose vouchers (such as the Minnesota PTA, League of Women Voters, Elementary and Secondary School Principals, and Minnesota Association of [public] Alternative Programs) endorsed more options among public education.

A second justification for options recognizes that there is no one best kind of school for everyone. Over the last twenty years, there has been a quiet alternative school movement in public education. In some cases, these schools were started to help young people who had been disruptive in traditional schools. In other cases, alternative programs were the results of efforts of teachers and parents to create schools within the public system that corresponded to their philosophy about how some children learned most effectively. These programs ranged across the educational spectrum, from "open" or progressive education to "fundamental."

I had the opportunity to help start the St. Paul Open School, a K–12 public school in St. Paul, Minnesota. The school began in 1971 and exists today. Key features included development of an individual learning plan for each student, use of the entire North American continent as a place to learn, graduation based on demonstration of required competencies, rather than accumulation of credits, and an adviser-advisee system. The school received an award from the U.S. Office of Education because federal officials concluded it was "a carefully evaluated, proven innovation worthy of national replication." However, although it is a great place for some students and educators, it is not a good place for everyone.

Several years after the Open School was founded, a group of St. Paul parents and teachers convinced the board to open a much more traditional program, called the Benjamin E. Mays Fundamental School. Both Mays and the Open School accept a cross section of students who apply, and each operates at the average allocation per pupil. Both schools have above-average test scores.

People who work in such programs learn that there is no one *best* program for all students or all teachers. Although each helps students gain basic and applied skills and a positive attitude toward themselves, the parents and educators in these programs often disagree strongly on how schools should be organized and how instruction should be provided.

This variation helps explain why permitting choice complements "school-based" management programs, and why neither choice nor school-based management is sufficient. Teachers and parents with strong ideas about how schools run resist compromising many of their ideas. It is relatively easy to have several different kinds of schools within a building (as East Harlem does so well); but it is very difficult to have one school that at the same time is an open, fundamental, Montessori, language immersion, and performing arts-centered school. Trying to be many things at one time produces bland mediocrity that satisfies very few people.

There are other reasons to combine site-based management and public school choice. What happens if some parents, teachers, and students do not like the kind of program that the majority establishes? Without options, there can be continuing, frustrating conflict.

The final rationale for more choice involves use of controlled competition. Research cited later in this chapter shows that controlled, not unregulated, competition can help stimulate widespread improvement in public schools.

WHAT DOES THE GENERAL PUBLIC THINK?

National Gallup polls show what people think about allowing families to select among public schools: there is widespread support for the idea. In 1986 a national Gallup poll asked, "Do you wish you had the right to choose which public schools your children attend in this community?" To this question 68 percent answered yes, and 25 percent answered no. A year later (1987), another national Gallup poll asked, "Do you think that parents in this community should or should not have the right to choose which local schools their children attend?" To this question, 71 percent answered yes, 20 percent said no and 9 percent did not know; 70 percent of whites and 77 percent of minorities agreed families should be able to select among schools (Gallup, 1986; Gallup and Clark, 1987).

Another example of this trend occurred in Minnesota. In 1985, Governor Rudy Perpich recommended that families should have the option to send their children to various public schools, so long as the receiving district had room and the students' movement did not have a negative impact on desegregation activities. Two months after Perpich made his speech, a statewide poll found 33 percent in favor, 60 percent opposed. Nevertheless, parts of the governor's proposal were adopted during each of the next four years. As the state gained experience, support grew. In 1987, a statewide poll found that support for Perpich's proposal had increased to 56 percent with 39 percent opposed. A 1988 statewide poll found that 63 percent then supported the idea, with 33 percent opposed. Thus, in four years, opinions had changed from about 2–1 against, to 2–1 in favor of parental choice among public schools (Craig, 1987; Minnesota Business Partnership, 1988).

The national press, sensing public interest, discovered the issue. The *Wall Street Journal, New York Times, Boston Globe,* and *Philadelphia Inquirer* ran front-page stories on Minnesota's new public school program during the summer of 1988 (Putka, 1988; Fiske, 1988a, 1988b; Cohen, 1988a, 1988b; Cassel, 1988). *Newsweek* and *U.S. News and World Report* (Leslie et al., 1988; Rachlin, 1988) published major stories on the subject during September 1988.

STATE AND FEDERAL INITIATIVES

Governors and legislators of both political parties noticed that more than 70 percent of Americans supported choice among local schools. Edward Fiske of the *New York Times* described an emerging national consensus of the value of expanding choice among public schools: "Liberals and conservatives are backing the same policies on a broader scale for widely different reasons. . . . Conservatives have always liked voucher schemes and magnet schools because they promote competition between schools. Now liberals are joining the bandwagon as a way of giving the poor what the wealthy already have" (Fiske, 1988a, p. B6).

In the last several years, fifteen states developed new programs or increased financial support for existing public school choice programs. These programs are not identical, but show that choice can be applied to help solve specific problems in a state or region.

SUMMARY OF STATE ACTIONS PROMOTING PUBLIC SCHOOL CHOICE

The following information regarding the status of programs in the various states where public school choice has been promoted was gathered by phone calls I made during the first and second weeks of December 1988 to state departments of education and governors' offices. It has been supplemented with contacts made during the first three months of 1989. I have sought to be accurate and consistent.

In the category of "postsecondary options," I found many states that said students may take postsecondary courses and receive dual credit if they (the students) pay for it. Most of these states say the district may decide to pay for postsecondary courses if they think the student is ready. I do not consider either of these options to be real encouragement from the state for more choice, so they are not included in the summary.

Note that the following summary does not list states in which these ideas are being discussed. As of March 1989, various public school choice plans were pending in eighteen state legislatures.

1. *Local magnet and/or alternative schools*
   Except for Delaware, New Hampshire, North Dakota, and Vermont, all states (including the District of Columbia) report that some local public school districts offer some magnet and/or alternative schools from which families may select.
2. *Specialty schools* (statewide or regional magnet nine-month school, drawing from several districts, funded by the state)
   Alabama. (High school for the performing arts)
   Alaska. (Residential boarding secondary school in Sitka)
   Illinois. (Statewide school for mathematics and science)
   Indiana. (Passed enabling legislation [without funding] for a statewide magnet secondary school)
   Lousiana. (Statewide school for mathematics and science)
   Michigan. ($1 million in state funds allocated to help start approximately six regional magnet secondary schools for science and mathematics)
   Mississippi. (Statewide magnet school for mathematics and science)
   North Carolina. (State support for two residential magnet schools)
   South Carolina. (Established residential magnet school in mathematics and science)
   Virginia. (Helped fund development of five regional magnet schools)
3. *Open enrollment*
   • *Limited open enrollment.* (Certain students may attend public schools outside their resident district with state funds paying the cost and without permission of the resident district.)
   Arizona. (Districts may establish covenants prohibiting inter-district movement, and nonresident families may be charged more than state funds provide.)
   California. (Allows elementary students to attend public schools in districts where their parents live or work, so long as the movement does not have a negative impact on desegregation activities.)
   Colorado. (Students who have dropped out for a semester may attend a locally designed alternative public school in another district with state reimbursement and without permission from the resident district.)
   Iowa. (Students may attend public schools outside their

district in a course or program not available in their
resident district.)

- *Comprehensive open enrollment.* (K–12 students may attend
public schools outside their resident district with state funds
paying the costs and without permission from the resident
board of education.)

  Arkansas. (Beginning September 1990, K–12 students can
  move across district lines if the receiving district has room
  and the movement does not have a negative impact on
  desegregation efforts.)

  Iowa. (Beginning September 1990, K–12 students may move
  across district lines if the receiving district has room and
  the movement does not have a negative impact on desegregation.)

- *Metropolitan open enrollment.* (The state permits one- or two-way
movement between an urban district and surrounding suburban districts in order to promote desegregation and integration and higher-quality education.)

  Arkansas. (Under court-ordered desegregation, the state
  helps support a Little Rock area desegregation program.
  Students from suburbs may attend Little Rock magnet
  schools, and the suburban districts continue to receive
  funds from the state for those students.)

  Connecticut. (A funded magnet program in Bridgeport to
  promote desegregation in suburb and city began in the fall
  of 1988, but so far no suburban students are participating.)

  Massachusetts. (Minority students in several cities may attend school in the suburbs with the state paying the tuition.)

  Missouri. (The state has provided funds for development of
  magnet schools in St. Louis and for transportation of
  students. The state provides double funding of suburban
  and urban students whose movement back and forth between St. Louis and suburban districts promotes desegregation. The state has also paid for development of magnet
  schools in Kansas City.)

  New York.

  Wisconsin. (To promote desegregation, state provides double
  funds for students moving between Milwaukee schools and
  suburban district schools.)

- *Statewide open enrollment.*
  Minnesota.

4. *Postsecondary options*
   - *Limited postsecondary options.* (Students may attend postsecondary programs with permission of the local district, with state or local funds paying all or part of the costs, or with the state requiring some formal action of the district.)
     Arizona. (Students may take courses for high school gradua- tion credit at community colleges if they pay for them; community colleges must accept these students and can receive state funding for them.)
     Florida. (The state pays for students maintaining a certain grade-point average who take courses at community col- leges that are not available in their high school.)
     Iowa. (Public school students may take one or two courses not available in their high school, up to a limit of $200, with state funds paying tuition.)
     Kansas. (High school seniors may take community college courses they select for high school credit. Students must pay tuition and other charges. Both systems can collect reimbursement for these students.)
     Maine. (The state has allocated additional funds that pay for students to take courses at postsecondary institutions if the local district approves.)
     Oregon. (The 2 + 2 program brings together high schools and community colleges to plan cooperative projects that sometimes involve students taking community college courses.)
     Rhode Island. (Every district must develop a concurrent enrollment policy that permits high school students to attend postsecondary institutions with tax funds paying their fees; districts may retain the power to decide who participates in this program.)
     Utah. (Students may take postsecondary courses with some state reimbursement and with some cost to the student.)
     Washington. (A very small program allows high school stu- dents to take courses at the University of Washington. Some dollars follow students, and families must pay some costs.)

- *Comprehensive postsecondary options.* (Students may attend post-secondary programs with state and/or local funds paying all the tuition and fees, and the local board may not decide which students may participate or which courses they take.)

    Colorado. (A statewide program permits public high school juniors and seniors to attend public postsecondary institutions with state funds paying tuition.

    Minnesota. (A statewide program has been established.)

5. *Program development.* (State provides funds explicitly to help school districts plan and develop different kinds of full-day public school options.)

    Arkansas. (The state helps support a Little Rock area desegregation program involving an element of choice. Students from suburbs may attend Little Rock magnet schools, and if they do so, those districts continue to receive funds from the state.)

    California. (Helps support magnet schools for desegregation; funded twenty-five schools within schools for talented students.)

    Connecticut. (Funded planning for several cooperative interdistrict plans to promote integration between cities and suburbs using urban magnet schools.)

    District of Columbia. (Uses funds to establish magnet and alternative schools.)

    Illinois. (Some state funds targeted to help support development of alternative or magnet schools.)

    Maryland. (Helped some districts develop magnet programs.)

    Massachusetts. (Provides funds to help individual districts establish choice programs.)

    Minnesota. (Provided funds for a statewide performing arts magnet school.)

    Missouri. (The state has provided funds for development of magnet schools in St. Louis and for transportation of students. The state provides double funding of suburban and urban students whose movement back and forth between St. Louis and suburban districts promotes desegregation. The state has also paid for development of magnet schools in Kansas City.)

New York. (Provides funds to help establish urban magnet schools that promote integration.)

Wisconsin. (State helped pay for development of magnet schools in Milwaukee.)

As state governments took these actions, the federal government's role has been one of advocacy and limited financial assistance. The federal government has provided millions of dollars over the last eight years to help urban districts establish magnet schools. In the 1988 reauthorization of the federal elementary and secondary school program, Congress increased funding for urban magnet schools that are a part of desegregation programs.

In January 1989, then president Reagan, president-elect Bush, and Secretary of Education Cavazos spoke at a first-ever White House Workshop on Educational Choice. All endorsed the idea of public school choice. President Bush called expansion of choice among public schools "a national imperative," and said his administration would "provide every feasible assistance—financial and otherwise—to states and districts interested in further experiments with choice plans or other valuable reforms" (Bush, 1989).

RESEARCH ON PUBLIC SCHOOL CHOICE

With all this activity, information is available on the impact of different choice plans. The research shows that choice is a powerful tool, but that all plans are not equally effective. The details of plans are crucial, and failure to include certain features in a program could have unintended and unfortunate consequences. This section describes studies conducted on various programs over the last several years.

Minnesota Studies of Choice Options

Between 1985 and 1988, the Minnesota legislature passed several laws expanding parental choice among public schools.

Postsecondary Options. This legislation allows public school eleventh and twelfth graders to attend colleges, universities, and vocational schools. Participants increased by about 50 percent, from about 3,600 students in 1985–86, to about 5,700 in 1988–89 (about 5 percent of those eligible). First-year results showed that about 6 percent of the participants had dropped out of school; that two-thirds of the students had average grades of "B," "C," or "D"; that the high school students had done as well or better in postsecondary courses than the first-year class at most postsecondary institutions; that about half of the participating students lived in rural areas; that 90 percent of the parents said their children had learned more than if they had taken courses only at the local high school; and 95 percent of the students said they were satisfied or very satisfied with the program. A number of school districts have responded to this program by starting or expanding programs for students (Minnesota Department of Education, 1987). For example, without any new state funding or mandates, the number of advanced placement courses offered by Minnesota public high schools has quadrupled since Postsecondary Options began. University of Minnesota Twin Cities campus administrator Darryl Sedio says the number of schools working with the university to offer dual credit courses in the high school has increased from one in 1985 to twenty-four in 1989. He believes the Postsecondary Options program helped stimulate this interest (Sedio, 1989).

High School Graduation Incentives (HSGI) and *Area Learning Centers.* These options permit students ages 12–21 who have not succeeded in one public school to attend another public school outside the district, so long as the receiving district has room and students' transfer does not have a negative impact on desegregation. The Area Learning Centers legislation provided state funds to help twenty districts plan programs for these students, and then gave extra financial support to four of the programs judged to be of highest quality. Criteria used to determine which students are eligible to participate include low test scores or grades, chemical dependency, excessive truancy, or expulsion. The Minnesota Department of Education found that during the first year, about 1,500 students were enrolled in the program. Over 50 percent of HSGI students are re-enrolled dropouts. In its first six months, the program helped convince more than 700 young people that they should return to high school.

Enrollment Options Program. Parents of children ages 5 to 18 may transfer their children to public schools outside their resident district if both districts approve. Beginning in 1989–90, school districts lose the power to prevent students from leaving unless the movement will have a negative impact on desegregation plans. The initial law was passed late in the 1987 session, limited publicity was provided, and families had to apply during the summer of 1987 if they wanted to transfer. Approximately 20 percent of Minnesota's districts (95 out of 435 districts) agreed to participate during the first year. More than one-third (151) of the districts, which enroll 49 percent of Minnesota's students, participated in 1988–89. In September 1987, 137 students from 94 families used the law to transfer. About 440 students used the law in 1988–89. Although about 8.5 percent of Minnesota's students are "people of color" (Black, Hispanic, Native American, or Asian-American), about 10 percent of the students who used this law in 1988–89 are in these categories. The Department of Education surveyed parents who used the program in the 1987–88 school year. All the parents whose children were not graduating said they intended to use the program again the following year. Here are sample explanations parents gave for transferring:

> "My child needed a more flexible program that allows her to use the community extensively to pursue her many interests. Our home district has very rigid requirements not suited to her needs and abilities."
> "The resident district has no auto mechanics, welding, aviation, slow-learning English classes."
> "To meet child's needs for more accelerated art courses."
> "The new district has a larger school with more learning-disabled facilities and teachers."
> "We have a business in the nonresident school district where both my husband and I work. It's much easier for transportation."
> "My son has been attending the nonresident district for 4 years. He is black, and this option was open to us. We were *very* displeased with the resident school system. An older son graduated from the resident high school. We are *very* satisfied with the nonresident schools. We see a vast difference in quality of education."

Asked about their major reason for participating in the Enrollment Options Program, 44 percent of the families said better curriculum and academics, 26 percent said the location was closer to day care, job, or home; 23 percent said there were more options; 21 percent said there were social benefits or that social problems were alleviated; 16

percent said there was better teaching; 14 percent said there were more specialized classes; 7 percent said the parents had attended the school; and 7 percent said they wanted the student to complete high school or that they wanted to maintain continuity in schooling after the family moved (Zastrow, 1988).

Washington's Educational Clinics Program

Since 1978, Washington has provided state funds to help support "educational clinics" that work with students who have dropped out of high schools. All teachers in these programs must be licensed by the state. The clinics are located throughout the state. Most of the programs are run by nonprofit groups such as a "war on poverty" agency or a Native American tribe. Several have been established by a for-profit group. The clinics are intended to provide short-term services to students, rather than function as a substitute high school. Goals include helping students improve their skills and attitudes, preparing them to take the General Educational Development (GED) test, developing employment skills, and giving them opportunities to think about possible careers.

Washington State's Legislative Budget Commitee has evaluated the clinics several times. In one evaluation, the clinics were compared with public alternative schools: "Each type of approach appears to be valid and effective in its own way. Furthermore, each program produces outcomes which the Legislature has recognized as legitimate and desirable. On the basis of costs, outcomes and educational gains, the clinics make a good showing" (Washington Legislative Budget Committee, 1983). Two years later, another evaluation found that the clinics had helped students. "While there is some dropoff, educational clinics appear to have a lasting positive effect on a significant percentage of their students" (Washington Legislative Budget Committee, 1985).

Several states have adopted variations of the educational clinic theme, based on Washington state's programs. These include California, Colorado, and Oregon. However, no state has adopted precisely the same program.

St. Louis Desegregation Plan

In an extraordinary series of articles published in January and February 1988, the *St. Louis Post-Dispatch* looked at what had happened during the five years of the St. Louis desegregation plan using public school choice as a key strategy to promote integration between the city and its suburbs. Twelve reporters and three photographers visited 118 schools in 17 school districts and conducted more than 1,600 interviews. The newspaper also commissioned a series of telephone polls of more than 2,500 teachers, parents, and students in St. Louis and the suburbs. The plan has several key components:

1. Black students from the city are allowed to request a transfer to suburban districts. Suburban districts may reject students who have created discipline problems. Transportation is provided by bus or taxi from the city to the suburbs. The average cost of transporting a city student into the suburbs was $1,677 during the 1987–88 school year.

2. White students from the suburbs are allowed to request a transfer into the city. The average cost of driving a county student by bus or taxi into the city during the 1987–88 school year was $3,517 (Todd, 1988). The transportation costs for suburban students are more than twice those for urban students because relatively few suburban students are transferring into the city. Only 626 white suburban students attended St. Louis public schools in the 1987–88 school year, while 11,655 black students transferred to suburban districts.

3. Twenty-six magnet schools have been established in St. Louis to improve education for urban students and attract white suburban students. During the 1986–87 school year, the magnet elementary schools spent $5,590 per student, 42 percent more than was spent at neighborhood schools. Magnet high schools spent $7,602 per pupil, 27 percent more than the $5,403 spent on neighborhood high schools.

Despite the expenditure of more than $500 million in the last five years, almost two out of three black students in St. Louis attend schools that are at least 90 percent black. Many St. Louis black officials felt that the suburban schools were attracting some of the "best and brightest" black students. In 1986–87, the St. Louis city schools enrolled 46,636 students, of whom 35,280 were black and 11,356 were white.

Wisconsin Desegregation Choice Plan

The state of Wisconsin established a program in 1976 to encourage metropolitan school integration by enabling Milwaukee Public School students to attend suburban public schools, and vice versa. The program, called Chapter 220, pays both suburban and urban districts for each student who moves, in effect "double-funding" students who transfer. Moreover, suburban districts receive 20 percent basic aid increase if the number of minority transfer students they accept equals or exceeds 5 percent of their overall enrollment. Transportation is provided to all participating students.

A recent study strongly criticized the way this program operates. First, the state was providing an enormous amount of financial aid to suburban districts. On average, the state provided aid of $2,057 per pupil during 1986–87. For the same period, Milwaukee and participating suburban districts received an average of $8,737 for each transfer student. "Suburban districts, many with substantial ability to pay, receive state aid payments which exceed actual costs of educating Chapter 220 students," the study notes (Mitchell, 1988). The author recommended eliminating the "bonus" payments to suburban districts.

A second concern focused on the cost of transportation. The study found that the statewide average transportation cost per pupil in 1986–87 was $256, but that this program's average transportation cost per pupil was $2,100.

A third issue concerned overall increasing costs. Specifically, the costs are increasing faster than the number of students participating. "Between 1977 and 1982, participation increased 244 percent and costs rose 406 percent. Between 1982 and 1987, participation increased 226 percent and costs rose 328 percent" (Cole, 1988).

A final concern about the program involves a feature the Milwaukee and St. Louis plans share. In both cases, suburban districts are allowed to reject applicants from the city who have been involved in discipline problems. This permits suburban districts to take only certain students and appears inherently inequitable.

Four-City Magnet School Study

Many large cities have created a few magnet schools to promote integration, with most schools continuing to serve a certain geographical area. Districts often have allowed magnet schools much more flexibility, given them more financial resources, and allowed them to select faculty and students. Two Chicago-based researchers recently studied the impact of magnet high schools in four cities: Boston, Philadelphia, Chicago, and New York. This research is reported elsewhere in this volume (see Chapter 9).

Boston was the only one of the four cities that did not give extra resources and freedom to its magnet high schools. Researchers found a "six-tier" system in the other cities. The six kinds of schools included "nonselective low-income schools, nonselective low- to moderate-income schools, nonselective moderate-income schools, selective vocational schools, selective magnet schools, and selective exam schools." The researchers concluded that "many schools in the upper tiers operate as separate, virtually private schools, while those in the bottom tier, catering almost exclusively to low-income students, provide essentially custodial care" (Moore and Davenport, 1988, p. 3).

In these four cities, it was possible to predict which kinds of students would attend each kind of school. Low-income, black, Hispanic, special education students, and those with attendance problems were significantly underrepresented in academically selective schools, but heavily concentrated in low-income and low- to moderate-income nonselective schools. The selective schools have limited openings, and the majority of students were not able to attend selective schools.

These researchers urged changes in school district procedures so that "neighborhood" schools had more opportunity to compete with other schools. The results of this study "call into fundamental question the naive view that loosely structured choice systems will yield improved schools for all students through competition" (Moore and Davenport 1989, p. 10).

The report concludes with a series of recommendations about key features of choice plans which the authors believe must be included if the plans are to benefit the overall student body, rather than just a select few. These recommendations include suggestions pertaining to admissions policies, development of options that meet needs of a representative cross section of a school system's students, distribution of resources, granting of prerogatives regarding staff selection, staff training, upgrading of facilities, and discretionary funding.

Massachusetts Choice Plans

During the last seven years, the Massachusetts legislature has allocated more than $40 million to promote public school choice plans. The state has helped school districts and educators develop distinctive schools from which parents may choose. State funds have supported planning, building, and parent information activities. The funds have been allocated by the state's Department of Educational Equity. Recently the state studied the impact of expanding public school choice.

State officials pointed to Cambridge, Massachusetts, which five years ago eliminated *all* neighborhood schools at the kindergarten-to eighth-grade level. The state helped educators plan various programs, and then helped support a parent information center. This "controlled choice" plan allowed parents to select among various schools, so long as racial balance guidelines were followed.

State and local officials are delighted with the results of the plan. Since it was initiated about five years ago, average student achievement has *increased* every year. Moreover, the gap in achievement between black and white students has *decreased*. A state department official concluded, "The biggest impact is on school climate. . . . The policy appears to be stimulating positive educational environments, and it clearly reinforces the theory that socioeconomic mixing enhances school achievement" (Snider, 1988, p. 15).

East Harlem

It is a long way from Cambridge, Massachusetts to East Harlem, New York, in mind-set, if not in miles. While Cambridge is racially and economically diverse, East Harlem is one of the lowest-income areas in the country. Nevertheless, as John Merrow of the Public Broadcasting System's "McNeil-Lehrer Report," pointed out, "East Harlem is educationally rich." For the last eight years, the district has developed a system of choice among its public junior and middle school programs. For the last several years, there have been no neighborhood schools. Each school is available on the basis of choice.

East Harlem is a model of teacher empowerment. District administrators encourage teachers to develop distinctive, quality programs from which families may choose.

The district also works hard on parent information. Parents receive a variety of materials about the programs, and sixth-grade students study a decision-making unit that includes consideration of which school they will attend the following year.

When East Harlem started this program, about 15 percent of its students read at or above grade level and its students ranked thirty-second among the thirty-two community districts in New York City. Today, about 65 percent of the students read at or above grade level and its students rank, depending on the test, fifteenth or sixteenth. Vandalism is down dramatically, and the district has a waiting list of teachers who want to work in its schools. District administrators report a major reason for these improvements is their choice plan (Merrow, 1987; Fiske, 1988b, p. 13).

A Review of Studies of Plans for Public School Choice

Raywid (1989a) recently completed a review of more than a hundred studies on various public school choice plans. She concludes that when families have the opportunity to select among various public schools, students achieve more, like school and themselves better, parents have better attitudes toward school, and educators feel more like professionals (Raywid, 1989b). It should be noted that Raywid is a strong supporter of more choice among public schools, and a vigorous opponent of providing additional tax funds to private and parochial schools.

SUMMARY OF RESEARCH

The studies just cited, conducted all over the country, do not necessarily contradict each other. There is an emerging consensus about key features of public school choice plans. Although plans will differ, the most effective plans

- Include a clear statement of the goals and objectives that all schools are expected to meet, and their students to accomplish
- Provide information and counseling to help parents select among various programs for their children
- Include student assignment and transfer policies that do not discriminate against students on the basis of past achievement or behavior
- Avoid admissions procedures that are "first come, first served"
- Encourage and assist most schools within a given geographical area to develop distinctive features, rather than simply concentrating resources on a few schools
- Provide opportunities for building-level educators to help create programs
- Make transportation within a reasonable area available for all students, with a priority given to those coming from low-income and non-English-speaking families
- Require that dollars should follow students; sending and receiving institutions should not both receive funding
- Develop and follow procedures that promote more desegregation and integration
- Include provisions for continuing oversight and modification

Failing to include these features will result in programs that expand choice for some (especially affluent, well-informed families), while increasing the achievement gap between the affluent and the poor. However, well-designed choice plans can and have helped to narrow achievement gaps, and have had a dramatic positive impact on youngsters from low-income families.

PROSPECTS FOR EXPANSION OF THE STATE ROLE

In a democracy, it is not enough to have popular support for an idea; the idea must have advocates. New, often unusual coalitions are promoting public school choice throughout the country.

Minnesota is one example. The governor was joined by the League of Women Voters, Minnesota PTA, Elementary and Secondary School Principals, as well as the Minnesota Business Partnership. MBP members are the "CEOs" of the seventy-five largest companies in the state (3M, Honeywell, Pillsbury, and so on). Hundreds of individual educators supported the legislation, although powerful education groups such as the Minnesota Education Association, Minnesota Federation of Teachers, Minnesota School Boards Association, and Minnesota Association of School Administrators used their influence and resources trying to defeat it. Several studies of the Minnesota experience have now appeared, although none is recent enough to have followed political activity through 1988 (King and Roberts, 1987; Mazzoni, 1988). Each analysis agrees that development of coalitions, including both educators and those outside the profession, was central to the adoption of legislation in Minnesota.

Similar coalitions are emerging in states such as Colorado and California. In Colorado, liberal and conservative state legislators agreed to a postsecondary options plan recommended by a liberal state board of education member who spent years opposing voucher plans (funding private and parochial schools) and a conservative "think tank," the Independence Institute. A K–12 open-enrollment bill, similar to Minnesota's law, also was introduced in 1988, but was defeated. It was reintroduced in 1989. In California, the Business Roundtable recently adopted a series of reform recommendations that included allowing eleventh- and twelfth-graders to choose among various secondary and postsecondary schools, as well as promoting more choice within individual school districts. The California Business Roundtable is beginning to work with public alternative school educators to win support for this program. For the last several years, California public alternative school teachers and administrators have been trying to win support for legislation that would authorize public school educators to establish a school if parents of at least thirty students said they wanted their children to attend the program. Any program established under this legislation would have to meet all state standards. A variety of California reform reports issued over the last several years recommend expansion of choice among public schools.

Efforts are continuing in other states. Governors in Arkansas, Illinois, Massachusetts, Michigan, New Mexico, North Carolina, and New Jersey suggested that their legislators take action in 1989 to expand the public school options available to families. In Massachusetts, for example, the governor has asked the Department of Education to develop an enrollment options program similar to Minnesota's. Governor Clinton in Arkansas recommended that his state adopt programs based on Minnesota's Postsecondary Options and Enrollment Options Act. In Arizona, Connecticut, Hawaii, Iowa, Michigan, Ohio, and Nebraska, coalitions are encouraging their legislators to adopt some form of expanded public school choice.

These recommendations have not been ignored by education leaders. Albert Shanker, president of the American Federation of Teachers, suggested in April 1988 that public school teachers be allowed to create distinctive programs from which families could choose (Shanker, 1988). The Minneapolis-St. Paul-based Citizens League used that recommendation as the basis for its recommendations on dealing with desegregation in a report issued in December 1988 (Citizens League, 1988). And the Minnesota Education Association lobbyist, acknowledging that his organization initially opposed Governor Perpich's open-enrollment proposals, says, "We are starting to see it as teacher empowerment" (Bencivenga, 1988, p. 20). The National Education Association points out that its members have participated in various public school choice plans throughout the country (National Education Association, 1986). It developed a series of features that should be a part of any choice plan and recommended them to the nation's governors. They were included in the 1986 report, *Time for Results* (National Governors' Association, 1986).

THE FEDERAL GOVERNMENT'S ROLE

The federal government can play and has played an important role in the development of choice plans at the state and local levels. This section describes what has been and might be done.

The first and perhaps best known role of the federal government has been to *support financially the development and expansion of public school choice plans at the district level.* Literally millions of federal dollars have been spent helping districts establish magnet schools. Some of the best local choice plans in the country, such as that in East Harlem, were established with federal assistance. However, some of the magnet school systems most frequently criticized, such as those in Chicago, were also developed with federal support. As noted earlier, the details of choice plans are crucial. In East Harlem, *every* school at the junior high level is a magnet, receiving approximately equal dollars per pupil, and admitting a cross section of students who apply. Some of the most popular schools in East Harlem have been replicated within the district in response to parent requests. In Chicago, there are relatively few magnet schools, huge waiting lists at the most popular, and enormous differences in funding between magnet and neighborhood schools. Moreover, Chicago magnet schools are allowed to pick and choose among students and educators. Not surprisingly, there is an enormous gap between the quality of education provided at magnet and at neighborhood schools.

Does this mean that the federal government should not support development of magnet schools? Not at all. However, I believe more attention should be paid to the details of choice plans, and to promotion of the East Harlem and Cambridge model, rather than the Chicago plan. In written testimony, I recently suggested to a congressional committee that the federal government use magnet school funds to encourage most or all schools within an urban area to be magnets, rather than creating a few "superschools" (Nathan, 1989b). The federal government also might require that school districts receiving magnet school funds establish parent information centers with aggressive outreach programs, and that schools developed with federal funds not be allowed to select among students on the basis of previous achievement or behavior (Nathan, 1989b).

A second role of the federal government has been to *support research about the design and impact of choice plans*. Portions of the studies carried out by Raywid and by Moore and Davenport, cited earlier, were done with federal assistance. Moreover, the federally funded study of Minnesota's Postsecondary Options program helped legislators understand the overall impact of the program. There remain important research questions to be answered about choice plans, and federal support in this area could be helpful. The federal government might ask researchers to look, for example, at ways technology could be used to help parents make more informed choices among schools, or what the impact might be of different approaches to racial balance guidelines for choice systems, or what standards states should require all schools to meet.

A third role of the federal government could be to *encourage attention of the nation on this issue*. Publicizing the value of well-designed choice plans and the problems of poorly designed programs, via conferences, publications, and speeches would help more people understand what is happening.

CONCLUSIONS

In the last five years, attitudes have changed. In a 1983 book published one month after *A Nation at Risk*, I recommended expansion of choice as a key part of school reform (Nathan, 1983). But until Minnesota's programs were adopted, evaluated, and determined to be successful, there was no substantial policymaker or media interest in the idea of expanded options among public schools.

Many states and school districts are looking closely at the research and details of public school choice programs. Scholars have determined that school choice is a powerful reform tool. Although there is no one best approach for each state, certain features ought to be included in any plan. There appears to be growing recognition that elements such as parent information, nondiscriminatory admissions policies, and opportunity for educators to create distinctive programs are not frills, but absolutely crucial to choice programs that will have widespread positive impact. Failure to include these features can increase, rather than decrease, achievement and opportunity gaps between affluent and low-income young people.

Today, a vast majority of the public supports the idea of more choice among public schools. More than twenty states have acted, in response to new coalitions of private and public sector advocates. Allowing families and educators to select among various public schools can have a rapid, dramatic positive impact. As educators, parents, and—most important—students, have testified, being allowed to select among public schools has changed lives.

Eighteen-year-old Chris Wilcox recently described the impact of Minnesota's choice programs on his life. These laws enabled him to attend an alternative public school and a local community college. He told several hundred people at a White House Workshop on Educational Choice that without the choice programs, "I probably would not have graduated. . . . Choice not only gave me a chance to personalize my education, but it also gave me the confidence that I can make something of myself and control my destiny" (Nathan, 1989a, p. 222).

REFERENCES

Bencivenga, Jim. "Multiple Choice: Minnesota Opens Enrollment and Eyes Reform," *Christian Science Monitor*, 10 June 1988, p. 19.

Bush, George. Speech to the White House Workshop on Education Choice, 10 January 1989. Quoted in William Snider, "Parley on 'Choice,' Final Budget Mark Transition," *Education Week*, 18 January 1989, p. 24.

Cassel, Andrew. "Minnesota's Free Market in Education," *Philadelphia Inquirer*, 27 June 1988, p. 1.

Citizens League. *Chartered Schools = Choices for Educators + Quality for All Students*. Minneapolis: Citizens League, 1988.

Cohen, Muriel. "Minnesota Experiments with Open Enrollment," *Boston Globe*, 29 May 1988a.

Cohen, Muriel. "Minnesota Bolsters Open Enrollment with Funding," *Boston Globe*, 6 June 1988b, p. 1.

Cole, Jeff. "Reform Urged for Financing of Chapter 220," *Milwaukee Sentinel*, 31 October 1988.

Craig, Will. "Open Enrollment in Public Schools," *CURA Reporter*, December 1987.

Fiske, Edward. "Lessons," *New York Times*, 22 June 1988a, p. B6.

Fiske, Edward. "Parental Choice in Public School Gains," *New York Times*, 11 July 1988b, p. 1.

Gallup, Alec M. "The 18th Annual Gallup Poll of the Public's Attitudes toward the Public Schools," *Phi Delta Kappan* 68 (1986): 56.

Gallup, Alec M., and Clark, David. "The 19th Annual Gallup Poll of the Public's Attitudes toward the Public Schools," *Phi Delta Kappan* 69 (1987): 20.

King, Paul J., and Roberts, Nancy C. "Policy Entrepreneurs: Catalysts for Policy Innovation," *Journal of State Government* 60 (1987): 172–178.

Leslie, Connie, et al. "Giving Parents a Choice," *Newsweek*, 19 September 1988.

Mazzoni, Tim. "The Politics of Educational Choice in Minnesota." In *The Politics of Excellence and Choice in Education*, ed. William L. Boyd and Charles T. Kerchner. New York: Falmer Press, 1988.

Merrow, John. "Choice in Education." "McNeil/Lehrer Report," PBS. March 1987.

Minnesota Business Partnership. *Minnesota Public Attitude Survey: A Citizens Prescription for Opportunity*. Minneapolis: Minnesota Business Partnership, 1988.

Minnesota Department of Education. *Postsecondary Enrollment Options Program Final Report*. St. Paul: Minnesota Department of Education, 1987.

Minnesota Department of Education. *Enrollment Options Program, Parent Survey 1987–88, Overall Results Summary*. St. Paul: Minnesota Department of Education, 1988.

Mitchell, George. *A Study of Chapter 220*. Madison: Wisconsin Policy Research Institute, 1988.

Moore, Donald R., and Davenport, Suzanne. "School Choice: The New Improved Sorting Machine." Presentation to the National Invitation Conference on Public School Choice, 24 February 1989.

Moore, Donald R., and Davenport, Suzanne. *The New Improved Sorting Machine*. Chicago: Designs for Change, 1988.

Nathan, Joe. *Free to Teach: Achieving Equity and Excellence in Schools.* New York: Pilgrim Press, 1983.

Nathan, Joe, ed. *Public Schools by Choice: Expanding Opportunities for Parents, Students, and Teachers.* St. Paul: Institute for Learning and Teaching, 1989a.

Nathan, Joe. "Testimony to the House Committee on Elementary, Secondary, and Vocational Education," February 1989b. Available from author at Humphrey Institute of Public Affairs, University of Minnesota, Minneapolis. Mimeographed.

National Education Association. "NEA Agrees with State Governors: It's Time to See Some Reform Results." Washington, DC: National Education Association, 1986. (Mimeographed.)

National Governors' Association. *Time for Results: The Governors' 1991 Report on Education.* Washington, DC: National Governors' Association, 1986.

Putka, Gary. "Choose-a-School: Parents Are Getting to Send Kids Where They Like," *Wall Street Journal,* 13 May 1988, p. 1.

Rachlin, Jill. "When Parents and Students Give the Grades," *U.S. News and World Report,* 12 September 1988, pp. 60–61.

Raywid, Mary Anne. *The Case for Public Schools of Choice.* Bloomington, IN: Phi Delta Kappa, 1989a.

Raywid, Mary Anne. "The Mounting Case for Schools of Choice." In *Public Schools by Choice: Expanding Opportunities for Parents, Students, and Educators,* ed. Joe Nathan. St. Paul: Institute for Learning and Teaching, 1989b.

Sedio, Darryl. "Presentation to the Citizens League." Minneapolis: Citizens League, January 1989. (Mimeographed.)

Shanker, Albert. "Remarks to NGA Education Task Force on Parent Involvement and Choice." December 16, 1986 (Mimeographed.)

Shanker, Albert. "Opting Out of the Old Stuff," *New York Times,* 3 April 1988. (Paid advertisement.)

Snider, William. "Massachusetts District Backs Plan to Integrate Its Students on Basis of Language, Not Race," *Education Week* 7, No. 34 (18 May 1988).

Todd, Cynthia. "Bus Companies Are Paid Millions," *St. Louis Post-Dispatch,* 2 February 1988, p. 8A.

Washington Legislative Budget Committee. *Report on Educational Clinics Program Years 1980–82.* Olympia: Washington Legislative Budget Committee, 1983.

Washington Legislative Budget Committee. *Report on Educational Clinics Program Years 1982–84.* Olympia: Washington Legislative Budget Committee, 1985.

Zastrow, Ken. "Enrollment Options Parent Survey." St. Paul: Minnesota Department of Education, 1988. (Mimeographed.)